USA Wrestling

Coach's Guide

to Excellence,

2nd Edition

USAwrestling

On the Cover

Cael Sanderson, the United States first wrestler to go undefeated in college winning four NCAA Titles, captures the gold at the 84 kgs weight class in freestyle at the 2004 Athens, Olympic Games. Sanderson is lifted in the air by USA Wrestling's National Teams Coach Kevin Jackson, a 1992 Olympic Gold Medalist at the Barcelona Games. Sanderson's collegiate Coach Bobby Douglas is also pictured in the celebration.

Library of Congress Cataloging in Publication Data:
    USA WRESTLING COACH'S GUIDE TO EXCELLENCE, 2nd Edition

Publisher: I. L. Cooper

Library of Congress Control Number: 2005908040

ISBN: 0-9769303-1-5

Developed and published with Cooper Publishing Group LLC. For more information about this and other publications, contact the Publisher: Cooper Publishing Group LLC, P.O. Box 1129, Traverse City, MI 49685. Email: ICOOPER100@aol.com

10 9 8 7 6 5 4 3 2 1 0

The Publisher disclaims responsibility for any adverse effects or consequences from the misapplication or injudicious use of the information contained within this text.

Contents

Acknowledgements

The scope of content of this book would not have been possible were it not for the help and assistance of many persons which contributed to its completion. USA Wrestling would like to say "Thank You" and acknowledge all of the professionals and organizations that gave of themselves, and their time for the benefit of the great sport of wrestling.

Included in the writing team that helped produce the second edition of the Coaches Guide to Excellence are Danny Struck, Gold Certified Coach, who has shown great leadership in grass-roots program development. Dave Curby, Gold Certified Coach, whose wide array of knowledge on physiology and strength training leads the way in wrestling research. Ben Stehura, Gold Certified Coach from Limestone University, provided strong knowledge in the development of wrestlers. Katie Downing, Gold Certified Coach and 2005 World Team Member, developed information on the addition of Women's wrestling into the NCEP curriculum. Gary Abbott, Director of Special Projects for USA Wrestling, leads the wrestling community in research on Title IX as well as many other areas in the sport. Eileen Bowker, certified athletic trainer, compiled the most up to date information on skin infections as well as nutrition and weight management. Kyle Fellure, Head Coach for the University of Indianapolis, provided excellent insight into training collegiate athletes and developing a coaching philosophy. Randy Hinderliter, Gold Certified Coach, is a leader of certifying coaches nationally and provided great leadership for the overall direction of the curriculum. Beasey Hendrix, Gold Certified Coach, developed excellent information on mental skills. Isaac Ramaswamy provided great technical knowledge and writing skills. Tyler Brandt, Gold Certified Coach, gave great information for periodization and peaking of athletes. And, special thanks goes to John Sachs of www.tech-fall.com for the use of the great wrestling photos provided for the updated book.

Special thanks go to fellow staff members at USA Wrestling under the direction and leadership of Rich Bender. Specifically, the State Services division under the direction of Mark Scott was a great joy to work with while the book was being developed. Thank you to Marge Civil, Shonna Vest, Ted DeRousse, and Kevin Hansen. Jamie McNab, with National Teams, volunteered freely of her time for editing and organizing the book.

We thank Olympic Coach magazine for the Sidebar "Applying Sport Psychology to the Real World of Athletes" in chapter 13. For more information about Olympic Coach magazine go to http://coaching.usolympicteam.com/coaching.

This book was put together with the great help of Butch Cooper and his fantastic staff at Cooper publishing.

Sincerely,

Ted Witulski
NCEP Manager
USA Wrestling

Foreword

The sport of wrestling is ever-evolving. A successful coach is a person that constantly seeks the most current and useful knowledge in the sport of wrestling. A while ago a coach asked, "Why would I need coaches education? . . . . I've been coaching for twenty-five years."

Certainly, twenty-five years of experience is valuable, in a profession where longevity is often short. But, the fact remains wrestling has changed and if we want it to reach the masses of youth that need to experience its character building traits, then America's coaches must persist in their willingness to learn.

As coaches we often see that the hardest working wrestlers are the ones that step out of obscurity and into greatness. When this occurs it is usually because a knowledgeable and dedicated wrestling coach has made it their mission to help a wrestler pursue their dreams on a difficult path.

America needs to develop more great wrestling coaches that are dedicated and motivated to keep our sport strong. The way we will build the sport of wrestling is by making sure that USA Wrestling's National Coaches Education Program succeeds by connecting America's grass-roots with America's elite wrestling stars to make the United States the greatest wrestling nation in the world.

The continued improvement and development of wrestling coaching in America is an essential ingredient in elevating the standard of wrestling in our country.

Dan Gable
Olympic Champion

Preface

For years, the wrestling community will remember the dramatic victory of Rulon Gardner, a self-proclaimed Wyoming farm-boy, over the Russian legend Alexander Kareline, a three-time Olympic Gold Medalist who had never been defeated in more than a dozen years of senior level competition.

When Rulon Gardner achieved the seemingly impossible he was greeted at the edge of the mat by a host of Olympic coaches, celebrating the shocking upset. As Rulon stepped on top of the highest platform of Olympic achievement to receive his gold medal every coach that ever worked with Rulon from the Olympic level, through the college and high school ranks, down to the first coach who ever talked Rulon into trying the sport of wrestling must have swelled with pride. Great coaching at every level is the backbone of every great athlete's success. The path certainly wasn't easy and at times it had to seem like a distant pipe-dream but Rulon Gardner with the help of dedicated and determined coaches stayed the course and will forever be remembered for his incredible victory.

USA Wrestling's National Coaches Education Program plays an integral part in the mission of possessing the most powerful and successful wrestling program in the world. The four-tiered program delivered through volunteers for the NCEP can make a dramatic difference the direction of wrestling in America and the world.

This newly designed and restructured Bronze text targets the essential subjects and skills necessary for coaches to succeed in assisting their athletes towards great achievements. We sincerely hope that the text will provide coaches with the information they need to help propel their programs forward, making the sport of wrestling stronger and more readily available to every youth in America.

Ted Witulski
NCEP Manager
USA Wrestling

Code of Conduct for Coaches

As the subsequent chapters will attest, the coach has a number of responsibilities to a variety of groups. The following *Code of Conduct* reflects a summary of these responsibilities.

1. The coach shall strive to acquire and implement the most current knowledge of the rules, strategies, and teaching methods of the sport.
2. The coach shall strive to structure a safe environment for the athlete during practices, matches, travel, and other team functions.
3. The coach shall strive to work closely with parents and community members to promote an understanding of the role of athletics in the total educational experience.
4. The coach shall strive to have the welfare of the athlete as the primary concern when making decisions that relate to the care of injuries, rehabilitation, and return to activity.
5. The coach shall strive to promote effective communication with wrestlers, officials, fellow coaches, parents, school administrators, and community members.
6. The coach shall strive to serve as a leader and model in the development of appropriate conduct for the athlete both within and beyond the sport setting.
7. The coach shall strive to use strategies in practice and competition that reflect a standard of fairness to all competitors and that are designed to encourage competition within the letter and spirit of the rules.
8. The coach shall strive to keep the concepts of winning and losing in proper perspective.
9. The coach shall strive to enforce team policies with fairness, consistency, and an appreciation for individual differences.
10. The coach shall strive to be knowledgeable of the state association's policies pertaining to the sport and shall ensure that the regulations governing eligibility are upheld.

The joy of coaching is epitomized as a coach congratulates his athlete.

1
Role of the Coach

Danny Struck, Kyle Fellure, Randy Hinderliter, Ben Stehura

QUESTIONS TO CONSIDER

- What is the primary role that a coach should seek to fulfill?
- What are the potential benefits of participation in athletics?
- What are the potentially detrimental effects of participation in athletics?
- What are the principal goals a coach should seek to achieve?

Roles of the Coach

As a coach not only are you responsible for teaching technique, your duties extend beyond the mat. You are called to fulfill many different roles such as being a leader, administrator, counselor, and mentor.

Leaders assume what others have to say is valuable, and therefore, actively seek out others ideas and opinions. As a leader you must always be willing to listen and be open minded enough to change what you do. Leaders must be creative in finding new ways to accomplish goals whether it be by adapting your methods or by delegating to others. Being knowledgeable about what you are teaching and always looking to expand on what you already know is a characteristic of a leader. A leader has to be a visionary, mapping out a clear path to accomplishing desired goals. Most importantly being sincere and caring to your wrestling family including, athletes, parents, administration, coaching staff, and community. To become an effective leader good communication skills are a must.

Most coaches believe that administration is only a small part of coaching. Administration is in fact a very large part of a coaches responsibility. As an administrator you will be responsible for making travel plans, scheduling practices and meets, equipment purchase, budgeting, and overall coordination of the wrestling program. If organization is not your strong suit don't be afraid to delegate to others.

Working with wrestlers is not always an easy thing to do. As a coach you must be ready to meet the needs of a varied group of athletes. The intensity of wrestling produces the highest of highs and the lowest of lows. This will be further addressed in the chapter on interpersonal relations and developing psychological skills in young athletes.

Being a mentor is setting an example of how to conduct yourself in different situations. Mentors help develop character and guide wrestlers on and off the mat. They are compassionate, caring and are consistently a positive influence in the lives of their athletes.

"Do as I do, follow me."
Tom Erickson,
Purdue University on Leadership

Getting on the mat is a great part of being a coach for a wrestling program. Whether working with a tots team or the local high school, demonstrating technique and working with kids one on one is an exhilarating part of coaching. But, it is not the only part.

In fact, the role of a wrestling coaching is deep and wide. If the program is to flourish and fulfill its mission of bringing the age-old tradition of wrestling to young people than the wrestling coach must look beyond the best part of coaching, getting on the mat.

The role of the coach seems to be constantly expanding. Coaches are expected to be mentors, promoters, technicians, counselors, video experts, journalists, athletic trainers, and even janitors.

Whether it is cleaning the mats or making sure that the matches get video taped a coach has a host of roles that he must fill, or find someone to fill them for him.

For a coach to truly succeed in the sport, it is necessary that they develop the ability to work through people. Coaches that micromanage every detail of wrestling may actually fail at filling all of the roles of a coach or worse yet, may face burnout from the laundry list of responsibilities that must be taken care of.

While coaching on the mat is a high priority, it is also imperative that a coach take a serious role in developing upcoming assistants in the program. These future coaches in the program must be given real and realistic duties that the lead coach of the program needs to monitor to assure their completion.

A head coach needs to make sure that the assistants understand all aspects of the program and learn the skills that will help make them a productive head coach eventually. Working through people, delegating responsibility and monitoring completion of tasks will help the head coach lead the program while building the next generation of coaches.

Participation

Participation in athletics can exert an important positive influence on young people. The high rate of participation in athletics and the broad community support these programs receive suggest that this belief is shared by many individuals. However, mere participation does not ensure that athletes will obtain all of the potentially beneficial effects. In fact, without proper coaching, positive parental support and guidance, there is a risk that the detrimental effects of participation may outweigh the beneficial effects. Therefore, the quality of adult leadership provided by coaches as they direct their practices, contests, and special events is the primary factor in determining the degree to which beneficial or detrimental effects occur.

Beneficial Effects of Participation in Athletics

The benefits of participation are numerous and many occur within the context of a good program. Wrestling is a sport that teaches important life skills. Benefits include:

- developing appropriate skills;
- developing physical fitness;
- learning appropriate conditioning techniques that affect health and performance;
- developing a realistic and positive self-image;
- enhancing the likelihood of participation in physical activity throughout life;
- learning the rules and strategies of sport;
- developing a respect for rules as facilitators of safe and fair competition;
- obtaining enjoyment and recreation;
- developing positive personal, social, and psychological skills (e.g., self-worth, self-discipline, team work, effective communication, goal-setting, self-control); and
- denouncing drug use as the way to recreate, escape from reality, or enhance performance.

Many wrestlers achieve significant benefits in at least some of the components listed previously. The extent to which the benefits are obtained depends upon the quality of coaching leadership and the frequency, duration, and intensity of participation.

Ineffective Coaching of Participation in Athletics

When coaches identify appropriate skill, knowledge, fitness, and personal and social objectives for their athletes and employ suitable teaching methods, their athletes are likely to obtain the benefits previously listed. If, however, the coach selects inappropriate objectives or uses ineffective teaching methods, no benefits (or even detrimental effects) may result.

When incorrect techniques and/or negative behaviors are learned by young athletes, it is difficult and time-consuming for the next coach to extinguish these inappropriate actions and attitudes and then to teach for appropriate outcomes. Therefore, ineffective coaching, whether intended or not, can result in detrimental outcomes for the participants. The value of a good coach can be placed in perspective by contrasting the beneficial effects of participation with the following detrimental effects:

- developing inappropriate physical skills;
- sustaining injury, illness, or loss of physical fitness;
- learning incorrect conditioning techniques;
- developing a negative or unrealistic Self-image;
- avoiding future participation in sport and physical activity for self and others;
- learning incorrect rules and strategies of sport;
- learning to misuse rules to gain unfair or unsafe advantages;
- replacing the enjoyment of participation with a fear of failure; developing negative or antisocial behaviors;
- taking drugs in an attempt to enhance performance; and
- wasting time that could be devoted to other activities.

The benefits of athletic participation are directly related to the quality of the leadership provided by the coach. Participation in wrestling is positive by nature. Ineffective coaching can lead to detrimental effects in wrestling.

Athletes and parents desire good coaching. Although many guidelines for effective coaching exist, they are commonly violated. It is important to remember, therefore, that beneficial and/or detrimental effects of participation in athletics can occur. The degree to which beneficial rather than detrimental effects occur is related to the quality of your coaching leadership. Accordingly, it is important for you to clearly understand your role as a coach, make correct choices, and take appropriate actions to maximize the beneficial effects and minimize detrimental effects of participation. This chapter, as well as other chapters in this USAW manual, will provide guidance in assisting you to make these choices.

GOALS FOR THE COACH

If your primary purpose is to maximize the benefits of participation while minimizing the detrimental effects, then important goals include:

- effectively teaching the physical skills, rules, and strategies of the sport in an orderly and enjoyable environment;
- appropriately challenging the cardiovascular and muscular systems of your athletes through active practice sessions and competitions; and
- teaching and modeling desirable personal, social, and psychological skills.

The contribution you make to your athletes is directly related to the degree to which you are effective in these three areas.

Winning is also an important goal for coaches and participants on athletic teams. Winning depends in part, however, on the quality of the opposition, calls made by officials, or extenuating circumstances. These are all factors over which you, as a coach, can exert

SIDEBAR: The Dad—dash—Coach

Ted Witulski

It is a phenomenon that has become more prevalent in the sport of wrestling. With the idea that wrestling is an individual sport and national travel becoming more a part of wrestling for younger and younger age groups, the age of the Dad—Dash—Coach seems to have arrived.

Gather at any "big-time" youth tournament and people are more likely to see small tribes of parents with their kids as opposed to the large youth clubs that once dominated the landscape. Parents now seem intent on filling a dual role in wrestling proud supporter of their youth, and purveyor of the keys to success in the sport of wrestling.

It is a difficult role for any parent to assume, and evidence of that can often be seen in the dustups that occur at youth events. More than a few times the dad-coach has been accused of living out their success and failures vicariously through their own wrestler. And, more than a few times tournament organizers have had to deal with nasty situations where a parent crossed the line of abuse towards their own child. Being the dad-coach brings out a whole string of topics that the wrestling community needs to consider. Undoubtedly, the dad-coach phenomenon is not something that will be done away with, but in the interest of the kids and the sport that we cherish there are ways to improve upon the role of the dad-coach.

Probably the over-arching concern that comes with being the dad-coach is the ability to maintain proper perspective. Wrestling coaches in general are an intense lot; however, the dad-coach role seems to even intensify the situations. A bad call isn't just a mistake against a kid on the team, now it becomes a slight to one's own flesh and blood. The intensity most certainly goes up a notch.

The dad-coach must look for a way to balance duel roles parent and coach. On the mat it is necessary for coaches to keep perspective and treat officials, opponents and tournament staff with respect. Bad calls and tough losses are bound to occur; instead of allowing thinking to degenerate into conspiratorial scenarios the coaching role must prove to be the stronger influence.

The dad-coach must maintain the level-headedness of a coach. Tough breaks are times to showcase the work that needs to be done for a wrestler to ascend to a higher rank. Even the youngest wrestler must be readied to accept both winning and losing with maturity. When a call in the match changed the course of who won and who loss, it is a prime example of when wrestlers need to shoulder the burden. Mark Perry a red-shirt freshman from Iowa lost a tough match in his hometown of Stillwater Oklahoma wrestling against the top-ranked Oklahoma State Cowboys—a team coached by Perry's own uncle, wrestling legend John Smith. After the loss Perry had the maturity to say, "I don't like to make excuses."

Dad-coaches would do well to remember that statement. The strongest advice most coaches give their wrestlers is to not make excuses, don't look to put the blame on others, shoulder it, it will make you stronger. Dad-coaches are going to be susceptible to inflamed passions, but they have chosen the role of a coach. The best advice may be for the dad-coach to teach their children-wrestlers to follow legendary Coach Dan Gable's advice, "Make Your Own Luck".

Sometimes for a well-trained coach it can be a little maddening when they watch a youth match. Recently a good example occurred at one of the Ultimate Challenge events. Two young scrappers were out on the mat, both sides coaches were of the family variety, moms and dads serving that duel role. As one wrestler worked a half, the defending wrestlers' corner could be heard yelling, "grab his head".

Trained coaches know that "grab his head" isn't the sound way to defend a half. Sound advice though may not always be given from parents who are also coaches. It is somewhat of a myth in wrestling that only really high-level athletes need high-level coaching. The dad-coach, the parents, should make it a challenge upon themselves to excel in the field of coaching.

Just going off of the knowledge that they had when they were wrestlers, or what they picked up at a couple local tournaments, doesn't exactly model the excellence that they are trying to instill into their own child that they are coaching. The parent coaches should seek out coaching clinics and real mat-time where they are on the mat working the moves with a partner their own size. This on the mat real wrestling education will also give them a new found respect for how difficult and tiring the sport of wrestling can be. Parents must be prepared to build a strong foundation of wrestling skills for young wrestlers so that when they move on to higher levels the next coach can truly advance the wrestler-child's learning.

Finally, another important thing for the dad-coach to remember is that the younger ages of wrestling are meant to engrain the enjoyment of the sport into the wrestler. If the young son or daughter isn't having fun in wrestling, then it does not matter how badly the parent may want them to continue wrestling. It is bitterly disappointing to see good young wrestlers quit the sport of wrestling because it became a chore instead of inherently fun.

Many outstanding American wrestlers started their careers relatively late compared to the tots and pee-wees that now chase around on the mats prior to tournaments. Olympic Silver Medalist Jamill Kelly did not start wrestling until the 9th grade. So, what's the rush to indoctrinate into the militaristic discipline of wrestling at a young age?

Making sure that young kids love the sport of wrestling will go a long ways in keeping them in the sport until they are ready to light their own fires of determination and self-discipline.

Another important way that the dad-coach can make sure that their youngster is enjoying the sport of wrestling is to make sure they are surrounded by friends that love the sport as well. The dad-coach and son often travel to tournaments alone by choice. However, if the dad-coach would take a leadership role in getting more of the clubs kids to a major event the memories would certainly be even more memorable. Who doesn't look fondly on the relationships that they built in wrestling while traveling to a tournament?

The dad-coach can still coach their own kid, but it would be a tremendous service to the sport of wrestling if even more dad-coaches grew the sport by reaching out to the other kids in the club like the single-mom that wants her kid to love wrestling but doesn't have the ability to do it on her own. The best dad-coaches are the ones that are selfless not just for their own flesh and blood; they are ready to move beyond being a coach of their own and just be a coach.

The dad-coach is a growing segment of the wrestling community in America. Passions have to remain in check, and professionalism must be a priority. Finally, young wrestlers must build on the feeling of overwhelming enjoyment on the mat and not suppress that sense of fun. The ultimate goal of the dad-coach should be the guy that loves the sport so much and succeeded in coaching his own kids that he is determined to become just a coach—the guy that will build a local club so that all young people have the opportunity to get to know the sport of wrestling.

little or no control. It is important, therefore, to concentrate on factors over which you have control (e.g., teaching physical skills, rules and strategies; developing physical fitness; cultivating personal, social and psychological skills; and creating team cohesiveness). As you become effective at these components of coaching, the elements that contribute to losing or winning a contest will occur naturally.

A large amount of time is invested by athletes and coaches irrespective of whether the benefits to the athletes are small, moderate, or great. Parents and administrators should demand that coaches continually focus on improving the ratio of beneficial to detrimental effects for their team by learning and applying principles of effective coaching such as those described in the various chapters of this USAW manual. The following paragraphs summarize the content of this USAW manual.

Philosophy

The attitude you and other members of the athletic staff have toward sports programs will have a significant impact on the way you coach. The mere fact that you are enrolled in the National Coaches Education Program (NCEP) reflects a commitment by you to enhance your coaching competence. Your role as a coach is to maximize the beneficial effects of participation, while minimizing potentially detrimental effects. Your athletic philosophy should be based upon the premise that athletic programs exist for the welfare of the athletes.

Positive interactions with the people you come in contact with are extremely important components of coaching. Good working relationships with the parents, athletes, fans, faculty, custodians, officials, and other coaches are important not only in establishing a successful season but also in modeling proper personal and social skills for your athletes.

Growth and Development

Effective coaching implies that coaches know how growing, maturing athletes are affected by the stresses of competition. Coaches must understand and deal with physical changes, maturing cognitive capacities, and gender differences. Basic knowledge of physical conditioning principles will help you design effective practices and training sessions.

Weight training has been used by athletes in an effort to improve performance. A coach must know how to administer and supervise an effective weight training program while being cognizant of the potential risks involved. Proper nutrition is another important factor that affects an athlete's performance. Caloric requirements along with specific nutrient needs should be conveyed to the athletes, not only in an attempt to improve their diets, but also to improve performance. The components of vision and their relevance in athletic performance are also important.

Sports Medicine

One of the potentially detrimental effects of athletic participation is risk of injury. As a coach, it is important for you to take steps to prevent injuries by providing a healthy and safe environment. However, injuries will occur even if every precaution has been taken. Sport injuries require immediate attention to help prevent further injury; reduce the risk of excessive blood loss or swelling; promote quicker recovery; and, in extreme cases, prevent permanent damage or even death. Rehabilitation may be necessary before an injured athlete can reenter practice and competition. General guidelines exist that describe who is responsible for the rehabilitation, what are the criteria for reentry, and who decides when the athlete returns to competition.

Many calisthenics and stretching exercises have been found to be detrimental to the anatomical structure and function of the athlete. A coach must use only safe physical activities. Finally, pre-participation athletic examinations and proper medical records are necessary components in a comprehensive and cohesive program for taking care of your athletes' health.

Psychology

The extent to which benefits are gained from sports participation depends largely on your ability to effectively plan and evaluate instruction. Your ability to communicate, both as a speaker and listener, will aid you in maintaining discipline and motivating your athletes. During instruction, a coach should concentrate on desired objectives and reward and reinforce efforts to achieve these outcomes.

Your athletes are likely to model many of your traits and actions. Therefore, it is critical that you act as an appropriate role model and create an atmosphere in which you can positively shape the personal and social skills of your athletes. You should never lose your temper, yell at officials, or break rules to gain an unfair advantage. In essence, "actions speak louder than words" and you must "practice what you preach" if you hope to positively influence your athletes' behavior.

Substance abuse is an increasing problem in athletics to about the same degree as it is in current society. The accessibility and popularity of alcohol and other drugs highlight the need for preventive action by parents, teachers, administrators, and coaches. Sharing accurate information about drugs, increasing awareness of the pressures experienced by athletes, and teaching students to properly deal with situations where drugs are used are critical actions that a coach should perform.

Litigation/Liability

The potentially detrimental effects of athletics can extend from athletes to coaches as well. Knowledge of your legal responsibilities and rights as a coach will help you avoid lawsuits and, if practiced, protect you if litigation does occur. Appropriate insurance (medical and liability) is needed to provide for expenses and/or judgments if injury or litigation occur.

Sports Management

One of the first steps a coach should take is to identify goals and objectives for the season. Earlier in this chapter, broad goals were mentioned such as teaching physical skills, rules and strategies; challenging the cardiovascular and muscular system; and molding desirable personal, social, and psychological skills. The content of much of this USAW manual should help you in identifying objectives to meet the needs of your athletes. Next, these objectives should be organized into a plan from which practices, contests and other events can be managed efficiently.

Scheduling of facilities and transportation for practices and contests should be based on sound principles and procedures that are fair to all parties concerned. While the budget is usually allocated through negotiations with the coach, the ultimate responsibility to allocate resources within the budget falls to the coach. Therefore, it is necessary for the coach to learn as much as possible regarding budget management.

SUMMARY

The roles of a coach are to be a leader, administrator, counselor and a mentor. The sport of wrestling is positive in itself. The goals of a successful coach is to maximize the positive aspects of participation in wrestling. Coaching wrestling is a great tool for teaching young athletes life skills and create positive experiences not only in the sport but beyond. A coach needs to be aware of the influence he or she is having in the life of a young wrestler. The aforementioned principles will help to provide a foundation for you to begin your career as a successful wrestling coach.

2
Philosophy of Coaching and Goal Setting

Danny Struck, Kyle Fellure, Randy Hinderliter, Ben Stehura

QUESTIONS TO CONSIDER

- What is the one common aspect of successful coaching philosophy?
- How is a philosophy of coaching developed?
- What is in a philosophy?
- What is a goal?
- What is the difference between abstract and concrete goals?
- What are the three types of goals?
- What are the four areas of goal setting?

Your philosophy of coaching will determine your response in critical situations.

DEVELOPING A COACHING PHILOSOPHY

"A philosophy is like a mental steering mechanism. It guides you in the decisions you make. If you don't have one or if yours is faulty, you'll go nowhere or get lost trying to go somewhere."

Dan Gable, Legendary Coach

As a coach begins his/her career, one of the very first questions that must be answered is "What is my philosophy of coaching?" The development of a coaching philosophy will lay the foundation for everything you do as a coach both within and outside of your program. It must be thoroughly understood that regardless of the sport, there are numerous coaches that achieve success with entirely different methods and philosophies. However, the one similarity that all of these great coaches have, is an unshakeable belief that what *they* do to achieve their success is the best possible way to build their athletes, coaches, and program.

The development of a coaching philosophy entails many different components. Many coaches, especially in the beginning, coach in the same manner in which they were coached as competitive athletes. Many coaches model their style and philosophy after coaches they admire and respect. Still other coaches follow the steps and ideals of a mentor or head coach they worked under. All of these examples are commonplace and accepted methods of coaching. However, it is the superior coach who learns to combine many aspects of the aforementioned methods and then use and adjust them according to *his/her* strengths and weaknesses. In so doing, the formation of an individual philosophy is formed.

The fact that there are some basic principles that the best coaches center their methods around does not diminish the point that there is no "right" or "wrong" philosophy of coaching. The development of your own individual coaching philosophy will be the result of time, trial and error, mistakes, education, experience, and upbringing. The most important factor to remember and apply is to use and believe in a philosophy that works for you and fosters the success of your athletes and wrestling program.

"I would say that my philosophy in coaching is one that has developed my entire life. My philosophy probably began as a teen and my mother recalling times I would help my brothers with their sport skills. My philosophy grew in my career as a law enforcement officer in striving to make a difference. And it was my passion of working with youth wrestlers where my philosophy may have taken its last evolution. My philosophy…making positive differences in the life of kids through wrestling. In this book you will learn how wrestling teaches life skills. Wrestling is not alone as a teacher and there are tons of lessons to learn, some good, some bad. But wrestling is unique in its emphasis on teaching positive lessons."

Randy Hinderliter
Coaches Certification and
Education Director
USAW Kansas, Gold Certified Coach

WHAT IS IN A PHILOSOPHY?

The best coaches model their coaching philosophy to compliment their personalities, strengths, and overcome their weaknesses. This includes everything from the disciplinary measures they enforce to the style of wrestling their team will exhibit. A few examples of some questions you may want to ask are, "What style (takedowns, mat wrestling, counter attack) of wrestling do I feel is most successful for my athletes to perform?"; "What are my policies regarding weight loss?"; "What is my philosophy regarding athletics (winning) vs personal growth?"; "What is my position on academics as it relates to athletics?"; "What is my opinion on training wrestlers for competition?"; "What are my thoughts on winning?" These are just a few areas that would be considered a part of a coaches philosophy.

There are many different successful styles, personalities, and philosophies in coaching. The most important aspect to remember, is to develop a style and philosophy that works for you, your athletes, and the program. **You must believe in what you are doing with unwavering commitment.**

"The hardest thing to do in life is to be able to rectify a situation that's negative while it's spiraling downward."
Tom Brands, Head Coach Virginia Tech

What Are Goals?

Goals are measuring sticks of success. They can be either abstract or concrete. An abstract goal is not easily defined or measured. It is often a feeling or an overriding principle which may not be tangible. Some examples would include the desire to improve every day, work harder today than I did yesterday, develop team unity, be a person of good character. These are the goals that every coach and athlete at every level can achieve and obtain. These are the goals you are always striving towards and is what defines the great sport of wrestling. Concrete goals are easily defined and can be easily measured by a simple yes or

---

SIDEBAR: Setting Goals as a Team
Kyle Fellure

As a coach I am always looking for new ways to motivate my team. I feel that setting short term goals that my wrestlers can see and achieve, help them stay motivated. I use a team goal sheet for each competition we have throughout the season. We go over it on our Monday team meeting so the wrestlers can have something to work toward in practice during the week. After the competition I give them the evaluation of the goals we either achieved or failed. I can see them working harder during the week and also at the site of competition to accomplish the team goals. Following is an example of a goal sheet for an open tournament at the beginning of our season

Open Goals

	Win	Tie	Lose	
Win	XXXXXXX			55–50
No Pins			XXXXX	
4 Placers	XXXXXXX			10 placers
Champ			XXXXX	1 2nd place
Over Time			XXXXX	
Stalling	XXXXXX			
Unsportman Like		XXXXXXX		
Near Fall	XXXXXX			
MVP _____				
Practice _____				

We have certain categories we looked to improve on from the same tournament last year. First, we want to win. I look to see if we won more matches than we lost as a team. For this particular meet we went 55-50. As any coach I hate getting pinned. Although a very lofty goal I don't want to give up any pins. We gave up a few so we lost that column. Last year at this tournament we had only 4 placers. This year we had ten. A great improvement from last year. The team was very excited to accomplish this goal. We didn't have a champ last year as we did not this year. We did have a freshman in the finals. Hopefully next year! Something we are always saying in practice is to win every overtime match. We lost only two out of 7. We still lost though. Something I was very proud of was not giving up a stalling point, we were always aggressive and always looking to score. When we are at a competition we are representing the University of Indianapolis and want to conduct ourselves in a respectable manner. We had one unsportsmanlike conduct call. Sometimes guys get frustrated and things happen but I always want my wrestlers to play by the rules. One thing we worked on a lot in practice this particular week was being able to turn while we are on top. We did an excellent job and recorded more near fall counts than we gave up. I also like to recognize guys who worked hard and did well. I name an MVP for the tournament and a guy who worked hard in practice but didn't necessarily do well in the tournament. Overall it was a good weekend, but still a lot of room for improvement. As we went over this sheet for the open the team felt good about what they accomplished and were motivated to accomplish every goal for the next competition.

(Kyle Fellure, Coach, University of Indianapolis)

---

no question. These goals could encompass many different areas from individual goals, to team and program goals. Some concrete goals would be: Did your athlete get the first takedown? Did the athlete or team win a state championship? Did the athlete make it to the second period of wrestling? Some program goals would be: Did we increase booster club membership? Did we increase athlete participation? Was our retention rate improved? Has attendance at meets and tournaments gone up? Has booster club revenue increased?

GOAL SETTING

Goals should be specific, challenging, realistic and attainable. They can begin with short term goals that lead to long term objectives. Goals should always be stated in terms of controlled behaviors, rather than uncontrollable outcomes, and they should always be positive in nature. When setting goals it is important to keep in mind the age and skill level of the athletes you are working with. Goals can be grouped into three types: short, medium and long term goals. There are four specific areas for goal setting: Athlete, Team, Coaching, and Program goals. Goal setting requires commitment on the part of the coach as well as the athletes, but its rewards are well worth the effort.

A. Short Term Goals

Short term goals cannot be defined by a certain time table. These are the first steps or building blocks to meet the long term objective. Short term goals allow athletes to experience immediate success and helps them stay motivated. Short term goals help athletes and coaches stay focused on the long term objective. Short term goals are constantly achieved, assessed and reset.

B. Intermediate Goals

Intermediate goals are a benchmark for your progress up the ladder of completing your long term goals. These goals are important for helping you asses your progress toward the long term objective. They also help you set new short term goals.

C. Long Term Goals

Long term goals are your ultimate objectives, your target that you shoot for. They are attainable but require maximum effort, and long term dedication.

1. Athlete Goals

As a coach, you are responsible for the development of your athletes in many areas. Regardless of whether it is athletically, academically, or socially, you must set the goals for your wrestlers to work towards and standards by which they must adhere. Though wrestling is an individual sport, it is your leadership that will determine the goals and success that your wrestlers will set for themselves. The best way in which to have both you and your athlete understand each other and have some agreement in objectives, is to discuss this with them one on-one in private. It is important that as the head of your team you know the goals of your athletes, and in turn they know your expectations of them. This process will enable both of you to work together, not in conflict, towards the accomplishment of the understood goals.

Examples of Effective Goal Setting

Short	Medium	Long
Learn a double leg takedown	Execute a double leg takedown in practice	Score a double leg takedown in competition
Wrestle entire first period	Wrestle an entire match	Win a match
Get first takedown in match	Win the match	Place at the tournament
Earn varsity spot	Qualify for nationals	Become an All-American
Win a state title	Win a national title	Win an Olympic title

SIDEBAR: Don't Screw Up. This is the Big Leagues

Ted Witulski

For parents and coaches their competitive zeal sometimes leads kids to the wrong conclusion. No doubt many of us have seen someone at a youth wrestling tournament that has lost a healthy perspective on winning and losing.

Of course, wrestling is not alone in this struggle to keep sanity in the midst of competition. When it comes right down to it, our society very often rewards the winners and the rest are just losers, even if it's a hard fought second place finish.

Stand at the side of any mat at a youth tournament and the energy and excitement surrounds you. Coaches, parents, moms and dads are there and they want the win. It is not just a selfish desire. The ones there to cheer on their wrestlers want their kids to win because they no losing is tough, and they certainly don't want their kids to have to learn the tough lessons in losing.

With that desire for victory, the mature adult can also quickly lose perspective. "It's go-time." "Don't give him anything." "Don't screw up. This is the big leagues."

We want our kids to love winning, but as the people that influence the next generation of wrestlers we need to get the kids to love the sport of wrestling. Across the country and even the continent parental sportsmanship has come under fire.

A few short years ago, one hockey parent beat the team's coach to death.

In the northeast some soccer leagues have gone to the drastic step of instituting "silent sidelines"—in other words if a parent so much as cheers for their own team giving a heartfelt "that-a-boy" to their own kid they are escorted to the parking lot and told to leave.

Thankfully, wrestling hasn't had to institute drastic steps to maintain decorum. When things go awry usually some coaching of the coaches or parents to remind them of the important positive role that they need to fulfill gets everyone back on the right track.

Recently, the Canadian Hockey Association has turned heads with a new series of public service announcement in the hockey-crazed country. These radio, print, and TV announcement turn the ordinary parent-youth athlete relationship on its head.

One announcement shows a young child screaming through a megaphone as his father attempts to sink an important putt, another shows a father on the clock as he takes care of business in the bathroom, son watching with stop-watch in hand.

Obviously, the Canadians needed to return to a healthy perspective on winning and losing. Something that we all need to routinely do is revisit why we love the sport of wrestling.

Young wrestlers are highly motivated to learn the sport and succeed; negative coaching will eventually turn them off to the competitive atmosphere. Wrestling is fun to kids. They'll scrap on a patch of grass with no referees if given the chance. The pressure and negativity can chase them away from a positive life-altering experience.

Young wrestlers want to make their parents and coaches proud. Kids aim to please but sometimes things, like winning, are out of their control. Make sure they know you are proud of them.

Young wrestlers often enjoy the tournaments and competitions not just for the matches that they wrestle but for the time spent with friends, coaches, and parents. They see a bigger picture other than just their wins and losses.

Young wrestlers maintain realistic expectations. They're in the mix of it all, sometimes they see that their abilities aren't where they need to be yet to get that gold medal. From there it has to be the youth's choice on just exactly what he/she is willing to do to succeed.

Young wrestlers in losses know when they've given their best. As parents and coaches we need to reward the effort, not just the outcome.

Young wrestlers love the feeling of learning the technique. Very often in matches there is the one shining moment when the young wrestler hits a move that will surprise even his coaches. Those gems are times when parents and coaches should recognize the performance and not just the outcome.

We love the sport of wrestling for the good that it teaches young people. When coaching and cheering is done in a positive and productive manner young people are more likely to reap those benefits because they will stay with the sport. It is a tough battle to maintain that good balance, because we care deeply about our wrestlers—our sons and daughters. We want them to achieve, and sometimes our zeal can get in the way of the big picture. In those times take a deep breath, and remember why we led them to the sport of wrestling in the first place.

SIDEBAR: Coaching Coaches ... Ten Things To Think About

By Chuck Wielgus, Executive Director of USA Swimming

I have spent the past thirty years working in the sports business. I have coached basketball, lacrosse, soccer and swimming ... and I have had the opportunity to work with many other sports, including baseball, canoe/kayak, golf, running, snowboarding, tennis, triathlon and volleyball. I have observed coaches at all levels; young coaches and experienced coaches, lazy coaches and dedicated coaches, troubled coaches and wise coaches. Like every other profession, the ranks of coaches offer a full spectrum of personalities and styles. Recently, I was asked to offer some advice to a group of young coaches. For better or worse, here were my ten tips.

1. BE SERIOUS
Serious people are taken seriously. Be a thinker, a doer, and a leader. Take things seriously and treat all others with respect. This doesn't mean you shouldn't show a lighter side of yourself, but don't be silly. Silly people aren't taken seriously.

2. BUILD YOUR REPUTATION ON THE FOUNDATION OF ETHICAL BEHAVIOR
The absolute worst part of my job is being the recipient of Code of Conduct complaints against coaches who have been charged with abusing their position of authority and trust with young athletes. Coaches who cross the line have their reputation tainted forever. You can never undo a conviction for sexual misconduct or financial improprieties. Your reputation is the most important part of your resume ... protect it for life.

3. TAKE A BROAD VIEW OF YOUR ROLE AS A COACH
I've heard many coaches say, "I just want to coach" implying that they don't want to be bothered with all the "other" things that interfere with their on-deck duties. This is a narrow and naïve view. Mature, professional coaches understand that while they are a specialist in the particulars of their chosen sport, they must also be a knowledgeable generalist as a community relations ambassador, financial planner, fund raiser, guidance counselor, human resources coordinator, media relations specialist, politician, parent advisor, salesperson and strategic planner. Ignoring these other roles will limit your professional growth.

4. BE COGNIZANT OF THE OVERALL EXPERIENCES OF YOUR ATHLETES
When you're working with young athletes, be aware that there are many things that impact their life. Be interested in their world and try to recognize the other things that are impacting the way they think and feel. Engage them in ways that broaden not only their physical skills, but challenge their mental participation. As a coach, you are going to have an enormous impact on a young athlete's life, so think carefully about how you can foster an environment that will give each athlete the opportunity to grow as both an athlete and a person.

5. BE POLITICALLY AWARE, BUT POLITICALLY CAUTIOUS
In many ways, navigating your way through life is very much about political awareness. Keep your antenna up and be cognizant of the issues and relationships that can impact your ability to do your job. And while it's very important to be politically aware, it's equally important to be cautious about getting politically involved. Pick your issues and your battles carefully. Keep yourself and others focused on philosophies and principles, as opposed to personalities and people.

6. GET INVOLVED IN THE COMMUNITY
If you're an isolationist, then you'll be isolated ... get involved! Cultivate friends and supporters in your community. As a coach, you are absolutely helping to improve the quality of life for young people in your community. Find ways to share the successes of your athletes with local business and civic leaders, and then find ways to give these same leaders an opportunity to contribute to your program. If others understand that you are doing things to improve the quality of life for others, they will naturally want to help you and your program ... but, you have to go find them and you have to ask for their help!

7. FIND A MENTOR

We all need mentors … people we can look to for guidance and inspiration. It has been said that the best way to be a good conversationalist is to ask somebody else to talk about him or herself. Identify the people you admire most and then seek them out. Call up an older coach and offer to buy them breakfast in exchange for the opportunity to ask them some questions and to talk about different teaching techniques. This is such an easy and effective way to expand your personal horizon, improve your knowledge and develop new relationships. You'll be surprised how receptive others will be, but you have to initiate the invitation … so just do it!

8. BE A LIFELONG LEARNER

The day you stop learning is the day you start treading water … and that's when others will pass you by. Perhaps the most common characteristic I've seen in all our top coaches is that they never cease to stop looking for ways to add to their base of knowledge. They are always looking for that next little nugget of information that they can use to help them improve the way they can help their athletes. Lifelong learners are always growing and evolving.

9. BE PROFESSIONAL

Be proud of being a coach. How you present yourself to others will determine how others will view you. If you're sloppy in dress, manner and speech that's how most people will perceive you. On the other hand, you can't expect to compensate for a lack of competence and substance simply by looking sharp and talking smooth. Be yourself and be proud of what you do for a living … and then consistently present yourself to others with those thoughts in mind.

10. HAVE FUN

The #1 reason kids quit sports is because it no longer is fun. You can be fun without being silly. Fun and interesting people are magnets; they attract others and keep the big ball of life rolling along. If you're the kind of person who really loves what you do, then share that love with others. As the old saying goes, "life's too short" so make the most of it for yourself, your family and the athletes with whom you work.

Thanks for reading … and thanks for being a coach!

Here are some examples of athlete goals:

- Get the first takedown
- Not get pinned the entire season
- Earn a varsity spot
- Place in 5 tournaments
- Win a state championship

2. Team Goals

The dynamics of a group working together towards a unified goal creates a powerful effect. With a team of athletes it is important to share your goals with each and every member. The effort and focus of your third and fourth string wrestlers is just as important as that of your starters to create unity of vision and purpose. Without this combined effort of all involved, you will greatly diminish the possibility of achieving your goals.

Here are some examples of team goals:

- No stalling calls
- No forfeits
- Team GPA 3.0 or better
- Attend all practices
- Never be late to a practice
- Built team unity

3. Coaching Goals

Just as your athletes and team must set goals, you must also hold yourself accountable for the achievement of your goals. Coaches, at times, can get an athlete to do things that even parents can't. You are in a position to have tremendous influence, both positive and negative. Don't miss this opportunity by holding yourself to a standard lower than that of what you are asking of your team. As a coach, your

4. Program Goals

Program goals encompass the total development of your organization. Your program could include the youth program, middle school program, high school program, charter USA Wrestling 501C-3 club, booster club, alumni supporters, etc. Your program is like a family. In order to meet the various needs of a program delegation and collaboration are paramount. The program and everyone involved at all levels need to work together for the betterment of the wrestlers.

Here are some examples of program goals:

- Improve retention rates of wrestlers
- Increase booster club revenue
- Gain more positive media exposure
- Establish a board of directors for your club
- Supply all wrestlers with appropriate facilities and equipment

SUMMARY

The development of a solid coaching philosophy is a task that takes years, experience, modeling, education, and trial and error. There are many different coaching philosophies that can produce positive results. Remember, you must believe in what you are doing with unwaivering commitment.. However, there are some basic principles of coaching that, when applied correctly, will greatly enhance your chances for success and the realization of your goals. The aforementioned principles will help to provide a foundation for you to begin your career as a successful wrestling coach. It is important that your beliefs, coaching philosophy, and your goals coincide so that your vision is clear and complete.

"In order to be an effective coach I have to earn the trust of an athlete."
" When an athlete trusts us, they will do virtually anything for us."
Ray Brinzer, Angry Fish Wrestling Club

"To achieve victory, your goals must be set for victory."

athletes will emulate and copy what they see you do more than any other single person in their athletic sphere of influence. It is for that reason that you must set the example for what you expect them to do. When they see you *doing* what you have told them to do, your guidance and knowledge will carry much more authority, and in return your athletes will follow your instructions and the desired effect will be accomplished.

Here are some examples of coaching goals:

- Be a good role model
- Attend 5 techniques clinics
- Become a USA Wrestling gold level coach
- Coach a world team
  BE A POSITIVE INFLUENCE

3
Effective Teaching and Risk Management

Ted Witulski

QUESTIONS TO CONSIDER

- What should the coach know in order to be an effective teacher?
- What guidelines should the coach follow when teaching young athletes?
- What are the characteristics of a good practice?
- Identify qualities of a "good" drill.
- What should the coach know in order to conduct safe practices and matches?
- Identify the seven components of risk management that are required of all wrestling coaches.

Properly training and teaching athletes is a learned process of coaching.

19

INTRODUCTION

The modern day wrestling coach is called on to fill many roles, but none is more important than that of being a good teacher. In fact, if the coach is not a good teacher, all of the other roles will be diminished, too. The coach's effectiveness as a counselor, substitute parent, role model, friend, and mentor is increased if the coach is a good teacher.

Good teaching is the foundation for successful coaching.

EFFECTIVE TEACHING GUIDELINES

There are many ways in which you, as a coach, can impart information to young athletes. There are also many styles or methods that have been shown to be effective. Despite the variety of styles that coaches use, certain rules or guidelines are common to all good instruction.

To be an effective teacher a coach must:

- Clearly communicate what is to be learned
- Be able to evaluate the athletes' abilities
- Use a coaching style that fits the needs of young athletes
- Be consistent and systematic in teaching young athletes
- Be able to alter practice plans and match strategies on the basis of how effectively objectives are being met.

In the following section each of these guidelines will be discussed in more detail.

Communicate Clearly

The results that a coach expects young wrestlers to obtain can be placed into three categories:

Physical: pertaining to the development of the seven basic skills, as well as the physical conditioning that permits wrestlers to do these tasks without undue fatigue.

Mental: relating to the strategies, rules and responsibilities of the young athlete as a competitor and team member.

Social: referring to the personal characteristics of wrestlers, such as loyalty to a common cause, supporting team members, respecting opponents, official and spectators, listening to the coach's instructions, and conducting oneself as a responsible citizen.

You, as a coach, are responsible for identifying precisely what is to be learned by the athletes within each of the previously identified categories. **Athletes will not learn desirable skills, values, and attitudes simply by exposure** or by having adults wish that certain fundamental laws of good citizenship will be acquired. Learning requires instruction, practice under realistic situations, corrective action and then more practice. This cycle should be repeated until the desired outcome is attained. For this reason, clearly stated objectives by you as the coach are essential prior to the time when you initiate any instruction. Failure to define your objectives will lead to chaos in your instruction.

Taking Advantage of the Teachable Moment

Though we coach wrestling because of the inherent excitement of the sport, there is also the ever-present opportunity to reveal the deeper meaning to young athletes. Off the mat, in the time where coaches and athletes are in social settings a coach can take advantage of situations at hand that will make an impact on the young athletes' lives.

Dr. Steven Carr Reuben author of Children of Character offered these six points about seeking out the teachable moment.

1. Recognize that your athletes often learn moral lessons unconsciously, in casual moments.
2. Be aware of situations that represent moral choices.
3. Talk with your athletes about the ethical challenges represented in everyday situations, the media and popular culture.
4. Praise your athletes for their ethical choices.
5. Point out ethical behavior in others.
6. Let your athletes see your own thought processes regarding ethical decisions.

A coach does not have to be heavy handed in trying to strengthen the athletes' character; rather, small individual conversations can go a long way in developing the social skills of athletes while eliminating undesirable behavior.

For example, a coach after witnessing one of his athletes "picking on" another younger wrestler can quietly pull the offending athlete aside, choosing to start a conversation about the difficulty of developing a wrestling program.

The coach can lead the conversation about the importance in keeping as many kids out for wrestling as possible to build the best team possible. The teachable moment was there because of the actions of the individual, and without a hard-nosed authoritarian lecture the coach could show the athlete that better social skills will help reach that desired goal. Later, the coach may catch the athlete treating a teammate with respect, using that as a teachable moment to praise the athlete will reinforce that desired behavior.

The wrestling community often takes pride in the life-lessons that the sport teaches young people. Taking advantage of teachable moments can be an excellent way for a coach to assure that these character building lessons are learned.

Evaluation of Athletes' Abilities

The coaches should be able to assess the abilities of all wrestlers **prior to** determining the instructional objectives for the year. The accurate assessment of wrestler's abilities determines a coach's instructional strategies, as well as the expectations and goals that can be set for the season.

Assessment should include each athlete's status in the areas of physical, mental, and social skills. For example, a wrestler with excellent physical skills, but who has a bad attitude, could cause major disruptions on the team if the coach does not address the deficiencies in the wrestler's social skills. Conversely, wrestlers who have excellent social and mental skills will not be able to realize their potential as competitors if they are unable to translate these abilities because of underdeveloped physical skills.

The assessment of athletes' abilities is essential to a good beginning in the wrestling season, but assessment by the coach must also occur practice-by-practice, throughout the season. In fact, accurate assessment of wrestler's needs is one of the most essential components of good teaching. All good coaches have the ability to assess a situation and then take corrective action during the teachable moment when instruction has the greatest chance of being effective.

Assessing Needs and Taking Corrective Action

Physical Skills

Coaches can learn much about their wrestlers' physical skills by observing them in drills and matches. The assessment of physical skills depends on:

- knowing the correct way to perform a skill
- knowing the sequence of actions that result in the correct performance of the skill
- being able to detect your wrestlers' correct and incorrect actions
- being able to tell your wrestlers how to correct their faulty performance

Once again, the judgment of the coach is the key to improving your athlete's performance. If you are inexperienced in the analysis of skills there are many valuable resources available to help you. The National Coaches Education Program has a variety of videos available contact the National Office to purchase these. The study of advanced technique by the coach will help reveal ways to improve any team.

There is no substitute for experience when you attempt to identify errors and correct the physical techniques of your wrestlers. However, inexperienced coaches have learned that the process of observing and correcting mistakes can be enhanced by the following guidelines:

- choose a vantage point so that you can see the entire skill being performed.
- observe the entire skill before dissecting it into its parts; then have the wrestler attempt to correct only the one part or seg-

SIDEBAR: You have three seconds

Ted Witulski

Times have changed. When TV was first introduced to the American culture the popular sit-com at its inception was the Honeymooners. The Honeymooners, in retrospect, is far removed from today's TV programming. "Pow right in the kisser", the often delivered line was about the only eye popping excitement from the show. Especially when viewers consider that each of the half-hour Honeymooner shows was filmed with one stationary camera.

Then along came Gunsmoke, it was revolutionary because it used multiple cameras. Of course the multiple camera angles, of between three to the late episodes of seven, is hardly revolutionary anymore. Most football games on television have more cameras covering a single play. From the quarterback's reception of the snap from center, to the one-on-one battle between the receiver and the d-back, every aspect of a single play is covered quickly.

Have you ever watched a child watch MTV? Eyes barely open, bodies slouched, even when they are interested in the show, they appear disinterested. MTV long removed from the days of the Honeymooners has taken TV to a whole new level. Forty years ago teenagers watched the Honeymooners and were satisfied with the lone camera angle. In today's fast paced society MTV changes the camera angle on average at least once every three seconds.

The blur of images and sounds is what the coach is up against when organizing a two-hour practice after a long day of school for the students. Every practice is another challenge to sharpen these athletes mental edge and draw them deeply into the sport.

Unfortunately, to reach those athletes, it seems you only got about three-seconds.

Don't just throw your arms up in disgust. Each coach needs to recognize the necessity of a well organized and ever changing practice routine to keep wrestlers attention. The infectious enthusiasm of the start of the new season will eventually dissipate. A practice that always follows the same routine will eventually become monotonous. Always look to make the greatest impact on wrestlers at each practice.

There are many ways the coaches can assure that the impact that they want to have on their team remains strong. USA Wrestling's National Coaches Education Program encourages coaches to seek out and use a variety of methods in obtaining the attention of its athletes during a season of practices.

Warm-ups often become a routine that varies little throughout the season. The team warm-up sets the tone for the practice. If wrestlers only go through the motions then the risk is that a sub-par warm-up will lead to a disappointing and emotionless practice.

A practice routine shouldn't just be a tired and slow jog in a circle. There are literally hundreds of ways wrestlers can warm-up to start a practice. Encourage the team leaders to take charge in pacing wrestlers through different beginnings of practices. Possibilities might include a warm-up based on crawling drills and tumbling drills. A warm-up for another day might include hopping and jumping drills. A strength building warm-up using buddy carries is another way to get the juices flowing. Coaches that setup a practice with a fun and varied warm-up will capture the team's attention with greater ease.

Remembering that the time coaches have to make an impression on the wrestling team is exceedingly short and unfortunately dictated by a declining attention span. Coaches should front-load the technique that needs to be emphasized. When wrestlers need to learn technique from a coach, often the coach relies on a lecture model that is commonly used in the classroom setting. The danger inherent in this is that kids have gone through a day of classes that similarly have used this format.

When a coach needs to lecture his team on the specifics of technique it is strongly suggested that the coach use visual-aides, to help "entertain" the team by holding their attention longer. Coaches will often demonstrate the technique on a wrestler, but other visual-aides such as video of a team member in a match using the technique can help hold the team's attention. Further the use of a dry erase board gives the wrestlers another way to focus on the technique at hand.

To heighten the impact of the technical demonstration coaches can write a precise phrase on the chalkboard to serve as a backdrop. If the team is learning the importance of moving off the bottom, a coach might write, "COIL UP—YOU'RE A SPRING". Keep in mind that these wrestlers are the same kids that average better than five hours of television watching a day. It is imperative for coaches to consistently work to capture and hold their attention in practice.

Another common mistake made by coaches is to try to teach too much in that short fifteen to twenty minutes where the wrestlers are tuned in. Don't try to cover a concept of neutral wrestling and then switch to a reversal technique. If it is necessary to teach both techniques in the same practice separate the technical lectures at different points in the practice. Coaches might even need to go as far as teaching the bottom technique in a different area of the wrestling room as an unconscious way of breaking from the previous technique lecture.

Many study shows that adult learners can keep tuned in at best for 15 to 20 minutes at the start of a class or in this case a practice. During a two-hour practice, coaches should accept and adjust to the fact that their wrestlers attention span will have dropped to, less than three to five minutes by the end of practice.

When a coach truly considers the message in attention span, late practice live wrestling for extended times such as thirty minutes will have less meaning. Especially late in a practice, wrestlers will need to constantly refocus on the objective of a drill. Having athletes wrestle live for a long duration, may serve as a conditioning element, but it will do little to provide the learning needed to improve technique.

The art of coaching wrestling at times will have to bend to the science of today's society. Attention spans for youth are increasingly short. To help a coach reach the members of his team, he must be prepared to have variety throughout the season. Additionally, coaches should think about how they can effectively instruct their athletes during practices. As we try to sharpen the skills of athletes, we are increasingly on the clock to capture their interest. Coaches no longer plan practices for the generation that watched the Honeymooners; instead, the youth of today grew up on the ever-changing images on MTV. Work hard and hold the wrestler's attention. It's a tough job. Remember you got about three seconds.

ment that is most important to success. When this segment has been corrected, then proceed to the next most important segment.
- have the wrestler practice the essential component until the correct motor pattern has been achieved.
- be ready to encourage the wrestler while the new pattern is being learned; remember that the speed and total coordination with which the old pattern was performed will be reduced while the wrestler is learning the adjustments.

Assessing the physical conditioning of athletes in wrestling does not require sophisticated laboratory equipment. As a coach you will be able to determine which wrestlers have the stamina to consistently perform throughout an entire match or those who cannot finish moves due to lack of strength and power. Although improved techniques will assist wrestlers who are in position to perform their skills, success in the sport of wrestling depends on an athlete's ability to maintain good position and execute correct technique throughout

the duration of a match, even when fatigued. Remember that skillful techniques are not a substitute for physical conditioning. However, in wrestling, physical conditioning is most effectively achieved by having the athletes practice the real-match situations and carefully selecting drills in your practices.

Assessing Mental Needs

Young wrestlers will learn the rules and strategies of wrestling most effectively by having you, the coach, anticipate what is to occur during matches and then ensuring that you construct similar situations in your practices. The "sixth sense" that some young wrestlers possess comes from having been in similar situations before, then recognizing the options available to them and choosing the correct course of action under the circumstances. Only if young wrestlers have experienced an identical situation in previous matches and practices can you expect them to make the correct decision. Therefore, your teaching in practices must be based on the situations that you expect them to encounter in matches. How they resolve these dilemmas will be directly related to their understanding of similar situations in practice and matches.

Assessing Social Needs

The interaction among your wrestlers will provide you with an indication of their social needs. Often, the most skillful wrestlers are also the most popular. Their social needs are likely to be met by the recognition that they receive from teammates, parents, and fans because of their wrestling abilities. The coach should ensure that the recognition for skill and ability should not overshadow the need to acquire the social skills of good citizenship. Too often skillful wrestlers are treated as though the rules of the team and society do not apply to them, only to find that they are societal misfits when their sports skills no longer shield them from the application of equal treatment.

Coaches should be particularly alert to the special problems of social development that are often present in immature wrestlers whose skill level is consistently below the average of his/her team and age level group. These underdeveloped wrestlers face the constant challenge of being unable to compete on an equal basis in the drills, and perhaps equally as important, they are frequently excluded from the camaraderie that develops within a team.

It is often a difficult situation for a coach to interject himself into. Many times there are kids that seem to be the outcast of the team. Their social skills are negligible and they seem to crave even the negative attention that leads to the other more popular kids picking on them. This challenge can be difficult to overcome, but coaches and athletes must remember the many important life lessons that participants gain from being a part of a wrestling team. It is not uncommon for that social outcast that is on the receiving end of jokes and petty torments actually **needs the sport of wrestling more than the sport probably needs him.** A coach of character will recognize this and do whatever he can to get the team members to recognize this so that the young athlete of questionable social skills can feel that he is part of something bigger—being a valued part of a team.

The coach is the essential promoter of social development within a team and is the one who must recognize the contributions of the immature, underdeveloped wrestlers by praising their successes and placing them in situations where they are likely to succeed. When wrestlers recognize that the coach values the contributions of all team members, then the leaders of the team are also more likely to accept those whose contributions to team goals are not consistently evident.

GUIDELINES TO GOOD TEACHING

Although there are many ways to instruct young wrestlers, the inexperienced coach will find the following sequence easy to use and effective in teaching and refining skills. As you begin your instruction, it is best to remember that young wrestlers learn best by participating. They do not learn well by sitting and listening to coaches' lecture about topics that too often seem abstract, but which adults think are concrete. **A good rule may be, "When I speak, I want you to stop what you're doing and listen."** Do not violate your own rule by continuing to talk when wrestlers are not paying attention.

Prior to your instruction:

- be sure you have the attention of all wrestlers
- tell them precisely what you want them to learn; do this in one-minute or less, preferably with a physical demonstration of the skill
- have wrestlers practice the skill while you observe them and provide feedback
- have wrestlers come back to a group setting and discuss the adjustments that are needed for improvement
- place the wrestlers into groups by size and ability; continue to practice and provide feedback
- repeat the last two steps as frequently as needed until the desired level of competence is achieved.

The following ten steps to good teaching have been shown to be effective in a variety of settings, including the teaching of young athletes.

1. Be Realistic About Your Wrestlers' Abilities

Wrestlers will respond to realistic and challenging expectations. Conversely, expectations that are beyond their achievement will decrease the motivation of even the most skillful wrestlers. Set short term goals on an individual basis and adjust them when they are achieved. Wrestlers tend to achieve according to their coaches' expectations if the expectations are realistic.

As a coach you should expect to significantly improve the skills, knowledge of rules and strategies and attitudes of each of your wrestlers during the course of the season. Make a commitment to help each of the wrestlers realize these goals.

2. Structure Your Instruction

Your wrestlers' progress will be directly linked to how clearly you communicate and teach toward your intended outcomes. This means that every practice must have well defined objectives and a systematic plan of instruction. The critical steps to a structured lesson are:

- select the essential skills, rules, and strategies from the many options available
- clearly identify elements of acceptable performance for each skill you include in practice
- organize and conduct your practices to maximize the opportunity your wrestlers have to acquire the skill(s) by using the effective teaching techniques contained in this chapter.

3. Establish an Orderly Environment

The achievement of objectives by coaches is directly related to the learning that takes place in a safe, orderly, and business-like environment, with clear expectations of what is to be accomplished at each practice. Wrestlers must be held accountable for being on time and coming to the practice ready to learn. Young wrestlers do not learn effectively in long, boring practices that involve drills that do not relate to their understanding of the sport of wrestling. Keep your practices organized, personalized, and pertinent to the needs of your team.

4. Maintain Consistent Discipline

You will find that keeping control of your team is much easier than regaining control once problems with misbehavior have disrupted your authority. Thus, your role is much easier if you can prevent the types of misbehavior that arise when coaches do not anticipate and avoid problems with discipline.

Preventing Misbehavior

Although threats and lectures may prevent misbehavior in the short-term, they create a hostile and negative atmosphere and, typically, their effectiveness is short-lived. Moreover, this type of relationship between a coach and team members does not promote learning the sport of wrestling nor does it motivate the wrestlers to accept the coach's instructions.

Sound discipline involves two steps that must be in place before misbehavior occurs. They are:

A. Defining how wrestlers are to behave and identifying misbehavior that will not be tolerated.
B. Identifying the consequences for individuals who do not behave according to the rules.

Preteen. and teenage athletes want clearly defined limits and structure for how they should behave. This can be accomplished without showing anger, lecturing the wrestlers, or threatening them. As the coach, it is your responsibility to have a systematic plan for maintaining discipline before your season gets underway. Coaches who have taken the time to establish rules of conduct will be in a position to react in a reasonable and fair manner when team members misbehave.

Defining Team Rules

The first step in developing a plan to maintain discipline is to identify what you consider to be desirable and undesirable conduct by your wrestlers. This list can then be used to establish relevant team rules. A list of potential items to consider when identifying team rules is included in Table 3-1.

Enforcement of Rules

Not only are rules needed to maintain discipline, but enforcement of those rules must be carried out so that reoccurrences are prevented. Rules are enforced through rewards and penalties. Wrestlers are rewarded when they abide by the rules and penalized when they break the rules. The next step, therefore, in developing a plan to maintain discipline is to determine the rewards and penalties for each rule. Your wrestlers can be asked for suggestions at this point because they will receive the benefits or consequences of the decisions.

When determining rewards and penalties for rules, the most effective approach is to use rewards that are meaningful to your wrestlers and appropriate to the situation. Withdrawal of rewards should be used for misconduct. A list of potential rewards and penalties that can be used in wrestling is cited in Table 3-2.

The best way to motivate wrestlers to behave in an acceptable manner is to reward them for good behavior.

Remember that penalties are only effective when they are meaningful to the wrestlers. Typically, the types of penalties that are used for rule violations are ineffective because they are not important to the wrestlers. Generally, they do not leave room for positive interactions

Table 3-1. Items to consider when defining rules for your team.

Examples of Desirable and Undesirable Conduct in Wrestling	
Desirable Conduct	**Undesirable Conduct**
Attending to your instructions	Talking while you are trying to give instructions
Full concentration on drills	Inattentive behavior during drills
Treating opponents with respect	Fighting with opponents or using abusive language
Giving positive encouragement to teammates	Making negative comments about teammates
Avoiding illegal moves	Intentionally trying to hurt someone with use of an illegal move
Being prompt to practices and matches	Being late or absent from practices and matches
Helping to pick up equipment after practices	Leaving equipment out for others to pick up
Bringing all your equipment to practices	Forgetting to bring a part of your equipment or uniform to matches and practices

Table 3-2. Example of rewards and penalties.

Examples of Rewards and Penalties That Can Be Used in Wrestling	
Rewards	**Penalties**
Selected for varsity	Being taken out of the lineup
Elected Team Captain	Not being allowed to compete
Leading an exercise or activity	Assessing janitorial duties: cleaning mats, cleaning locker room, etc.
Praise from you	Dismissed for
Decals	1. next practice
Medals	2. next week
	3. rest of season

between you and your wrestlers. Examples of ineffective penalties include showing anger, embarrassing wrestlers by lecturing them in the presence of team members or adults, shouting at wrestlers, or assigning a physical activity (extra sit-ups, extra pushups). Assigning a physical activity for certain misbehavior may develop a negative attitude toward that activity. Avoid using physical activity as a form of punishment; the benefits of wrestling, such as learning skills and gaining cardiovascular fitness, are gained through activity.

Adolescents should not associate activity with punishment.

Although threats, lectures and/or yelling may deter misbehavior in the short term, the negative atmosphere that results reduces long term coaching effectiveness. A more positive approach to handling misbehavior is to prevent it by establishing, with wrestler input, clear team rules. Use fair and consistent enforcement of the rules, primarily through rewarding correct behavior, rather than penalizing unacceptable behavior.

5. Group Your Wrestlers According to Ability

Your wrestling team will most likely have wrestlers at various levels of ability. For effective learning the wrestlers at times need to be divided into smaller groups. The critical consideration for grouping wrestlers effectively is to have them practicing at a level that is needed to advance their wrestling ability.
The general guidelines to effectively group wrestlers are:

● when a new skill, rule, or strategy is being taught that all your athletes need to know, use a single group instructional setting
● as you identify differences in ability, place wrestlers of similar ability, maturity and size in smaller groups
● when a skill, rule, or strategy is being practiced where individual athletes are at several levels of ability (initial, intermediate, or advanced), establish learning stations that focus on specific outcomes to meet these needs.

Organize the groups so that there is a systematic order in which wrestlers take turns. Each group must know precisely what is to be learned. Supervise each group by rotating and spending short periods of time with each. Avoid the temptation of spending all of the instructional time with one group. If any group is favored during small group instruction, it should be those wrestlers who are the least skillful because they are also the ones who are least able to diagnose and correct their own errors.

6. Maximize Your Wrestlers' On-Task Time

Progress in skill development is directly related to the amount of time that wrestlers spend practicing these skills in match-like situations. Practices provide the opportunity to attempt a specific skill repeatedly under guided instruction. Coaches should anticipate match situations and then conduct their practices to simulate match situations, while still being able to adjust the environment to meet the developmental levels of the various athletes. **Practices are the most effective learning environment for perfecting physical and mental skills.** In order to ensure that practices are conducted wisely you should consider the following timesaving techniques.

● Reduce the number of athletes who are waiting by using smaller groups in drills.
● Provide sufficient equipment so that wrestlers do not have to wait for their turn to use it.
● Schedule your drills so that one leads into the next without major setup time.
● Clearly outline and/or diagram each portion of practice and communicate as much of that information as possible before implementing it on the mat.
● Delegate assistants (coaching staff and volunteers) to help you with instructional stations under your supervision.

7. Maximize the Wrestlers' Success Rate

Successfully achieving a desired outcome and the motivation to continue to refine the desired outcome are highly related. Therefore, coaches must structure their practices so that

SIDEBAR: Coaching Youth Wrestling
Age range: Kindergarten through 4th grade

Ted Witulski

Recommended Objective: minimize the risk of injury and exclusion and maximize the benefits of participation by offering an active and enjoyable practice setting

Setting: a well-supervised high school wrestling room of thirty or more kids

What can coaches expect when they take to the mat to run a wrestling practice for that K-4th grade age range? For certain, the coaches can expect to be kept on their toes because the unforeseen is bound to happen. A majority of the young people will likely have less than a year of experience on the mat, and even the ones that have wrestled for at least a year studies show have a bare knowledge of the rules of an actual match and tournament.

Though these young people are enthusiastic wrestlers, and may have even won a gold medal or two they have not yet internalized the rules of the sport regardless of style they are participating in. More importantly, education studies show that most children under the age of eight do not have the mental ability to understand competition, handling both winning and losing.

Going off of these basic facts for this age range what type of practice is appropriate? And, how can a coaching staff run an effective practice that will encourage youth to stay with the sport of wrestling.

First, the staff must adhere to a set time length for practice. Parents need to know when to pick up kids, but another important consideration: how long can youth of this age stay engaged? It is relevant to note that shortened attention spans make the coaches jobs more difficult. Also, as the season progresses and the kids gain understanding of the sport practices may grow longer in duration. Ideally, coaches should look to run a practice of seventy-five to ninety minutes in duration as the season is introduced to young participants. Eventually, coaches may find it possible to run practices up to two hours in length. However, exceeding two hours probably will not produce added enjoyment for kids involved in the sport.

Next, while many coaches would love to mold their group of post toddlers into wrestling terrors of the mat, studies show that heavy emphasis on technique, competition, and winning is counterproductive for this group. The translation is that the kids of this age group have very **different priorities from their coaches and parents**. They are involved in this sport primarily for **social activation**; it is likely they came to a practice because a friend asked them to join the squad. They know **winning is good, but they can't explain why exactly**; therefore, the kids are looking for direction towards this goal and should begin to be introduced to competitive games and situations, but not necessarily dropped into local tournaments or competitions. They are seeking a practice setting that places a high priority on **active involvement and fun**; thus, a practice centered on technique study and drilling does not meet their expectations. In fact, clearly, practices in this mold have a much higher dropout rate than games based practices. A high loss of potential wrestlers will make a staff's job harder at succeeding levels as the prospective participants move on to other sports. In the United States the average length of time that a participant spends pursuing one sport **is less than five years**.

What does this mean for coaches as they try to meet the needs of this wrestling age group?

First, the practice must be highly structured and organized. The kids in this group have short attention spans and are filled with energy and excitement. Coaches should know precisely what activities the kids will be involved in and move from activity to activity quickly to maintain interest. Coaches should use the "on the clock" approach using a visible countdown clock that all participants can see. Also, a dry erase board is useful in showing the kids the direction of the practice. Using visual resources like these gives the practice a professional feel, and can help provide a serious tone when needed. Coaches should also recognize that use of video in the practice can be exciting and enjoyable for the kids. Seeing an actual high-level sequence of wrestling or even a complete match may be the first chance that these young wrestlers ever see real wrestling on television.

While many coaches nationally tell the young wrestlers that if they are good there will be a game at the end of practice, this thinking does not reflect the coaches willingness to meet the needs of this age group. Instead the entire practice should be the game!

Promoting the end of practice with the game, runs counter to the kids excitement for wrestling and actually produces a feeling of drudgery as kids take part in the "menial" tasks of wrestling in the practice. Coaches for this age group must take extraordinary steps to use the "Games Approach" to coaching wrestling.

The kids in this age will begin to develop understanding of the rules of wrestling and the need for technique through this approach. Also, the coaches will meet the needs of the age group by providing a fast moving and energetic practice, sending the kids home tired and excited that they are a part of the sport of wrestling.

- Coaches should keep time of activities to between three and seven minutes in length. Telling kids that they have to drill a move a thousand times before they know it, and giving them twenty minutes to drill only promotes disorder in the room and apathy towards the sport. A fast paced practice is exciting for this age group.
- Coaches should keep warm-up time to no more than ten minutes, utilizing high energy activities that include tumbling, crawls, and carries. (Stretching at this age is a secondary emphasis since most kids' body framework is still flexible; instead, coaches should help kids develop control over their body as it moves through space.)
- Coaches should include a short lesson time of about three to five minutes that introduces kids to age appropriate lessons and words such as unity, hard work, respect, sportsmanship, etc.
- Coaches should attempt to involve as many kids as possible throughout the practice. (A game that has two kids wrestling and twenty kids watching is not as good that has five groups of kids with the entire team participating at once. Remember to still provide effective supervision though!

- Coaches should effectively use role models as a part of practice introducing kids to legendary and collegiate wrestlers by just telling about them, or even having wrestlers visit their practice. Note that even having a successful high school wrestler come and give encouragement to the squad is very meaningful.
- Coaches should look to expand the ranks of the staff by asking interested parents to become involved youth coaches and go through the process of NCEP certification, giving the staff another effective coach to help the club.
- Coaches should look to the kids as allies to promote more membership in the club. Having the kids invite their friends to join and even providing an award for getting another member such as a t-shirt can be a tremendous asset in growing a program. Remember coaches are in the sales business! Positive word of mouth will make a difference!
- Coaches should fill the practice time with high energy activities. Focusing on conditioning as a work-out will have a negative connotation to kids of this age. Instead, teach them how to do a pushup and have a pushup contest. Look for innovative ways to keep the practice active.
- Coaches should slowly introduce kids to the concept of drilling a move. Proper use of the games approach to coaching leads kids to see how a move helps kids succeed in the game. Showing the kids how to practice the move in a short time frame in a controlled setting leads to the recognition for the need for drilling.
- Coaches should focus the entire structure of a practice around a basic part of the sport of wrestling. For example, coaches may work on hand control in one practice, or even focus on one of the basic skills. Guard against trying to introduce too much in a practice to get kids ready for the next meet. If that is the goal of a practice, then you may not be meeting the needs of the age group.

SIDEBAR: Coaching Youth Wrestling
Age range: Middle School fifth-eighth grade

Ted Witulski

Recommended Objective: minimize the risk of injury and exclusion and maximize the benefits of participation while moving participants to a deeper commitment to the sport.

Setting: a well-supervised high school wrestling room of thirty or more kids

Few coaches will deny that this age group gives parents their most trouble. As kids move into the middle school and their early teen years they are literally inundated with a variety of choices: some good, some bad. Kids in this age group are given greater freedom by their parents and can drop activities that were once dear to them at the drop of a hat. Sometimes this is made easier now that the kids do not have constant parental supervision and are allowed to stay at home alone.

A coach that faces a wrestling practice for this age range will encounter an even wider variety of kids with many different needs. While the younger age group may only have a couple of kids with a year or two of wrestling under their belt, this age group is quite different. Some kids will have been "wrestling all of their life" others may be a wrestler for a year or two, and still others might have come to the realization that soccer and basketball aren't their things and they want to try wrestling.

While the younger age division has less understanding of winning and is less motivated by winning as a goal, socially winning in this age range takes on a much greater importance. Increasingly, kids are singled out as being "terrible" or being a "loser", which is translated into active discouragement leading to the loss of more and more potential wrestlers.

Coaches again will have to make adjustments to the needs of this age group. In many ways it is natural to assume that the fun-loving coach of the youth kids must now turn into a hard-nosed street cop coaching the early teenagers. Of course, a wider range of discipline problems may occur but no studies show that strict discipline alone will lead to greater cooperation, greater involvement, and greater enjoyment of the sport of wrestling.

Coaches will encounter discipline problems, and coaches are encouraged to refer to the chapter on maintaining discipline for greater guidance. Coaches of this age will find that young kids are looking for more involvement from their coaches as mentors and practices need to include time to fill these roles.

Previously coaches probably felt up against the clock trying to fit a variety of activities into short practices. For the middle school range practices can be as short as ninety minutes or as long as $2^{1}/_{2}$ hours provided that the practice is broken into appropriate chunks. While real young wrestlers have short attention spans and need a constant flow of activities the middle school range can stay on task for a longer time (five to seven minutes). But, because the practice is longer in duration the coaching staff should look to have parts of the practices in distinct "chunks" of twenty to twenty-five minutes. While a youth practice may focus on one basic skill, a middle school practice might focus on the skill of level change, and then move to the teaching of duckunders that incorporates some drilling, followed by active wrestling drills and live wrestling that refocuses on the prior chunks of the practice.

Warm-ups for the athletes at this age again should aim to be highly physical and active utilizing running, jumping, tumbling, crawls, carries, and even resistance training like pushups and sit-ups. The time for these warm-ups should be about twenty to twenty-five minutes, and include thorough stretching of joints and muscles, paying particular attention to knees and shoulders where injuries begin to be more common in this age range.

Technical teaching of skills, strategies, and rules is relevant at this age. Middle school wrestlers share a nearly even ability to analyze wrestling as high school aged wrestlers. However, it is necessary to note that wrestlers at this age aren't prepared to endure twenty and thirty minute "show-us" technique sessions. Rather, demonstration and practice of a particular skill should be in the three to five minute range. A coach that is speaking on points of skills, strategies, and rules for longer than five minutes without refocusing the wrestlers is probably not meeting the needs of the age group.

Practices again should be structured and the use of the "on the clock" system as well as visual aids and live action footage is profoundly useful. Within the practice plan coaches should work greater character building times in between the chunks of wrestling skills and activities. The teaching of character building does not have to be preachy or overbearing, but the needs of this age group require coaches to help the participant gain greater understanding of how wrestling will help them succeed in life.

Don't assume that the wrestlers understand proper nutrition or that wrestling is a tremendous builder of successful personal traits. Kids at this age are searching for meaning for what they are doing and coach must be prepared to answer the inevitable question, "why is wrestling important?".

Coaches will also find that kids at the middle school level are very in tune with a social hierarchy and left to their own devices can be brutally tough on one another. It is commonly at this age where the problem of hazing begins to form. A coach that ignores "put downs" and sarcasm directed at members of the squad will find that this only leads to greater problems and difficulties in the future. By no means should coaches join into this hierarchy making some members of the team feel welcome and leaving the others to fend for themselves.

Coaching at the middle school level can be very rewarding as these kids remember the time and attention that they were given by their volunteer coaches as they progress to high school and even college. Coaches get more opportunity to coach kids on technique and strategy as a competitive environment becomes a part of the wrestling structure. However, coaches still need to work with young wrestlers who aren't succeeding on the mat in competition. It is too early an age for kids to decide to drop from a sport because they are not winning. Instead, coaches must focus the wrestler on the other benefits of the sport that may include physical wellness, team unity, and character building. Coaches that dedicate themselves to promoting their middle school program get the reward of knowing they are the feeder for high school programs and can see young people that they brought to the sport of wrestling achieve great things.

- Coaches should be comfortable lengthening the time of activities but still realize that attention spans will play a role in practice. Break the practice up into wrestling chunks and learning activities.
- Coaches should actively prepare to deal with discipline problems that include singling kids out and even illegal hazing. At this age coaches can lose wrestlers because the best wrestler on the team aggressively taunt or humiliate teammates. Take care to educate this wrestler about the downsides to bullying that include loss of respect, as well as degrading the coaches' ability to form a good wrestling team.

- Coaches should prepare to teach on a wider range of topics like nutrition, women's wrestling, strength training, hydration, and even hygiene.
- Coaches should guard against liability concerns like letting an unqualified adult or former wrestler be a part of practice without proper training or prior legal authorization.
- Coaches should look to deepen wrestlers' commitment to the sport by planning a schedule that leads them into regional and even national wrestling events. A weekend trip to a major wrestling event can be a terrific way to keep kids excited about being a part of the team.
- Coaches should prepare to deal with social concerns such as drug and alcohol abuse with this age group. Again, coaches are important mentors in the minds of the participants of this age group. Being able to deal with issues like these in individual and group settings is important.
- Coaches must prepare to balance the needs of first year wrestlers with those of experienced wrestlers, since it is likely both will be intermixed in the practice room. This can lead to risk management concerns; particularly if coaches are trying to get the inexperienced wrestler to keep pace by practicing moves that are too advanced.
- Coaches must deal with hygiene and skin infections effectively. While younger wrestlers have less exposure to skin infections, these problems begin to appear more readily with the middle school group. Knowing how to properly treat and more importantly properly prevent skin infections by good hygiene is a must.
- Coaches must still make enjoyment a priority in practices. Just because the kids are no longer in the youth group does not mean they are fully committed to the sport, prepared to endure an authoritarian style practice. The games approach and team games are still relevant at this age range.
- Coaches must deal with age groups separately. Too often wrestling programs fail because the youth age group is intermingled with the middle school team. The middle schoolers inevitably are short-changed and find other activities besides wrestling to pursue.

wrestlers are successful in lessons to be learned. This relationship between attempts and successes mandates that coaches structure their practices so that wrestlers will succeed on a high proportion of their early attempts. The following hints have been used by successful wrestling coaches:

- reduce each skill, rule, or strategy into achievable sub-skills and focus instruction on those sub-skills
- provide feedback to the athlete so that, on most occasions, something that they did is rewarded, followed by specific instructions about what needs more work, ending with an encouraging, "Try again.'

8. Monitor the Wrestlers' Progress

Wrestlers learn most effectively during practices that are accompanied by meaningful feedback. In wrestling, the meaningful feedback is most frequently provided by the coach or assistant coaches. The old cliché "Practice makes perfect" is only true if athletes are practicing appropriate skills in the correct manner. If left to their own agendas, young wrestlers may practice inappropriate skills or they may practice pertinent skills inappropriately. As their coach, you must be sure that the practices are conducted with the correct balance between feedback and independent learning.

9. Ask Questions of the Wrestlers

Young wrestlers generally enjoy their relationships with their coaches. Asking them questions is an ideal way to build the coach/athlete relationship. Questions should be designed to provide insight into: Why the athlete is involved in wrestling? Who are the significant persons in his/her life? What are his/her goals for the season? What parts of the match are personally satisfying? Coaches who know their wrestlers are most likely to be able to meet their needs by placing the wrestlers into situations that will enhance their self-esteem. Ultimately, the coach should have the goal to promote a positive personal relationship with all of their members on the team.

10. Promote a Sense of Control

Coaches must be in control of their teams, but control is not a one-way street. Wrestlers, too, must feel that they have some control over their own destiny when they attend practices and matches. They must feel that they will be rewarded for hard work, that their goals will be considered, and that their role on the wrestling team is valued and essential to the welfare of the team. As a coach you can promote a sense of control by:

- organizing your instruction to result in many successful experiences (i.e., opportunities to provide positive feedback).
- teaching your wrestlers that everyone learns various wrestling skills at different rates. Many of our World and Olympic wrestling team members started their careers on J.V. and lost more matches than they won. Teach young wrestlers to use effort and their own continuous progress as their primary guide. They should avoid comparing their skill level with that of other wrestlers.
- encouraging individual wrestlers to put forth their best effort. Reward such effort with a comment, pat on the back, thumbs up sign, or other means which will communicate your approval.

EFFECTIVE PRACTICES

Effective practices are those sessions that meet the needs of the wrestlers to carry out the objectives that are listed in the plan for the season. The keys to effective practices are **careful planning and sound instruction.** Both ingredients are under the control of the coach. It is absolutely essential that coaches go into all practices with a pre-determined and sound practice plan. Coaches that exude professionalism do not "wing it". Rather, they make a commitment to the kids of the team just as coaches preach that the kids need to make a commitment to the sport of wrestling. An unorganized, rudderless practice is a disservice to the sport of wrestling. Therefore, each of your practices should:

- be based upon previous planning, seasonal organization, needs of the team, and needs of the individuals
- list the objectives and key points that will be the focus of instruction for that practice
- show the amount of time allotted to each objective during the practice
- identify the activities (instructional, drill, or scrimmage) that will be used to teach or practice the objectives
- apply the guidelines for effective instruction included in this chapter
- include an evaluation of the strengths and weaknesses of the practice to the team.

PRACTICE TIME NEEDED

The amount of time that wrestlers can attend to your instruction depends on their ages and developmental levels. Generally, wrestlers aged ten and under cannot effectively tolerate more than one hour of concentrated practice. As age advances and the abilities of wrestlers improve the practices, too, can be slightly longer. **A primary problem in youth wrestling is to use effectively the time that is available.**

Another common problem in youth wrestling is to define far too many objectives and then teach for exposure rather than mastery. The most important part of wrestling is understanding the basic skills. Make sure your athletes understand these skills first. When insufficient time is devoted to basic skills, the result is incompetence and frustration. A good rule is to distribute your practice time across several objectives. Then devote sufficient time to each objective so that a meaningful change in the performance of 80 percent of the wrestlers has occurred. Devote time in additional practices to the objective until the wrestlers are able to transfer the skill into match-like drills. At that point, they can be expected to transfer the skills of practice into their matches.

CHARACTERISTICS OF A GOOD DRILL

The two most important components of your practices are the **development of individual skills** and the translation of these **skills into match-like situations through drills.** Therefore, the drills that you select must be related to your objectives. Too often coaches use drills that are traditional or favorites of the wrestlers but that have no relevance to the skills to be learned. Such drills waste valuable time. Drills should be selected or developed according to the following features. Drills should:

- have a meaningful objective
- require a relatively short explanation
- provide an excellent opportunity for wrestlers to master the skill or concept
- keep wrestlers "on task" during the drill
- be easily modified to accommodate skilled and unskilled wrestlers
- provide opportunity for skill analysis and feedback to wrestlers
- the drill should be challenging and fun

Write your drills on single sheets or cards. After the practice, write your comments about the drill's usefulness directly on the card and file the card for future use. Good drills can be used many times during a season. Share your drills with fellow coaches. Such activities promote fellowship among coaches and provide the beginning coach with a repertoire of useful teaching tools and techniques.

Incorporating Effective Teaching Measures

1. **Teach after a pre-practice meeting:** Because every practice should be thoroughly pre-planned, it is important to share the plan for the days practice with the assistants. The coaches and parents that will assist in practice need to know what the approach to practice is. Also, athletes that will be demonstrating drills and techniques should also have the opportunity to practice these ahead of time with the coaching staff. A pre-meeting will save practice time and help assure a more consistent flow of events.

2. **Teach on the clock:** One of the most effective pieces of equipment a coach can invest in for his practice room is a visible score clock with timer. Keeping all activities timed to the second will give the practice a strong sense of purpose. If a coach consistently teaches by putting all drills and activities "on the clock", then they will soon find that the practices are more efficient as well.

3. **Teach using Dry Erase Boards:** Having dry erase boards for use in the wrestling room provides another valuable way for wrestlers to internalize technique and the different parts of practice. Dry erase boards give coaches space to write out moves series, and keep a list of drills so that visually all wrestlers are engaged in the practice.

4. **Teach to an announced focused objective:** Every practice a coach can focus the participants into a specific area of wrestling. For example, if the team overall is having difficulty clearing hips from bottom the coach should announce improvement in this area as the focused goal for the day. It can be written on the dry erase boards and constantly referred during the practice. Additionally, the drills and technique should be centered on that focused goal.

6. **Teach by discussing the future direction:** At the end of practice an effective coach will tune the participants into the future direction of practices. Ideally the practices should have a "building block" feel where skills and technique build on each other. When it is necessary to start working on an entirely new skill the coach should make it clear to the athletes that a new skill or technique is being focused on. This will mark an end to one area of focus and move to the next.

PROTECTING THE SAFETY OF WRESTLERS

In addition to providing effective instruction, the coach has the responsibility of ensuring that all practices and matches are conducted in a safe environment. Therefore, the coach's primary responsibility can be summed up in this statement: **Teach for improved competence and safety every day.**

For over a decade courts, lawyers, and professional associations have been establishing the legal responsibilities of the youth sports coach. These responsibilities include providing adequate supervision, a safe environment, proper instruction, adequate and proper planning, adequate evaluation for injury or incapacity, appropriate emergency procedures and first aid training, adequate and proper equipment, appropriate warnings, and adequate matching of wrestlers and competitors. These duties are to be met by the coach while he/she is involved in any supervisory situation related to his/her coaching responsibilities.

A coach must know how to handle potentially dangerous situations by making correct decisions for the athlete.

4
Risk Management

Ted Witulski, Randy Hinderliter

QUESTIONS TO CONSIDER

- What is risk management and why is it relevant to coaches?
- What are the three parts of developing a risk management program for coaches?
- What are the legal qualifications or competencies that coaches should have?
- How are the "reasonable expectations of wrestlers' parents" related to risk management?
- What are the management practices that will help coaches achieve their risk management objectives?
- What are the three steps coaches should take to implement their risk management program?

The ability to effectively communicate to many different groups is a common trait of the best coaches.

INTRODUCTION

Protecting the Sport With Proper Choices

It happens every year across the country. While his friends decided to go off to college after graduation another young man decided to stay close to home and work. As the football season ends and the kids in high school gear up for the start of wrestling practices the young man decides to go talk to his high school coach.

The young man is actually only about six months removed from being classmates with some of the wrestlers. He just turned eighteen, but he was a great wrestler, a good kid, and he loved the sport.

He goes to the coach and says, "Coach, I'd like to help out this year with the wrestling team. Can I help you coach this year?"

Of course, it would be great to have another assistant in the room. It might be good to have a young guy that could still get on the mat with the wrestlers. He might be able to help a couple of more kids become state medalists.

As a coach what is the proper answer? Should this young man be allowed to join the coaching staff? Or, are there steps that he should have to take before he can be a coach?

It is a tough decision to make. The excitement of having another coach in the room probably needs to be tempered with providing competent assistants that will work for the betterment of the wrestlers and program. More and more, coaching decisions have to be viewed through the prism of liability and risk management. It is imperative that coaches across the country make proper choices that protect the sport of wrestling from embarrassing, unnecessary, and in some cases very expensive situations.

The Exposed Coach

In our society, it has become apparent that people are more willing than ever to use the legal system as a remedy when they feel they have been injured, harmed or treated unfairly. The result has been steady rise in sport liability cases, many of which focus directly on coach conduct.

Because our judicial system is always active and hearing new cases, it is difficult to tell coaches exactly what is considered legal and what is considered to be negligent. Therefore, coaches must be vigilant in addressing risk management and safety issues, fully knowing that what was once legal may now be deemed illegal through the shifting nature of new court cases and past precedents.

Unfortunately, while many wrestling coaches volunteer their time for little or no pay, their role as a coach places a heavy responsibility on them as an adult that is acting en loco parentis—in place of parent. Even though a coach may not be profiting from his role as a coach, past precedents have proven that any volunteer's personal financial worth is at stake in case of negligence. This wide range of volunteers can include officials, parents driving wrestlers to events, mothers working at a concession stand, and even janitors volunteering time at a weekend tournament.

Previous court cases have shown a variety of ways in which coaches are sued. These include causing injury to an athlete through batter—where a coach acts inappropriately often in the heat of the moment when emotions are running high. Also, coaches have been found liable for battery by athletes where the coach has instructed their athlete to act in a manner that can cause serious risk of harm to an opposing player—for instance when a coach is taught a front headlock that chokes or asphyxiates an opponent. Another area of liability has occurred when coaches fail to instruct athletes in basic safety and warn of the inherent risk of injury in a contact sport. Finally, coaches in liability cases must also recognize that they must be prepared to offer higher standards of care than an ordinary person—in this regard coaches must be prepared to react properly when an injury arises be it minor or serious in nature.

Waivers Provide Little Cover for Coaches

A long held belief by coaches is that having participants sign a waiver of indemnity to a practice, tournament, or clinic will protect them from legal action and damage awards. Indemnity waivers at one time acted as a legal exemption from liability for damages. While waivers have had a long history of use in sport programs, it has become increasingly apparent that waivers do not offer the protection that they once had.

Recent court cases have set aside waivers giving plaintiff—injured parties—the power to pursue their legal remedies. These types of waivers do include cases where parents have signed in place of the minor child. Essentially, courts have ruled that parents cannot sign away the rights of a minor child.

The protection that waivers once offered should no longer be considered effective protection for coaches to rely on.

COVERAGE THROUGH INSURANCE

Coaches that run any activity whether it is a practice, tournament, or clinic must assure themselves that they are properly covered by insurance. Coaches must not assume that a school's insurance policy will cover a club practice. Nor, should coaches assume that because the participants in a small off-season workout are students in the building that the insurance that covered the athletes during the regular high school season is still in effect once the season has concluded.

Insurance companies facing tighter budgets has written more exclusions into the policies that they sell to organizations, an assumption of coverage in error, can easily lead to coach being held liable for damages that would have to be paid out of their own pocket. Even a minor injury such as a torn ligament or broken finger can lead to legal costs and damages that can run into the thousands of dollars.

Coaches by nature are altruistic and giving of their time. However, in today's society of lawsuits coaches must protect themselves and the sport of wrestling by investigating the facts of any assumed coverage, or in cases where it is found that no coverage exists coaches must exercise a leadership role in purchasing insurance coverage.

USA Wrestling, as the National Governing Body, provides insurance coverage as a part of the yearly membership dues to belong to the organization. More than 150,000 athletes and coaches, and over 3,000 clubs are covered by its insurance policy at the more than 1,500 events, and countless wrestling practices annually.

Coaches must seriously consider the responsibility of coaching, even when the duties are not the enjoyable ones like running a practice or warming kids up for a big meet. As a coach it is imperative that proper forethought go into protecting the athletes, volunteers, club, and coaches from the ever-present possibility of a lawsuit.

The Standard for Coaches

After looking at how often coaches actually leave themselves open for claims of liability, it is almost enough to scare a coach away from a sport he loves—a sport that can always use the help of another coach and volunteer. Coaches, however, should be assured that if they properly pursue and purchase quality sports insurance and faithfully follow the rules of the policy that there is still plenty of enjoyment left to be involved in the sport of wrestling.

The National Coaches Education Program constantly works to help coaches understand the standards that coaches must meet to properly perform their duties as a coach. Now, it is time to consider what are the standards and requirements that a coach must follow to manage risk and assure that his exposure to liability is minimal.

When all of the details are met a coach finally gets to take the mat and teach kids the sport he knows and loves. He is there for the kids, but whose standards must the coach assure that he meets? Is it the fellow teachers, the athletic director, the principal, the kids on the mat? Generally, the courts have applied one key standard to the conduct and actions of a coach.

Do his actions meet the reasonable expectations of the participant's parents?

Traditionally, teachers have been held to standards established by communities of parents. Many parents may never attend one of their children's practices, or even watch them compete in a tournament or scrimmage. Yet, coaches must pay particular care to meet the reasonable expectations of the wrestlers' parents.

In many ways, these expectations can vary from wrestler to wrestler. A coach should pay particular attention to individual parents who have specific concerns for their wrestler. Some wrestlers' parents for instance may have concerns for their child because of a breathing condition while other families do not have that as a worry. The result is that **the wrestling coach who understands that the requirements of the job will be measured by the reasonable expectations of his wrestlers' parents knows he or she must be an effective teacher.**

Coaches, in any sport, owe certain legal obligations to their wrestlers. The goal of risk management programs is to identify those legal obligations for coaches, then translate them into coaching conduct or behavior.

EFFECTIVE TEACHING
Legal Obligation: Coaches are supposed to be teachers first and foremost.
Coaching Behavior: Enroll in certification and continuing coaching education programs; and begin your own reading education program in coaching and communication skills.

EFFECTIVE SUPERVISION
Legal Obligation: Coaches are responsible for team supervision wherever and whenever the team meets.
Coaching Behavior: Hire competent assistants; and establish a plan of supervision for all team practices, meetings, games, and other events.

EFFECTIVE REACTION TO MEDICAL EMERGENCIES
Legal Obligation: Coaches are supposed to know medical emergencies when they see them; and to know how to respond quickly and responsibly as a staff.
Coaching Behavior: Take a certification course in emergency medical procedures, or at least first aid; and establish a plan for prompt reaction to medical emergencies.

PROVIDING SAFE EQUIPMENT
Legal Obligation: Coaches are supposed to know how to buy, fit, and maintain safe sports equipment.
Coaching Behavior: Establish equipment fitting, distribution, and maintenance plans in accordance with all manufacturer warranties, guidelines, and directions; take continuing education programs regarding equipment; and maintain records on equipment inspection and reconditioning.

PROVIDING SAFE FACILITIES
Legal Obligation: Coaches are supposed to know when surface conditions pose a danger to wrestlers.
Coaching Behavior: Take continuing education programs regarding facility operations; establish a plan for regular mat inspections, including quick repair of defects or problems and proper cleaning.

PROVIDING SAFE TRANSPORTATION
Legal Obligation: Coaches are supposed to know how wrestlers are being transported to away events, and with whom the wrestlers will be traveling.
Coaching Behavior: Use the league and parents to help establish transportation plans which should include approved drivers, vehicles, and stops; and establish a team code of travel conduct.

PROVIDING DUE PROCESS
Legal Obligation: Coaches have to establish fair rules and policies, and explain their reasons for suspending a wrestler from the team.
Coaching Behavior: Use the league and parents to establish rules and policies regarding team conduct; provide written copies of rules and policies to wrestlers and their parents; never suspend a wrestler without giving the wrestler and his parents the chance to explain their conduct.

PROVIDING COMPETENT ASSISTANTS
Legal Obligation: Coaches are supposed to hire or assign assistant coaches who are as competent as the head coach.
Coaching Behavior: Start a training program just for the assistant coaches; plan and organize the staff with continuing education and train-

SIDEBAR: Athletes Abusing Athletes

Ted Witulski

A long standing belief by many athletes and coaches nationally is that "initiation" builds unity. However, as more people come to understand the unwieldy power of the group mentality, coaches must become aware of the dangers of conduct that lead to hazing.

Alfred University conducted the first major study of hazing in the United States. Hazing was defined as, "any activity expected of someone joining the group that humiliates, degrades, abuses or endangers, regardless of the person's willingness to participate. This does not include activities such as rookies carrying the balls, team parties with community games, or going out with your teammates, unless an atmosphere of humiliation, abuse or danger arises."

Hazing is treated as a new phenomenon, but there have been reports of hazing going back to the late 1800's. The study of hazing took on new relevance in 1990 when Nicholas Haben, a lacrosse player at Western Illinois University, died from a hazing event as part of a team initiation that involved binge drinking.

Hazing is often an issue that people do not address until they have to. Coaches must take a proactive view at eliminating the traditions of initiation that fit the definition of hazing outlined in the Alfred University study.

A telling finding of the study was that only 12 percent of the respondents checked the "yes" box when asked if they had been hazed. Yet, when asked about specific activities they were asked to engage in when they joined the team—everything from physical abuse to forced consumption of alcohol to wearing embarrassing clothes—79 percent said they had been subjected to what the authors deemed questionable or unacceptable hazing.

To make the needed change to eradicate hazing coaches should:

1. Notice hazing.
2. Interpret hazing as a problem.
3. Recognize a responsibility to change it.
4. Acquire the skills needed to take action.
5. Take action.

Hazing can often masquerade as harmless conduct that many kids feel are important traditions to the strength of a program. Many kids feel that they have earned a right as an upper-classmen to revisit the indignity on younger athletes that was once directed at them in years past.

Coaches must prepare themselves to end wrongheaded traditions that can actually be a detriment to the program that they want to develop. Additionally, coaches risk liability when hazing rituals are allowed to continue with even limited knowledge of the students' intent.

Coaches should recognize common barriers to changing a hazing culture.

1. Denial of the problem.
2. Dismissing hazing as harmless.
3. Silence.
4. Fear.
5. Insufficient support for victims of hazing.
6. Cultural norms that promote acceptance of hazing.

Hazing has become a standard issue that coaches must deal with effectively as they involve themselves with any wrestling program. The sport of wrestling is challenging on its own merit. Coaches and athletes should not resurrect even more difficult barriers to be involved with wrestling, like those that often fall into the definition of hazing.

ing as a requirement; and require references from all assistants. Also note that there is a trend towards requiring background checks for individuals that work in a coaching capacity—make sure your team follows all of the required state mandates.

DEVELOPING A RISK MANAGEMENT PROGRAM

Coaching can be very frustrating when it involves being constantly second-guessed. Obviously, the coaching profession is one that has always suffered through hindsight. For that reason alone many coaches might prefer an evaluation standard based solely on their effort or time spent coaching. When dealing with volunteers, it seems fair to be evaluated on one's willingness to work with kids. The problem is that risk management cannot be successful if it measures effort alone. A successful risk management program has to evaluate coaching performance as "effective teaching."

Volunteer coaches who accept the teaching role also accept the role of a parent. And, thereby, they assume the standards of effective teaching. **Parents have the right to assume the coach has the ability to teach the sport or activity; to teach it safely; and, to teach it with the participation of their child in mind.** Obviously, it is expected that the experience will be fun. Those are the desired characteristics of an effective coaching risk management program.

Many risk management programs are developed simply by listing or identifying the legal competencies expected of coaches. The premise is that when a coach practices those legal competencies it results in an effective risk management program.

The problem is that merely identifying coaching competencies does not mean a coach knows how to practice them. Using "effective teaching according to the reasonable expectations of wrestlers' parents" as the risk management mission, we will develop the risk management program in three steps. First, we will identify the legal competencies required of coaches. Second, we will integrate those competencies into a management program. Third, we will offer three suggestions how to imple-ment the management program into an effective coaching risk management plan.

THE LEGAL COMPETENCIES EXPECTED OF COACHES

Legal experts all agree that the foundation of good coaching springs from **effective teaching**. Coaches are encouraged to constantly assess their abilities as an effective teacher. There is always room for improvement in this area, and there are always more effective techniques to use to improve participant learning. USA Wrestling encourages coaches to follow Dan Gable's advice "to be in the education business" for the betterment of the sport of wrestling.

Beyond effective teaching coaches should assure that they meet the following eight legal competencies of coaching wrestling.

- Effective supervision
- Effective reaction to medical emergencies
- Providing safe equipment
- Providing safe facilities
- Safe transportation
- Matching wrestlers according to size, skill, and maturity
- Providing "Due Process"
- Providing competent assistants

Effective Teaching or Instruction

The effective teacher knows that instruction means a great deal more than teaching moves or conducting drills. The wrestling coach has to learn that this competency demands a great deal of sensitivity, compassion, and patience; and, some specific non-instructional abilities. The coach, as an effective teacher, is in a position of leadership who can have a tremendous impact on the lives of young children.

Effective Supervision

Effective teaching includes the supervision of wrestlers. Effective coaching supervision has two primary components: *when* to supervise and *how* to supervise.

When to Supervise

Supervision is not strictly limited to the mat or to practice time. Supervision may be required when parents are late to pick up kids after practice. It may be required when kids are being transported under coach's direction to a match or practice. Or, it may be required during a team picnic outside of the training area. Any team function where wrestlers are required to attend should be supervised. Coaches need to also be prepared, however, to supervise those functions where attendance is optional, or even where the team just happened to be present without parental supervision. The coach is expected to know that greater supervision may be needed before and after practice, as well as when wrestlers are coming to or leaving practice.

Based on our risk management mission, the risk-conscious coach will not wonder if there is a responsibility to supervise in a particular instance. Rather, he or she will act according to whether, "It is reasonable for my wrestlers' parents to expect that I will supervise in this instance."

How to Supervise

There are three elements to "how to" supervise wrestlers. The first is to have a sufficient number of assistants to supervise. If the program provides assistant coaches, then this may not be a major problem unless the coaching staff's attention is solely directed to the area of activity. The greatest need for supervision usually occurs with wrestlers not directly involved with the activity, or who are away from the center of activity. Parents expect there will be sufficient help to supervise their youngsters during any phase of the activity.

The second element is location. **This means that the staff is located on and around the training area where they can see and readily react to any situations requiring supervision.** As noted before, supervision is not limited to the training area. Location and accessibility of supervisors includes locker rooms, showers and toilets, or other areas where team members are likely to congregate.

The final element is competence. One of the coaching competencies we will discuss is providing competent personnel. **It is reasonable for parents to expect that coaching assistants or aides are as well-qualified as the**

coach. It is not unreasonable for parents to expect their children to be supervised by a competent staff.

Are teenagers qualified or competent to supervise younger students or wrestlers? Age is not a legal bar to sage supervision if the teenager has experience and maturity. For example, it is common to leave public swimming pool supervision in the hands of teenagers. However, those youngsters have water safety certification, training programs, and some experience, before they are left to supervise pools. Similarly, the coach who relies on team dads or older brothers and sisters to supervise should be sure those parties possess the same degree of competence.

The failure to reasonably supervise is the primary allegation in most personal injury lawsuits filed against coaches and sports administrators. Our society has a deep-seeded belief injuries would not occur if proper supervision is provided. That surely is the attitude of many parents whether their children's injury was activity-related or caused by some risk other than wrestling.

Effective Reaction to Medical Emergency

Ideally, coaches should be certified in emergency medical treatment, or at least in first aid. Most injuries occur during practice, and safety experts have come to realize that qualified medical personnel are usually not available during the periods of greatest risk. **Many states now require that coaches have some minimal certification in emergency medical procedures.** Youth sports organizations and coaches should check for any local and state requirements regarding availability of medical personnel.

Parents expect that the coaching staff can recognize a medical emergency when it occurs. They also expect the coach to have a plan which can be immediately implemented to deal with the emergency.

There should be a plan for notifying emergency care providers; for providing emergency medical transportation promptly; and, for notifying a wrestler's parents and family physician as soon as possible. Clearly, a coach would be well-advised to have signed medical consent forms with medical history as well as appropriate addresses and phone numbers available at all times. When a medical emergency occurs a staff must act in unison to provide an effective reaction and still maintain appropriate supervision. Coaching staffs are encouraged to pre-plan and practice for a medical emergency prior to the start of a season.

Providing Safe Equipment

Teaching a sport or activity means that the teacher knows how to use the tools of the trade. There are a number of factors that coaches have to consider with equipment.

First, if the coach is directly involved in the purchase or approval of equipment, or has agreed to exclusively utilize a certain manufacturer's equipment, then the coach may have assumed the same legal responsibility as the manufacturer. This is referred to as products liability. It means that liability can attach to the coach for any equipment which is defectively designed or manufactured.

In most instances, however, providing safe equipment means the coach should make sure that it fits each wrestler correctly; that equipment is worn during activity; and, that the coach knows how to properly recondition and store equipment. Storage of equipment is an area that coaches should pay particular attention to. Open accessible wrestling rooms with mats are an inviting target for kids to roughhouse without supervision. Also, equipment like stationary bikes that are available outside of supervised times can be dangerous with young toddlers seeking them out as toys. **Plainly, it is expected that coaches will instruct their wrestlers on the proper means of equipment care and will watch for the misuse or abuse of equipment.**

A good coaching practice is to thoroughly read manufacturer instructions and guidelines. A coach can usually rely on those directions for maintenance or repair problems. Local youth leagues or associations can usually identify trade associations and journals which will provide up-to-date information regarding equipment use for their coaches.

PROVIDING SAFE FACILITIES

Providing safe facilities is similar to the safe equipment competency. It is based on a coach's ability to recognize dangerous wrestling surfaces and conditions. **Wrestlers should not be subjected to the risk of injury from improperly maintained mats, from unsafe surroundings, or even from poor equipment.** A coach should have knowledge of maintenance and repair processes. For example, coaches should learn about common problems with mat surfaces, protective barriers, and equipment.

Transportation

Generally, there is not an obligation to provide transportation. Often, however, coaches find themselves planning or organizing their team's transportation. In those cases, coaches assume the obligation to plan a safe means of transportation. While the type and condition of the transportation vehicle is important, the more critical consideration for the coach is approving who will drive team members. The major liability problem here is insurance coverage for the team. In many states, wrestlers who travel with friends or other team members by private arrangements may not be covered for personal injury due to the strict limitations of guest driving statutes. It is a good idea to have an organizational plan or policy which specifies who is permitted to drive the team; or, if available, which vehicles are to be used. Parental input should be included in any policy regarding transportation. Finally, it is important that the automobile insurance policies of the parents, coaches, and the youth sports organization be reviewed to determine where liability and medical coverage will be provided.

Matching Wrestlers According to Size, Skill, and Maturity

This competency has been addressed in the first part of the chapter, but it bears repetition. Good teaching requires coaches to advise their wrestlers of the risks of injury common to wrestling. Coaches should emphasize in a pre-season Parent Athlete Coach meeting that there is an **inherent risk of injury in any contact sport and injuries can range from mild contusions and cuts to serious injuries including paralysis and death.** Failure to warn of the possible dangers associated with a sport it is a common complaint in negligence cases.

It is important that size and experience differences be considered when organizing drills and scrimmages. In the best interest of safety for all athletes, wrestlers should be separated by size and/or skill levels. **Basically, this coaching competency recognizes that safe contact drills and exercises are an important part of effective teaching. Also, coaches should be prepared to forfeit a match when an immature or inexperienced wrestler faces an opponent that is "out of his league".** Coaches by nature are competitive and feel experience can improve an athlete; however, do not risk a complaint of negligence when a clear mismatch occurs. This competency recognizes that parents reasonably expect their inexperienced child will not face undue risks while learning wrestling.

Due Process

This is not easily accepted by many coaches as a competency. To a great extent, coaching has adopted the military style of command and leadership as the basis for its management method. In other words, providing reasons or explanations for coaching instructions are not characteristic of the profession. Of course, *due process* is also perceived as a legal tactic encompassing attorneys and second-guessing.

In fact, due process is an effective teaching method. It does not interfere with the decision making process, but it provides a level-headed approach to enforcement of rules and procedures. It does not, as popularly thought, mandate a forum where wrestlers will be represented by a lawyer. Simply stated, due process merely means that before a wrestler is to be suspended from a match or from the team, the coach will explain what rule was violated and give the wrestler the opportunity to explain his or her conduct. Due process requires that team rules have a legitimate instructional or supervisory purpose; and, that

the coach will enforce the rules fairly and consistently. Due process does not hinder a coach's right to discipline, or to require adherence to team rules. **Due process merely means that a coach will be fair with the establishment and enforcement of team rules which is another reasonable parental expectation.**

An effective way to avoid conflicts with irate or unhappy parents, are to utilize the due process competency to a coach's advantage. Often, parents will approach a coach looking to draw the coach into an argument, forcing him to justify a coaching decision. Coaches should recognize this early and instead of falling into the parental trap, lower the degree of emotion of the situation by offering due process to the parent. In effect, the coach by listening to the emotion of the parent responds in a non-defensive manner by saying, "I understand your concern and I may not agree with your assessment of the situation, but I would like to offer you our system of due process."

A coach acting in this manner can usually diffuse a problem. Many times a parent only wants to vent or feel that someone has heard their concern. They would rather blow off steam than to take time to go through a system of due process. Note that if a coach wishes to use this method a pre-established system of due process is a must. This may include a formal meeting with the club board of directors or the athletic director and principal for a high school coach.

Competent Personnel

Parents have the right to expect that assistant coaches or aides are competent. If teaching and supervision will be shared by more than just the head coach, then coaching competency requires that assistants be as competent as the head coach.

This obligates coaches to do three things: first, to recruit and select competent assistants; second, to plan a good training program for assistants that emphasizes the goals and objectives of the instructional program; and, finally, to perform a competency evaluation of assistants. It is common knowledge that getting good assistants can be a difficult chore. However, it is an easier task than facing legal liability for failing to provide capable personnel. Coaches are urged to check the references on all assistants, and to plan and implement comprehensive training programs. Most states provide coaching competency certification programs for coaching staffs. Finally, coaches are encouraged to lead coaches into involvement with USA Wrestling's National Coaches Education Program that offers sport specific education for wrestling.

THE "MANAGEMENT" PROGRAM FOR COACHING RISK MANAGEMENT

The basic functions of organizational management are **planning, organizing, staffing, leading, and evaluating**. They are important to the risk management because they help establish a competency program for the types of legal risks we identified.

Effective management, like effective teaching, begins with goals and objectives. The processes of planning, organizing, staffing, leading, and evaluating depend on established goals and objectives. We have already identified coaching goals and objectives in the first part of the chapter. They are enhancing kids' physical skills, teaching kids how to learn, and establishing good social behavior. It is important to remember that winning was not identified as a primary coaching goal. Unfortunately, in this day and age, winning is often mistaken as the primary goal of sport. However, just as the business organization risks its health by concentrating only on short-term profits, youth sports risks its credibility if it cannot see beyond winning.

The three goals specified (physical, mental, and social) are valuable because they not only serve as a foundation for sport, but they represent what most parents expect from their children's participation in sport. Certainly winning is a desirable and motivating goal of all sports. As a teacher of wrestling, you know that there are steps along the way that need to be emphasized over outcomes. Wrestling has the ability to develop and reveal character. Parents expect youth sport to instill confidence, teach sportsmanship, develop physical skill, and provide fun.

Planning

As noted, effective teaching requires planning. Using the three goals as a basis, a coach should plan how he or she is going to achieve those goals. A good teacher utilizes a lesson plan and a syllabus for achieving teaching goals. The effective coach should have a lesson plan which charts a path for wrestlers to achieve team and personal goals. A prudent coach will have plans for supervision, plans for reacting to medical emergencies, and plans for transportation issues. Planning is a critical function, and the planning process can be utilized as a valuable tool for training assistant coaches. From a parental point of view, most would expect that the coach has established goals or guidelines for the team and for their children.

Organization

Most organizations realize that establishing goals and objectives has little effect if the structure of the organization is not designed to meet them. Since the goals we have identified in the first part of the chapter are generally recognized in sport, you will not find many diverse organizational structures in youth sports. Many organizations have structured themselves along the traditional lines of the military command structure. A means of insuring that your team's organizational structure is effective is to examine how well you communicate the goals and objectives. For example, a principal means of good planning is to get feedback. In other words, how well a coach has planned can be gauged from the feedback of athletes and parents. By the same token, organizational effectiveness can be gauged from team and parental feedback regarding communication within the team structure.

Staffing

This again refers to the competent personnel issue. Since physical, mental, and social goals of sport serve as the basis for your plan-

It has been a long standing tradition in the wrestling community a coach taking to the mat to directly tutor the competitors in technique or live situations. While it would be peculiar to see a coach don football pads or put on the cleats for a soccer practice wrestling coaches for years have enjoyed the freedom to enjoy the rigors of wrestling with their team members.

However, with the advent of new and tougher interpretations for risk management coaches must note that the freedom once enjoyed to wrestle with their students is drastically being curtailed.

Injuries in the sport of wrestling are commonplace. The newest trend in litigation centers on negligent supervision cases. The courts have not supported coaches who have engaged in active participation that rose to the level on one-on-one competition. The courts have determined in such situations that the coach acting as a supervisor abandoned their supervisory role and became an equal competitor with the participant.

The courts have clearly ruled that is inappropriate for an adult supervisor to engage a student in a physical activity, believing that this is outside the reasonable expectations of a parent. Another important note is that coaches should not try to push the intensity of the activity in order to motivate.

Coaches that enjoy the competitor role in practice must be aware of the increased liability that they have when they forgo the supervisory role. Injuries are common in the sport of wrestling, but injuries to a minor competitor should never occur as a result of competition with a coach.

---

ning and organization, they also determine who you should hire. Will a candidate who sees winning as the primary goal of sport be a person who is likely to fit within the team organization? We already realize that planning and organization issues have to match the goals which have been established. From a staffing point of view, a coach is much better off hiring or accepting assistants who share the same goals and objectives.

Leading

This management function looks at leadership from two sides. First, why do people in an organization follow a leader? Second, how does a leader motivate people to perform with their best effort. There is no trick to understanding how this function works. When parents recognize that the coach can help their children achieve goals which the parents believe are important, they will support the program. When wrestlers see that their participation is more important to the coach than merely winning or losing, they will follow the program. Finally, when a coach, like the effective teacher, can show how those goals help the wrestlers become better, they will be motivated to perform better. Again, the emphasis is on the goals and objectives. A coaching manner may be charismatic, or it may be relatively passive. **Whatever manner or method is used to coach a team, adherence to goals and objectives will be the mark of the good leader.**

Evaluating

This management function is really called controlling, however, that term does not best describe the function. The purpose of controlling is to evaluate or measure how successful an organization has been in accomplishing its goals and objectives. Some coaches will measure success based on winning and losing percentages. Other coaches, like effective teachers, will measure success on the basis of retention. That is, did most of the kids retain an interest in the sport and return to wrestle the next season. In risk management, the measure of success is the safety of the program.

Again, this function is based on the physical, mental, and social goals of sport. From a risk management perspective, when an evaluation indicates that these goals have been largely met, then it is a good and safe indication that the coaching risk management program has been effective. By the same token, you cannot assume a coaching risk management program has been effective, if winning is the only measure of success.

IMPLEMENTING THE COACHING RISK MANAGEMENT PROGRAM

Implementing is the most difficult part of any management program. Many people who consider themselves "idea people" lack the ability to execute their plans. Experience persistently reminds us that ideas have little value if there is no capability to implement them.

We know that risk management starts with risk identification. Risk identification, however, has little effect in a risk management program if the program itself is not properly implemented. Often, organizations leave implementation to a risk manager whose function is to coordinate risk identification and elimination. In coaching, however, all coaches have to be risk managers. They cannot leave that function to others. That means that all coaches must have the ability to implement risk management goals and objectives.

There are three essential elements for the successful implementation of a risk management program: communication, working through people, and accepting change.

Communication

Like most of us, coaches probably would not admit they don't communicate well. As a matter of fact, many coaches exaggerate their oral communication skills. Since coaches rarely have their writing critiqued, many might also assume their writing skills are satisfactory. The reason for these false assumptions is that people believe that effective communication is in the message itself. In other words, if what is spoken or written is good, then the communication is good. That may be true in literature, but it is rarely true in organizational communication.

We now know, of course, that the key to effective communication in any organization is not the message, but the receiver. In other words, it does not matter how good the message may appear. If the message is not received and understood by the receiver, the communication has been ineffective. Coaching communication is compounded by the different ages, backgrounds, and experiences of other coaches and wrestlers. Therefore, it takes a very strong and understanding effort by a coach to be an effective communicator. The first step is to learn how to listen.

Be an Emotional Listener

The first lesson for the coach who wants to improve his or her organizational communication skills is to become a more effective listener. According to organizational management experts, there are two types of listening: rational listening and emotional listening. Most of us are rational listeners. That means that we tend to evaluate or judge what others have said to us. It is exemplified by our responses which either agree or disagree with what the speaker said. The rational listener judges others' communication, and is not prepared to change his mind or behavior as a result of what the speaker said. Emotional listening, on the other hand, means that you view things strictly from the speaker's point of view. It means that you can be influenced to change your mind or behavior. For the coach, it means the coach puts himself or herself in the shoes of the speaker, whether assistant coach or wrestler. This is a tough characteristic to learn because most of us are more interested in communication as it affects us, not how it affects the speaker.

Effective Teaching Requires Emotional Listening

The effective teacher knows that children see and understand things in different ways than adults. The teacher who is an emotional listener views things from the child's perspective. It is that ability which enables the effective teacher to communicate with children. The first step in effective communication for the coach is not speaking or sending a message; rather it is learning how to listen.

Teamwork: The Ability to Work Through People

Another organizational concept which has proved successful is teamwork. Teamwork, of course, is recognized as a critical element of success in sports. It is a quality upon which many coaches evaluate their team's performance. Also, it is a personal characteristic that coaches look for in their athletes. Unfortunately, it is not always altogether clear that coaches understand how to build teamwork, or how to participate as a team member.

Effective Teamwork Requires Commitment to Training

A goal of teamwork is to make your members as good as they can be, and to help them develop a feeling of satisfaction in what they do. Often, that goal depends on a leader's commitment to training. Today's effective organizations emphasize continuous training for their members, as well as cross-training to help members develop new skills and specialties.

Training is not merely something one learns to start a job, or a sport. It is a way of working; it never ends. It is a commitment which requires a willingness to train, retrain, and then train some more. Do the training practices of organizations have a place in youth sports? If organizations know that teamwork based on a commitment to training creates job satisfaction, it's safe to assume that wrestler satisfaction and retention will result from the same commitment to training. Can coaches become committed to that concept? It is difficult to gauge. For example, coaches often respond to losses in the following ways: "We did not execute" or, "We need to work harder" or, "We weren't ready to compete." The blame is placed on the failure of the wrestlers rather than the coach. It would be novel to hear a coach say, "I did a lousy job of preparing you for this match."

Successful organizations know failures in team performance usually reflect problems at the top, not the bottom. Likewise, the coaching commitment to training would require that coach to reflect on team performance from the top first. The training ethic is intended to make

assistant coaches more competent, help wrestlers continuously improve, and thereby create a sense of team satisfaction. If the training program is not doing that, the coach needs to first evaluate his or her performance. As noted, however, the popular excuse is that poor team performance is a result of player failure, not coaching failure.

Effective Teamwork Requires Emotional Listening

Working through people, like communication, requires emotional listening. Teamwork and the training ethic are based on the willingness to listen. Effective training requires input and feedback from the participants. A coach, therefore, must be an emotional listener to recognize whether or not the training is working. If the coach does not actively listen, it means the coach is making his or her own assumptions about the team. That is how the blame game starts.

The basis of teamwork is the capability to influence others, adapt to others, and be influenced by others. It is easy to see that emotional listening is its foundation.

The Ability to Accept Change

Many coaches model their coaching style on their own experiences. In management, it is an axiom that we manage as we were managed. In sport, many coaches coach as they were coached. There is nothing wrong with adopting some of your past experiences in sport. After all, the principal objectives (mental, physical, and social) are time-honored values. However, the effective teacher realizes that teaching those values requires change and adaption. The ability to change does not mean that you sacrifice values, it means you learn how to teach them more effectively than before.

Unfortunately, it is not easy to change even when team performance may be at stake. If your coaching experience is rooted in rational listening, as opposed to emotional listening, and team direction has always been simply left to the determination of the coach, then change will be difficult. Coaches, however, should consider that they utilize change all the time. Any special preparations for a specific opponent are changes. While many coaches may fear to change how they coach, they are, nevertheless, engaged in change and its effects every day.

The effective teacher seeks change. He or she is constantly searching for new methods and approaches to teaching. The effective teacher knows that "effective" is not a stationary concept. Effectiveness requires constant evaluation. Similarly, the coach must be able to adapt his or her methods in order to remain effective. And, the coach must be able to recognize that the role of sports has changed just as the wrestlers' abilities have.

5
Building a Wrestling Program

Danny Struck, Kyle Fellure, Randy Hinderliter, Ben Stehura

QUESTIONS TO CONSIDER

- What are the primary tools used in building a wrestling program?
- What is the most successful way to structure your goals?
- What are the seven principles of sound fund raising?

A successful program will foster enthusiastic support from all associated with it.

INTRODUCTION

Most of this country's greatest wrestlers were not only developed by excellent coaching and natural talent but were a product of very successful programs. The development of a wrestling program is a task that the greatest coaches have mastered. They are able to create an environment for their wrestlers to excel, regardless of the talent level within a room.

There are many basic principles that a coach must consider in the development and building of a wrestling program. Regardless of whether you are a club, scholastic or collegiate coach, the primary tools you will need are community support, a practice facility, a goal structure, reward system, planning, and follow-through.

COMMUNITY SUPPORT

Community support is the back bone of every successful wrestling program. This relationship creates support in every area that is important for a program's longevity and success. This includes support via money, access to needed venues or businesses, of fans and supporters, community pride, emotional support for the athlete, coaches and families, and kids' and parents' desire to be a part of the team which will draw the best athletes.

This type of support can only be fostered through the willingness of a coach to be able to work with several different types and levels of people in a professional and cordial manner. The coach must make the effort and take the initiative to introduce himself and work together with the community and its constituents to best meet the needs of all concerned and not just focus on the individual needs of the athletes and program.

PRACTICE FACILITIES

Once this working relationship is established, the focus can then be turned towards the specific needs of a wrestling team. The first need is a place to practice. Depending on your respective situations, there are several options that can be sought to best meet the needs of your program. Some ideal places to use for this purpose can be found in your local Boy's and Girl's Clubs, YMCA/YWCA, Community Centers, and schools. The practice facility must be large enough to accommodate a wrestling mat for the wrestlers to practice on. The size of the room will also be determined by the number of athletes that will be involved. An ideal situation would permit all of your wrestlers to practice at the same time with enough room to account for safety. However, if this is not the case, then you can be creative in using the facilities that you have (i.e., split your practice into two, only use half of your wrestlers at a time, use buddy drills, etc.).

For beginning programs, the purchase of a wrestling mat can be a hinderance. New wrestling mats run between $4,500 for a 36' x 36', $1\frac{1}{2}$" thick surface and $6,000+ for a 40'–42' x 40'–42', $1\frac{3}{4}$"–2" thick mat. Some other options that may be available are used mats and/or the reconditioning of a damaged one. These options can also cost thousands of dollars.

For schools or clubs without the funds to handle this type of purchase, there are some creative ways to work around the lack of capital. Some suggestions may be to split the cost with your athletic department or intramural clubs and share the use of the mat with other sports that would need its padded surface. This includes activities such as gymnastics, judo, tumbling, cheerleading, martial arts, dance, and many others. This option would lower the cost demand for your program and increase the demand for a school or athletic department to purchase the mat. Another possibility would be to raise the money through fundraising. There are many ways to do this which are outlined at the end of this chapter.

Upon securing a facility to practice in and a mat to practice on, it is imperative and strongly recommended that you and your program have liability insurance. If you are developing a program within a scholastic or collegiate program, your institution should already have coverage. If you are developing a club program, liability insurance can be acquired through a USA Wrestling Club Charter. This can be accomplished by contacting your respective state chairperson or the national office located in Colorado Springs, Colorado. Once all of these steps are accomplished, you are ready to set some goals and objectives for your wrestling program.

PROGRAM GOALS AND OBJECTIVES

The most successful wrestling programs are not a result of the best athletes, the most money, or the best facilities but rather a result of a specific goal structure and process to achieve it. Throughout this book you will find the specifics of training wrestlers such as practice planning, fundraising, weight training, and so forth. However, without a goal, these coaching skills are useless. Your goal structure is the most important part of a coach's job in creating success in all aspects of your program. This includes the physical, mental, and social development of your athletes both on and off the mat. It also includes creating community pride and respect for your athletes and wrestling program.

Most successful people believe that the best way to develop a goal system is from the end backwards. This means that you must decide what is your ultimate goal, whether for one season or many combined seasons, and then work backwards. For example, if your goal is to be state champions, then you will need to put a date on when you expect to achieve it. Upon establishing that objective, it is then necessary to break that down into short term goals. The more detailed a coach is in his/her planning, the better he will be able to measure his progress towards the pre-established long-term goals.

The detail planning of the best coaches follow a very similar pattern. That is, the breakdown of goals in the following manner: year end, seasonal peaks, monthly, weekly, daily, and individually. It must also be stated that your goal structure provides a road map for your destination. However, there are many ways to get from point A to point B, and many times you must allow for variation and flexibility in your planning.

Once your goals are established, it is important to make sure that they are shared and consistent with the goals of your administration, athletes, and community. This shared vision will create the powerful dynamics of a group working together toward a unified goal and not one coach or team working toward a goal in conflict with the necessary support group.

RECRUITING WRESTLERS

An often overlooked part of program development is the recruitment of wrestlers. Many people go with the philosophy of "if you build it, they will come." This may be true for a program with a strong tradition, or that has had recent success, but what about the smaller schools, or programs that are just starting. The coach must be willing to do more than just start the program. The coach must be willing to go out and "beat the bushes" to find those athletes that may not find you. No matter how well you coach your team, the fate of the team is in your athlete's.

When you are recruiting you must first decide what you want out of your program. Do you just want good individuals, a good team, or both? Are you trying to get as many kids involved as possible? Are you trying to offer opportunities for kids that might not be able to compete in other more popular sports? Whatever your reason for coaching, this must reflect in your recruiting tactics, so you can target the types of kids that will work best within your program.

For most coaches the name of the game is numbers. While some coaches just want to make sure their line-up is full. The dedicated coach sees that larger numbers can lead to greater success. The more wrestlers you have the bigger the talent pool, and the more likely it is that you will have a strong athlete in each weight class. The more wrestlers in the room, the more likely it is that you will have a good practice partner for your wrestlers. Games and scrimmages run better. For live wrestling there is more variety in the room. The more wrestlers the more likely you are to find more parent and community resources. Be careful, and remember not to sacrifice discipline, just to get out a large number of kids.

SIDEBAR: The Successful Team Climate
Ted Witulski

Some teams rise at the end of the year while other teams falter. Coaches always seek that little extra to get their team to take another step forward. More and more, coaches have come to the realization that their best years were when they had a united and tightly connected team.

To create a successful team climate sports psychologists have pointed to eight factors that affect a team.

1. **Autonomy:** the opportunity for the athlete to function independently of the group leader, and is able to make decisions on his/her own.

In a high school lineup there is a wide variety of weight classes, and on a high school team there is also a wide variety of personalities. Many time coaches want to use the "cookie-cutter" approach and have the athletes adapt to their coaching style. With experience, most coaches find this approach to be less than ideal.

Coaches should look to encourage autonomy in their wrestlers and actively give wrestlers the freedom and power to adapt their training as needed. Adapting training to fit the needs of different wrestling styles develops maturity in wrestlers and recognizes the wide range of techniques in the sport.

2. **Emotional Support:** the greatest need that an athlete requires from their fellow teammates or coach. Emotional support is most needed when the athlete is performing poorly. If this support is lacking, then the team climate will be affected negatively, athletes will feel abandoned and distant from the group.

Young kids often live in a world of self-doubt. Coaches that recognize the need to build emotional support in their athletes fill an important element in building a successful team. Coaches can model this behavior and teach the wrestlers on their team how to step up for each other and support them as needed.

Coaches should guard against poor treatment of the weak link of the team. Also, sarcasm can be a dangerous impediment for kids to truly feel the emotional support they need.

3. **Pressure:** can create a team environment where the athletes are scared of making a mistake or cause athletes to go beyond their means to defeat a superior opponent.

Coaches use pressure as a part of their practices and discuss it at different points in the season. Building towards major tournament goals will increase pressure, but a united team will respond positively to it.

At times during a season a coach may need to back the pressure off from the team, utilizing other training methods to break up the regiment of practices. Pressure, and the ability to respond to it is an important part of a successful team climate.

4. **Coach's Recognition:** an athletic effort, improvement, and performance are directly related to the athlete's self-confidence, responsibility and team worth. This in turn fosters a supportive and constructive team climate.

A coach has a tremendous ability to make every athlete feel as though they are an important part of the team. Coach's recognition will drive the younger athletes, even if they are not on varsity, to excel.

Coaches can use this ability to model positive behavior and attention for the athletes, in effect teaching the teammates on how to speak to each other in a way that will encourage the development of the team.

5. **Trust:** is important for developing a positive team climate. Coaches should explain to athletes that they trust the athletes' judgment.

In order for a team to succeed there must be a strong feeling of trust among the athletes. Additionally, the coach must encourage proper decision making by the athletes, and constantly reinforce that he/she trusts the athletes' judgment.

A strong sense of trust among the team will help drive the group on to higher accomplishments.

6. **Fairness:** an effective team climate must be based on the athlete's perception of "fair".

Coaches have to work hard at understanding where an athlete "is coming from." Kids will work hard for a program when they trust the decision making and judgment of the coaching staff. Recognize that athletes view every rule under the lens of fairness.

7. **Innovation:** allows the athlete to feel that the team or competition is his or her own. It promotes creativity and allows for the team individual flair to be shown (as long as it is not detrimental to the overall team goal).

Wrestling allows for a wide variety of athletic styles to be successful. Kids will want to feel the freedom to be innovative in their wrestling. Whether it is upper-body wrestling or shooting low-singles a wrestler can make a mark with his/her own style of wrestling.

8. **Cohesion:** a measure of a person's attraction to, sense of belonging to, and desire to remain a part of the group.

The chance for young people to feel as though they fit into the group is an essential part of creating a successful team climate. At every practice or competition all wrestlers should feel like they belong to this team. Work hard at making sure that the athletes aren't trying to single other kids out.

Listed are some ways to begin recruiting:
- Get a list of returning wrestlers
- Get names from teachers (use mass e-mailing to do this)
- Get a list of athletes from each fall sport; write them letters letting them know how wrestling will help them in their other sports.
- Try and introduce yourself, and be visible to as many kids as possible, especially the ones that the teachers write you back with.
- Write as many personalized letters as you can, this is a big task, but kids notice a mass mailing, and feel more wanted with a personal letter.
- Have seniors and juniors target these people on your list, as well as others they know
- Have seniors on fall sport teams recruit within their teams, have them tell "their story" to the younger athletes
- Put up posters in hallways, bulletin boards, fall sport locker rooms, local TV channels, or the schools' TV channel
- Make everything creative, MAKE THE SELL, and be a sincere "salesman"
- Get "popular" school faculty members to recruit
- Put highlight tapes on morning announcements, also place these highlight tapes in study halls or cafeteria's where kids can see them
- Call EVERYONE before the season starts (yes, this means everyone), get together a parent group and get the phone numbers of all the kids in the school that fall into the age group you are targeting, split those numbers up, and make personal contacts with those kids
- Send a letter to all potential wrestler parents—explain any academic, and personal improvements that wrestling can make, ask them to encourage their kids to wrestle

- Establish your rewards system and advertise it to potential athletes so they know what they may earn when they come out for wrestling

KEEPING KIDS OUT FOR WRESTLING

Once you have established ways to get kids out for wrestling, you have to find ways to keep them out. Coaches become frustrated at times when the attrition rate becomes high on their team. Coaches must understand that for the average team, it is always a struggle to keep kids out. Remember you are competing with jobs, other sports, video game systems, and girlfriends. Wrestling is a tough sport, and many times kids find out they do not want to put the work in. You must establish a reward system as well as create other incentives to keep kids active.

To keep kids coming back there are some simple things you can do. First, is keep a good database of kids in your program from the youngest to the oldest. This will ensure that you get the information out to the wrestlers that are already in your program. Each year mail out invitations to the kids, using a letter that lets them know you want them back again.

Create a "STATUS" for the wrestlers. Kids quickly put themselves in different peer groups. Whether it is the trouble making group, the academic group, the athlete group, etc… kids like to know that they have a role, and they like to stick with that role. Make sure you are putting the kids' achievements in the newspaper, in the school announcements, and keep their picture visible to the rest of the school in the form of some sort of bulletin board, so their fellow students know they wrestle. They will feel a sense of pride when the school community knows them as a wrestler, a hard worker, someone that is doing something positive.

You must be organized at practice, and other events. Kids and parents want to be involved with a well run program. Kids know if you are ready for practice or not, and they will have more fun dealing with something that they know you take pride in. Keep as many coaches around each kid at practice as you can. This keeps kids from feeling left out, and gives them more individual attention, which is something that kids crave. Post practices on a bulletin board so your team knows what to expect, and they can look forward to certain parts of practice.

Plan other outings, besides just wrestling. Even the best wrestlers need a break. Many kids will like wrestling, because they know they will get to experience other things in the world through wrestling. Take kids on bowling nights, paintball, indoor rock climbing, movies, dinners, camping, and sightseeing at tournaments. Kids will enjoy trying new things, and they will be excited knowing that when they are at wrestling events, instead of just sitting at hotels in the evenings, they will be able to do something new that they may not have done without wrestling. This also builds team unity, and helps your school administration know that you are trying to do more with the character make-up of your wrestlers, instead of just teaching them how to wrestle.

REWARD SYSTEM

One of the great motivators of mankind is the need for recognition. The knowledge and nurturing of this fact makes a very dramatic difference between good coaches and excellent coaches. The unified effort of parents, athletes, coaches, fans, businesses, administrations, and all support faculties are paramount in every model of excellence. This can be witnessed in the reward structure and recognition accorded to the members of a winning team.

Rewarding your athletes should always be done by the achievement of specific goals. It is important that they are not given incentives and rewards for doing nothing. This will counteract the effect that this recognition is meant to have. The actual substance of the rewards you give your athletes can be as trivial as extra rest during practice all the way up to trophies and plaques presented among a large group of people. The actual reward is not as important as the recognition among the wrestler's peers. When striving toward a worthwhile goal and

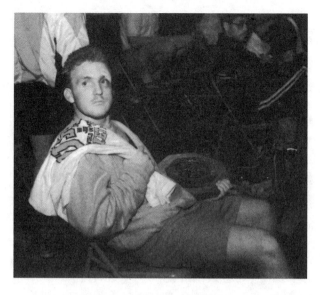

After years of hard work, this athlete's goal of winning a Junior National Championship was achieved.

the achievement of it, the recognition enhances the athletes' feelings of self-worth, self-esteem, and confidence. This, in turn, motivates the athlete toward greater achievement and success. This cycle is fostered by the establishment of the aforementioned goal structure. Within that structure are the targets for the athlete to shoot for daily, weekly, monthly, and seasonally. At the end of those targets is the recognition and reward that every person needs and desires.

There are many ideas that a coach may institute in designing and implementing a reward system for his program. Some time-tested methods are as follows:

- Listing the names of Conference Champions, State Champions, State Placers, All-Americans, National Champions, etc., in view of the public, school, and athletes.
- Establishing records in different categories of achievement, i.e., pins/takedowns, wins/ season, wins/career, tournament victories, etc.
- Developing a Hall of Fame with specific requirements to qualify.
- Having a year-end banquet for the wrestlers, their families, and fans in which the awards are presented.
- Rewarding the team members as a whole

regardless of whether they were the first team members or junior varsity.
- Having a wrestler of the week, month, or particular match.

These are just a few examples of the types of rewards the best coaches and programs use on a regular basis. The sky is the limit when a coach uses the imagination to develop a recognition system for his athletes and wrestling program.

FUND RAISING

The successful development of a wrestling program entails many components to be fulfilled by a head coach and his staff. Beyond the physical, technical, and training skills needed by a coach, it is also necessary to wear the hat of master politician and fund-raiser.

As wrestling is traditionally a non-revenue generating sport, it is crucial for the long term success of a program to have a plan and a means to generate the needed monies to run a team. The best wrestling programs have developed an extensive and detailed fund-raising plan designed to support the ever-growing needs of the athletes, community, and fans.

Though one of the most abhorred responsibilities of a coach, fund raising and promotion for your team is a vital part of creating a program that encompasses all of the components of the best programs.

The primary goal of fund raising is quite simply to raise money to pay for expenses incurred by a program that are necessary but not covered by your budget. The definition of "necessary expenses" will vary from program to program, but will grow as your program develops. For example, when starting a program from scratch, the most important items that may need to be purchased are a wrestling mat and uniforms for your squad. However, as your program develops, other "necessary" items that may be needed are promotional posters, media guides, and better facilities. Regardless of the level of your needs, it is important to understand the basics of how to go about raising money for the success of your program.

SIDEBAR: A Watchful Eye for Signs of Failure

Ted Witulski

Every year the sport of wrestling experiences a drop off rate. After speaking to kids that were once excited about the sport of wrestling, the National Coaches Education Program has identified some areas of concern that club coaches should keep a watchful eye on.

"Who is the coach?"

Many kids cited this as a concern. The coach-athlete relationship is a very important part of developing a strong wrestling program. The recognition that a wrestler receives from a coach can go a long way in keeping the athlete interested in being on the team.

Many former wrestlers noted that their club team did not have a strong coaching staff. In many cases, one coach was trying to do too much on their own. In other instances, the coaching staff was unstable and varied so that the kids could never count on who was running their program.

Of course, all wrestling programs will struggle with finding unpaid volunteers who can consistently put in time with the wrestlers. However, a coaching staff that is inconsistent to young wrestlers does not feel like a team. Instead, the wrestlers get the feeling that there are better things they should be doing with their time.

"We never knew when practice was."

Many former wrestlers and their parents noted that the clubs they joined did not have a well-defined season. As kids and their parents determine what sport and activities they will involve themselves with, one of the cornerstones that they are looking for is a clearly understood structure.

With wrestling clubs fighting to get time out of the ever busy schedules of young athletes it is important that the club has a consistent and clear practice plan. A club that is constantly shifting practice times or canceling workouts will have a difficult time convincing kids to join their program.

Another problem that kids and parents noted was the difficulty with wrestling season running over holiday breaks. If the club experiences problems with keeping a consistent schedule then the club may want to break a long season into smaller blocks: for example, having the clubs first training block running for six weeks in November and December, concluding before the holiday season.

Give the wrestlers and parents a structured program that they can trust. Wrestling clubs are the lifeblood of the sport of wrestling; make sure that the youth club reaches the community in a professional manner.

"Practices are boring. I liked it when we wrestled live, or played games."

Kids have an innate interest in the contact that makes up the sport of wrestling. However, many youth coaches attempt to teach the young wrestlers about the "details" of the moves and rules at the detriment of keeping the kids interested in the sport. A new wrestler wants to get on the mat and wrestle, just like a new basketball or soccer player wants to feel the exhilaration of competition. The lesson that club coaches should learn is that letting the kids dive into live wrestling is a good thing and can lead to teaching the technique and rules of wrestling.

To get kids quickly into the sport of wrestling, coaches are encouraged to use the games approach to coaching wrestling. The games approach encourages coaches to put wrestlers into small groups where the kids get to wrestle in controlled situations for a short time.

The wrestling is the game. The game is then used to lead kids in questioning to understand what technique would work best.

Left to their own devices kids will be drawn to the unique characteristics of the sport of wrestling. Let the young wrestlers experience wrestling as much as possible in the practices through the games approach. There will be time as kids advance in their interest in the sport to learn more technique and the intricacies of wrestling.

"I just felt too much pressure in wrestling."
The wrestling culture can bring with it a lot of pressure on to young wrestlers. It is not uncommon for kids to start wrestling and within a month be competing in a local tournament. In many cases, we may be moving kids too quickly from the practice room on to competitive matches.

Coaches and parents should pay a mindful eye to whether or not the athletes are truly ready to experience the pressure of wrestling competitively in match situations. To evaluate if young wrestlers are ready for competition the coach must be prepared to discuss why wrestlers compete in tournaments and what lessons are gained from the matches in competitions.

If the answers are focused on just winning and the awards given with becoming a champion at the local tournament then the coach may need to take the time to redirect the athlete's attention to other benchmarks such as performing well regardless of the outcome of the match, sportsmanship, and building the athlete into a better person.

"I quit wrestling because practices were always focused on the young kids just starting wrestling."
Nationally the largest drop out rate for kids is in the age range of 12-15 years old. At this age kids look to assert their independence and develop their individuality. Youth of this age are especially sensitive to being "babied". Programs that lump the youngest kids in with the middle school aged wrestlers often see a dramatic loss of these wrestlers.

Programs must look to be innovative by developing solutions to this problem. A good place to start is having practices separated by these age and skill levels. A wrestler who learned penetration steps last year does not look forward to going through the wait of moving on to more advanced skills. When kids feel like the practices are not advancing their skills or keeping them challenged they look to find other things to fill their recreation time.

Coaches must constantly work to make sure that kids of all ages feel that their presence is a valued component to the entire program. The wrestlers of the 12-15 year age range are prime candidates to leave the sport of wrestling if the program does not continue to reach them.

Seven Principles of Sound Fund Raising

1. Go where there is money to be given
2. Ask
3. Create a win-win proposition
4. Be professional
5. Work
6. Combine stability and creativity
7. Sincere verbal and written "Thank You"

1. *Go where there is money to be given*

With the understanding that fund raising is the solicitation of money, the first principle for a coach to know is to, "go where there is money to be solicited." This one principle, when used correctly, will save you time and generate more money than any other principle used.

In most situations, the places and people that may have money to be donated to your program are community businesses, doctors, lawyers, company presidents, business owners, community clubs and organizations, etc. Though there is no guarantee that one or all of these people and organizations will be able to meet your needs, you will greatly increase your chances by soliciting the highest percentage donor.

2. *Ask*

Though the fear of rejection inhibits many coaches from wearing the fund-raising hat, those that overcome that fear must do so by risking rejection and asking for money. In facing this most basic of fears, two things will happen. One, you will overcome your fear of rejection simply by doing that which you fear most; and two, you will raise the needed money for your program.

Businesses and people with money available to donate are most often happy and honored to be able to help support a worthy cause that they believe in. In many instances, the local athletic programs are one of the most recognized and respected organizations in a city or community. For a business or person to be directly associated with a winner and athletic team is a privilege and honor. Do not be ashamed or afraid to ask them to donate to your worthy cause.

3. *Create a win-win proposition*

When soliciting a business or person for a donation, one of the most important principles to remember is to put yourself in the position of the person being asked. When you do this, you can better formulate your approach and sales pitch to meet the needs of that person. Regardless of how much money one may have to donate, people in general will give based on how they can benefit from the transaction. You are soliciting them for *your* purposes but they will give for *their* purposes.

In designing your fund-raising plan and presentation, always think in terms of a win-win situation. How can the money donated benefit your program and how will the donator benefit from giving you the money? Many times this may be intangible such as the mere association with your program or it may be tangible such as advertising space allotted for the donator to help increase their business. Whatever the reward, it is imperative to create a win/win situation for both you and your prospective donor. This will insure a long lasting relationship and possible repeat donations.

4. *Be professional*

When approaching any type of donor, your professionalism will speak volumes about not only yourself but your program, institution, and athletes. Professionalism is no more than presenting yourself as the ultimate representative of how you perceive your program and all those persons associated with it.

This entails the way you dress, your hygiene, your spoken words, any presentation materials, your posture, and organization. All of these traits, when presented in a professional manner, will dramatically increase your chances of being successful in your fund-raising attempts. For most prospects, the only representative they will associate with your program is you. You only get one chance to

make a first impression. Be prepared to make the best presentation possible.

5. *Work*

When all of these principles are applied, you will put yourself and your program in a position to achieve the goals you desire. However, all of that will be useless unless action is put with your preparation. Fundraising is essentially you selling your program to a customer. One of the timeless principles of sales is that it is a numbers game. The more people you present with your product (your program) the more chances you will create in which they will buy it (donate). This can only be achieved by working.

One of the most dangerous mistakes a coach can make in this area is to limit the number of people they approach in hopes that those people will be able to fund your goals. When those few may be unable, for whatever reasons, to meet your needs then the likelihood that your goals will be met decreases dramatically. Put the odds in your favor and work the numbers.

6. *Combine stability and creativity*

Whether just starting a fundraising program or adding to an established one, this principle will have a dramatic effect on the amount of money you will be able to raise.

Stable fund-raisers are those that are developed and can be counted on year after year to generate money. Examples of these would be the formation of a booster Club, running an annual tournament, season ticket sales, wrestling camps, merchandise sales, etc. Creative fund-raisers are those that may not be used every year but help to generate funds for your program. Examples of these could include the sale of raffle tickets, car washes, special events, candy or food sales, specialty advertising, fan clubs, walk-a-thons, etc.

There are numerous ways to be creative in establishing fund-raising programs, and there are basically no limitations on the number of terrific ideas a club or program can use. An added benefit of creative fund raising will be the steady growth of your support group through new people and potential fans being exposed to your athletes, coaches, and program. The key is having a healthy balance of stable and creative money makers. The use of this principle will help to provide your program with both dependable "old" money (stability) and variable "new" money (creativity).

7. *Sincere verbal and written "Thank You"*

Upon receipt of the donation you have so diligently worked for and your donor has happily contributed, the power and effect of a simple "Thank You" cannot be emphasized enough. Too often, people are never thanked for the great job or philanthropy they exhibit on a daily basis. Do not make the mistake of putting yourself with the masses but rather separate yourself from them and sincerely thank your donors for their graciousness.

When thanks is being given in a verbal form, it is important to combine it with the physical actions of sincerity. These being a firm handshake, warm smile, and eye contact. When a written letter is being sent to a donor, it is very important to personally sign each letter and, when possible, write it yourself. This shows your donor that you respect them and their donation enough to take the time out of your busy schedule to write them a note of appreciation and not just send them a form letter that every other donor would receive with a copied signature. When this principle is used, you will create a strong base of loyal donors that will give to your program for years to come and generate a strong predictable income on an annual basis.

BE AWARE OF THE FOLLOWING

Many coaches will start out their career fired up, ready to take on all tasks. Remember to pace yourself, and only do what you can do well. Over extending yourself will only make you tired, leaving you bitter at the end of a day. Coaching is not easy, and you will need to make sure that you take some time for yourself. Be aware of the following items to ensure that you stay positive throughout your coaching career:

- Remember that wrestling does not have to be their favorite sport.
- Be sincere when you ask them to wrestle, and throughout every day of the year!
- Reach them in a number of ways until they understand you care for them.

- Some kids will only want to wrestle because of YOU!
- Do not ever talk bad about other coaches or sports in front of the kids on your team.
- Do not talk bad about kids, to the kids!
- Do establish that you are in a partnership with other sports, and that your primary goal is to empower them to be successful.
- Do know things about your athletes, and talk about other things than just wrestling.
- Do go to other events that your wrestlers participate in, let them know that you support them in all they do.
- Do remember to be prepared at all times, in class, in practice, and in camps. Your reputation will follow you!
- Everyday is a potential day to recruit a wrestler. You may just recruit some wrestler by your everyday demeanor.
- Do not ever get bitter, recruiting and building a program is hard work, and it is all part of being a coach.
- You are probably not the first to have the problems you may experience. Establish yourself in a coaching circle so you have others you respect that you can bounce ideas off of and learn from.
- Do not skip steps of building, or take short cuts. Only hard work succeeds.
- Make sure you coach your coaches. Make your own developmental video if you must so that your assistants know your wrestling vocabulary, and teach what you need them to.

SUMMARY

Fund raising, though one of the least liked aspects of a coach's job, is one of the most important components in developing a sound and perennially successful wrestling program. Its importance to a program is akin to the athlete with one weakness that he fails to develop, and, in turn, it becomes the very one that stops him from achieving his goals. The greatest coaches and programs in the world leave no weaknesses to destroy what they have so diligently worked to achieve. The use of these seven principles will put you and your program on the same level as the best.

6
Match and Program Promotion

Danny Struck, Kyle Fellure, Randy Hinderliter, Ben Stehura

QUESTIONS TO CONSIDER

- What is the most basic principle of promotion?
- What is a tremendous and potentially cost-free way to present your schedule?
- What is the most important aspect to understand when promoting to the media?
- What are the basics of promotion to the media?

A centered and raised wrestling mat is a tremendous way to attract and excite fans.

INTRODUCTION

It has often been said that "You don't play the sport of wrestling." Unlike other sports such as basketball, football, or swimming to name a few, wrestling is not an activity that you can casually "play." The physical, mental, and technical complexities of the sport demand too much for the layman to understand and perform. For those who participate in this great sport, it is precisely that aspect that attracts them. However, it is also this fact that prevents wrestling from being the spectator sport that other sports traditionally are.

Though these facts remain true, the best coaches overcome this apparent obstacle and attract large numbers of fans and supporters. Match and program promotion is a skill that is not an accident. It must be developed with an understanding of what the public and media desires and planning to fulfill those needs. Following are some basic principles for promoting your team to the public and media.

PROMOTION TO THE PUBLIC

Promoting your program and team to the public is one of the most effective ways in which to create a tremendous following. Regardless of how good your team may be, it will not draw people to watch if the public does not know about it. The most basic principle of promotion is to *inform the public.*

There are several steps that are necessary to get this very important information out in front of the public. You and your club must be willing to think outside the box. Wrestling has been around for thousands of years, yet due to the nature of it, the coach must be the person that pushes wrestling in the community over all others. The promotion of your program will not happen on its own. No matter how successful your program becomes, there are some things you will need to do every year to ensure this success. Do not expect others to do this. If you appoint someone to promote the program, oversee it to make sure it gets done.

One of the simplest, yet overlooked, promotional basics that can be done is to make sure a schedule of your matches is readily available and publicized. The time, date, location, and cost of your matches, and/or tournaments, is as important as any other promotional tool you use. Without this information, those that wish to attend your events will not do so due to the simple fact that they did not know about it.

A tremendous and potentially cost-free way in which to present your schedule is the formation of a poster/schedule. This not only notifies the public of your matches but it also gets the faces and names of your athletes in the public eye and conscience. The best way to cover the cost of this project is to solicit sponsors for the poster. In return, the sponsor's name or business can be placed on the poster which will provide them with a terrific vehicle for advertising. Many community businesses desire the advertising, name recognition, and reach that a poster/schedule of this type can provide them.

The distribution of this poster is also an important follow-up to its creation. The use of your wrestlers to distribute them to friends, family, and community businesses is a great publicity and marketing method. Besides creating these posters, you and your team must be the ones that get them out to the public. Start small and work your way out. Start by placing a schedule in every teacher's mailbox, ask them to hang them in their classrooms. Take a

Successful promotion to the public can result in outstanding attendance at your wrestling events.

Saturday off of practice or competition, and "plaster" the town with these posters. When this is done, people get the opportunity to meet the athletes and can then form a relationship with the team and associate the verbal and written information with the distinctive faces and personalities of your program. You may also expand this, and look into getting a local billboard rented during the season, and put your schedule and team picture up.

The use of special events throughout the season is also another way in which to draw attention and interest to your program. This can be done be designating specific matches as those in which discounts, coupons, or souvenirs are provided for special age groups or persons. Some examples of this may be having group nights where a group receives either free or discounted admission; poster night in which the first 50–1000 spectators receive free autographed posters; parents night specifically held to honor the parents of the athletes; theme nights where those dressed according to the particular theme receive free admission; raffle nights where prizes are drawn at the conclusion of the match or during a pre-determined intermission. The creative use of your imagination is the best way in which to devise different ideas that will meet the specific demands of your program, community, and public.

PROMOTION TO THE MEDIA

Wrestling coaches are often frustrated by a lack of coverage by the media. Many coaches become bitter, and blame the newspaper for their lack of coverage. This is a mistake! The most important thing to understand is that coaches should not expect the media to cover wrestling on its own. Like it or not, wrestling is not basketball or football, which receives automatic coverage from the media.

Wrestling people must work to get their local media interested in the sport. It must be both easy and fun for journalists to cover wrestling, or they may not bother.

The first rule is that coaches should not try to "do it all." It is the coach's job to train the athletes and supervise his program. A different person with an interest in the media should be specifically assigned to promoting the team.

This kind of person can be found for almost any program. For a college program, it might be a student sports information assistant, a volunteer journalism student, or an active alumnus. For a high school or club program, it could include a journalism student, an interested parent, even a member of the team. The key is to find somebody who is willing to put in the time and effort to make it work.

Your wrestling promoter only needs a few basic tools to get the job done. A telephone is a must, along with a computer. Many newspapers have press-release times, that they have to meet, and would like to just receive an e-mail from your club on how you did. Many local newspapers will even print your article if you write it, do not be afraid to type up what you want the article to say. You may be surprised to find out you have just created better relations with the newspaper as you save their writers some work. E-mailing in your results is perhaps the quickest and easiest way to get the word out on your teams success.

It should be the goal of your promotions volunteer to develop a regular following for your wrestling program in the local media. They should also try to excite other media to cover wrestling on special occasions.

Basics to Get Started

Create and expand a mailing list

Find the addresses for the journalists who cover wrestling now and those who might cover it in your community. Place the addresses on a label form or in a computer database. This should include newspapers, radio, and TV stations. Make sure to get the name of the person in charge. A letter addressed to "editor" may never reach the proper person. Other information to collect includes phone numbers and fax numbers. This list should be constantly updated, as media members often change jobs or get new assignments. E-mail can be your biggest ally. Don't just e-mail the media, write your own weekly or monthly newsletters. Send out e-mails before upcoming events, and send out results.

To get this e-mail list going, make sure you have a place for parents to place their e-mail on any pre-season registrations, or sign-in sheets you send out. Also make sure your e-mail is placed in highly visible areas on everything you send out. This will ensure that parents and fans can always keep in contact with you.

Work the mailing/target list

Create pre-event press releases, results press releases and feature story press releases. Make sure that wrestling is a part of the journalist's regular mail and e-mail.

Call selected journalists (personal contact is always best) with story ideas and invitations to attend events. Ask them how you can better help them cover the team. Be positive, no matter how badly you are treated. If you have journalists that can be especially useful make sure you send them a hand written note at the beginning of each season, and end of each season. Give them a t-shirt, and even take them out to eat one night before the season starts. Positive press can be one of your biggest recruiters, as young wrestlers and parents will read this and want to be a part of the team.

Create story ideas (find an angle)

Ask yourself: "Why should this be covered? What is interesting, new or exciting about this?" Don't expect journalists to fully research your story. Do as much of the work for them in advance. Make it easy to cover.

The best personal human interest stories are often locked in a coach's head. Tell your publicity volunteer about your athletes, team, and the competition. Before big events write in to the paper, not only things about your team, but other local wrestlers to watch for. Send in rankings, and other items of interest that the newspaper can use to create the interest in your upcoming meet.

Some journalists don't care about who beat who. They want feature material and interesting personal tidbits. Get to know your athletes as people and share that with the press. Wild hobbies, outstanding academics, big families, obstacles and handicaps over-

come . . . the list goes on forever if you are creative.

"Each year I e-mail the local news writers possible human interest stories. These stories could be things like: Brothers wrestling, a person overcoming a handicap, someone trying to fulfill the family legacy of wrestling, or a kid that has improved due to his hard work. You will also find that your school administration will like these stories, as it shows not just the winning and losing, but it shows what your program does for the kids at your school!"

Danny Struck—Indiana State Wrestling Association's State Coach Gold Certified Coach

Be available/make athletes available

Stories often die because journalists can't locate coaches or athletes for interviews in a timely fashion. Be available. If busy or traveling, let someone know where you are and how to reach you. Check in for messages. Return requests promptly. This is the biggest area of missed opportunities. Regularly invite journalists into your wrestling room, and let them know what is going on with your program at all times.

Create your own web-site

With the growth of the internet, many people don't get the daily paper anymore. Rather they get their news on the internet. If you can not create your own web-site, make sure you find someone that can. E-mail out notices each time you update the web-site. You can write your own stories on here, or post links to stories that have been written in the newspaper. Make sure you have a digital camera ready to keep pictures of your athlete's always changing on your web site. Kids love to see their picture, and this is a sure fire way to make sure they know they are being recognized.

With your web-site you can also have readily available your meet schedule, practice schedule, or have any other reminders posted that your athletes and parents need to have accessible.

Don't forget to add your school records,

favorite links, stats, and any other things that you want the public, and your kids to know. Showcase what you feel is most important!

Local/School Television

Most school systems, and towns have their own local stations now that play reruns of local basketball, and football games. While they might not come to record your match, you have to be willing to record your own! Get some past wrestlers to dress in a tie, and come in and do the mat-side commentary. Record, it and edit it. Most likely your school, or local station will be willing to play it, if you do the work. Try this with both high school an elementary wrestlers. If they see themselves wrestling on TV, the will most likely forever see themselves as wrestlers!

Also try giving them your highlight film, and having them run this on tv a few times, with your next wrestling sign-ups posted along with it.

Other sources of media attention

Besides the local paper, and tv keep in mind the following alternative media sources: school yearbook, school newspaper, school corporation newsletter, yard signs, bumper stickers, "fan club" t-shirts, marquee signs outside your school, and making personal appearances at other local youth sports to promote your program.

Create "The Big Event"

No matter how good or bad a team or schedule may be, there will always be at least one event which has special importance. It may be a meeting with an arch-rival, a match for a team championship, the regional or post-season qualifier, something that makes it bigger than the others. It could also be an individual match up, the two best in the league or region going for top rankings. Identify those and blow them up.

The final thing to remember is to treat the journalists well when they decide to cover your team. You must provide them a professional work situation, so they will be encouraged to come again. Remember—EASY and FUN.

Journalists need a few basics to do their job correctly. A place to sit, a place to work, a place to shoot photos and video tape, and access for interviews. For large programs, that means having a press row and work room available. For others, it may just mean giving the journalist a VIP seating location.

When the event is over, the coaches and athletes must be available for interviews, regardless of whether or not the team wins. If a journalist cannot get quotes after the event, which is part of their job, he/she may never cover wrestling again. The journalist may also need access to a telephone to file the story. Help them do their job.

After the event, the publicity volunteer should report the story and results to those not there. You might type up a small press release with results to FAX, e-mail or mail to local media. At the very least, it includes calling in the final result and highlights of the event to the media after every match.

This is a great place to be ready to think outside the box. We sometimes overlook professional wrestling as something that degrades our great sport. However, if we look at their marketing ideas it is easy to see why they are so successful. It isn't always the meet that is the center of focus but the show around it. At each home meet try to have something for the "non-wrestling fans." Have the dance team come in for a song and dance, or a local elementary school choir do your national anthem. Have "alumni-night" at your meet, and honor past greats of your program with some sort of special recognition. Have your middle school wrestle the opposing teams middle school, just before the high schools dual. Have free hot dog night for students with a high school ID.

The average person doesn't understand or even fully appreciate wrestling. In fact, most people had never attended a meet. You must create other angles to get the fans to come in. Above all don't be afraid to copy ideas that other sports, or organizations have used to get the fans in. Part of running a program is being a good marketer.

SUMMARY

There is no guarantee that doing this work will always result in receiving media coverage. However, if these basics are not covered, it is a good bet that there will be no coverage at all.

Most of this is not the job of a coach. Someone else should be doing the work. However, a coach must help make it easy for his promotions people to do their job. The coach should also follow up to make sure it is getting done.

SIDEBAR: What makes a successful high school wrestling program?
Tim Ottmann

There are seven basic elements to a successful high school wrestling program:

1. Great Coaching—At the root of all great wrestling programs are great coaches. They know how to teach sound fundamental techniques, organize excellent practice sessions, delegate to assistant coaches and motivate. In addition, many if not all, are excellent communicators.

2. Developing and Maintaining a Good Feeder Program—In order to reach the skill level necessary for championship performance, most wrestlers need to start wrestling before high school. A solid youth and middle school program provides the opportunity for kids to reach that skill level to compete for state championships.

3. Strength Training—Whether it's in the pre-season, post-season or during the season, strength training is essential to a wrestler's success. If both wrestlers are fundamentally sound, the stronger wrestler often comes out on top.

4. Off-Season Participation (Freestyle, summercamps)—Wrestling, like most sports, has become a ten month a year commitment. In order to get the "mat time" necessary to develop excellent technique and mat savy, wrestlers must train in the spring, summer and fall months.

5. Having a Tough Dual Meet and Tournament Schedule—"In order to be the best, you must beat the best". It's better to have a tough schedule and get beat a few times, than to have a soft schedule and have it catch up with you during Regionals and State. Quality programs are seen at the most competitive tournaments and duals.

6. Effective Use of Practice Time—Great wrestling programs don't waste time during practice sessions. Practice time should be scheduled with opportunities for skill development, combative matches, conditioning and strength training.

7. Dedicated Parents—Before high school coaches have an opportunity to begin working with freshmen, moms and dads have spent countless hours taking them to tournaments, motivating them to strive to be the best, and supporting them through difficult times. In high school, parental support is crucial to the success of high school wrestlers and the program in general.

7
Wrestling Club Development

Danny Struck, Kyle Fellure, Randy Hinderliter, Ben Stehura

QUESTIONS TO CONSIDER

- What do all successful wrestling clubs have in common?
- What are the six questions that need to be answered when starting a wrestling club?
- Is it necessary to have both medical and liability insurance for a wrestling club?

The development of a wrestling club can benefit many kids.

INTRODUCTION

Today, in one way or another, all kids face some difficult odds because they have to make daily choices about drugs, alcohol, and sex that can affect the rest of their lives. All too often, they have to make those choices when they are far too young to recognize the consequences of making the wrong decision.

Knowing that, responsible adults are willing to put in the time, effort and energy it takes to organize and run youth sports programs. They know that more often than not kids who get turned on to sports won't turn to drugs.

Consider the possibilities and remember that you, and adults like you, can make an important difference in the lives of youngsters in your community by giving them the opportunity to participate in wrestling.

Naturally, every town or community is different. In many communities, youngsters have very few opportunities to participate in well-organized and well-run youth sports programs. Perhaps yours is one of them. If that's the case, then it should be fairly easy to find other adults who are willing to join you in organizing a Kids Wrestling Club.

Maybe there are already several other ongoing youth sports organizations, but many kids still aren't involved in sports. Here again, it is not hard to point out how and why wrestling offers some benefits not to be found in other sports.

So, let's get specific. Answer the questions about youth sports in your community, and you will have a better idea about how a Kids Wrestling Club can become a success in your community.

GETTING ORGANIZED

The volunteer in any wrestling program, particularly in any youth wrestling program, is the heart and soul of any club. It's what makes the wheels go round and round.
Mark Scott, Director of State Services, USA Wrestling

Nearly all successful wrestling clubs have several things in common. They put the emphasis on fun and fundamentals and de-emphasize winning until youngsters are emotionally ready to accept both winning and losing.

Almost all wrestling clubs have something else in common; they all started small, sometimes with a tiny, but dedicated group of volunteers taking on all the different duties and responsibilities involved in running a Kids Wrestling Club.

In many cases, the idea to start a Kids Wrestling Club begins with one individual, who must then go about getting the help he or she needs to bring the benefits of this sport to kids in the community. If you find yourself in that position, then you probably have several questions:

1. *Who will organize the team?*
2. *Who will coach?*
3. *Who will pay expenses?*
4. *Where will they practice?*
5. *What will they wear?*
6. *What are the legal responsibilities?*

In looking at the answers to those and other questions, you will soon recognize that you are going to need the help of a group of adult volunteers.

Who Will Organize the Team?

Why not you? Usually a parent, high school coach or other adult with a concern for the well being of kids in the community takes the job. And often they have little or no previous experience in organizing a club for kids or adults. With this in mind, do not let any lack of experience on your part keep you from taking the steps that will get you moving toward a successful wrestling program.

Your first step is to ask around and find other people interested in helping you. Copy off others to come up with ideas to find people in your community that can pitch in. If your school has had any sort of tradition at all, there are probably past wrestlers that are just waiting for someone else to take the initiative to start the club, but if asked they will be willing to pitch in and help. Go back and look through past team pictures, and get a list of names, you may be able to look them up in a phone book and invite them to come in.

Getting an "alumni" meeting together may be another great start. Teams do this from the professional ranks, to college, and on down to high school. This keeps alumni excited about what you are doing, they keep pitching in, and they want to see the programs they came from succeed.

Organizational Meeting

Find a meeting place, such as a local YMCA, church, school, recreation center, or your home, and call a meeting of people who might be interested. Then send announcements about the meeting to local newspapers and radio station. Usually the news media is happy to give you free publicity for community projects like this. Remember to send out thank you cards, or give the media a t-shirt. They can be your biggest ally.

How you approach this organizational meeting depends largely on the people in your community and their current interest in and enthusiasm for wrestling. If you live in an area where wrestling is already very popular, then you will have little if any trouble "selling" the sport.

On the other hand, if you live in a community that isn't already well tuned in on the benefits of Kids Wrestling, you may need to take the time to explain the positive benefits of the sport. If you aren't a former wrestler, then you might want to get someone who is willing to talk about their positive experiences in the sport.

If you are not in an area where wrestling is popular, you may also need to hit getting parents together from another angle. The more parents feel a part of something, the more they will want to be there.

If you have a great deal of initial interest in the club, you will probably be able to find one individual to serve in each position. Of course, smaller groups of people can double up on some of the jobs. Following are the various positions that need to be filled:

The President; runs the meeting, appoints committees and oversees all the club's business.

The Vice-President; fills in whenever the president cannot make a meeting or other club business.

The Secretary; records minutes at each meeting, and maintains correspondence with other clubs and with USA Wrestling's state or national officers.

The Treasurer; has responsibilities that grow with the size of the club. In the beginning, with a very small club, operating on a small budget, one of the other officers might handle the money. But clubs can quickly grow to the point where keeping accurate accounts of revenues and expenditure becomes a time consuming job, and one best handled by someone with experience.

Depending on the size of the club, you might also need to set up committees to secure a place to practice, provide transportation to out-of-town matches, find equipment, and conduct your own tournaments. Many clubs create

---

IDEA

Have a "parent social." Have parents bring their favorite side dish or finger food to someones house. By having it at a house parents feel welcome, and feel a more family atmosphere to being involved in the club. Make this "social" something that doesn't necessarily have to be a meeting for anything other than to build camaraderie within your parent support group. You will find that the wrestling talk will develop on its own, and groups of parents will take off on ideas and get them organized on their own if they have a friend involved with them.

The main goal of the meeting is to enlist the help and cooperation of other adults and, if possible, to elect a slate of officers.

SIDEBAR: Helping the Coach Help You

Ted Witulski

Every wrestling coach in the country could use a little help. The title, wrestling coach, does not denote all of the tasks that have to be performed to just get through the day-to-day running of a wrestling team. A successful team is a goal for all coaches, but it is amazing how many things can get in the way.

The progress and performance of the program can be at risk when the coach has to do it all himself and is stymied by numerous situations that arise. Coaches are full of pride and hesitant to ask for help. However, a quality coach recognizes the need to get everyone invested in the program. Outlining expectations and ways that the athletes can help the team gives a clear signal on what needs to be done. Coaches are encouraged to integrate thoughts such as these in team discussions with their athletes.

Step one: Recruit hard for the team.

Every season the coaching staff of a team faces a new reality. Holes to fill, the four-year starter is gone, 14 weight classes to find a body for. The task is daunting, every weight from 103 to heavyweight has to have a wrestler. Of course the other reality is the sport doesn't have an easy sell to teenagers these days. Hard work and dedication doesn't scream fun to a high school kid who would rather spend their winter strengthening their thumb muscles playing video games.

So with that kind of reality in mind, help the coach out. Get out there each and every day and talk up the great side of wrestling to all potential participants. Don't size them up and think they don't have potential. The wrestling season and their desire will determine the outcome. Get your friends on the mats this winter, a growing team will signal to your school that something good is happening with wrestling.

When wrestlers make the "come out for wrestling" sales pitch, they should avoid the threatening language of tough practices and weight cutting. Instead sell the positives of the sport such as the values that it instills like commitment, and desire.

Every high school wrestler that loves the sport should push hard to build a bigger and better team and that means helping the coach recruit. Between now and the start of the season put the full court press on for athletes to join the wrestling team.

Step Two: No Team Member is a Punching Bag

High School is a tough time for almost everybody. Very often in schools a pecking order gets established. Unfortunately, it becomes acceptable to mistreat some guys on the team. Please remember that these teammates are out for wrestling for the same reason as everyone else. It's not an easy choice to become a wrestler, so treat all that take their passion for the sport experience to the mat with respect.

The coach can't be there to protect everyone at all times and of course sometimes it might seem like some kids are just asking for it. But if joking around turns into horseplay that singles out one kid or a group of guys then the dissension and hurt that is caused can be a real barrier for the wrestling team.

Leaders on the wrestling squad need to be the ones that tell teammates to "knock it off" and "we don't need that on our team." In today's society slip ups in judgment can lead to serious repercussion that even lurch into litigation.

Make a conscious effort to help foster the right environment amongst teammates, so that all participants will be proud of the time they spent on the wrestling team.

Step Three: Hit the showers.

Years ago a coach would end practice with the phrase, "hit the showers." With shrinking budgets for athletic teams, one of the first program cuts often made is a towel service for a high school team. More often than not, schools no longer provide essentials like towels and antibacterial soap to go with the phrase "hit the showers".

With these budget cuts many kids have decided that a shower can wait until they get home. In wrestling, the ultimate contact sport, this bad decision can give a coach nightmares.

"I shower when I get home", kids will say but in the meantime that choice leaves the team more susceptible to skin diseases. Once skin infections like ringworm, impetigo, herpes, scabies, and molluscum make their appearance, then the team can suffer all season long. For the coach it means getting kids to doctor's appointments, juggling lineups, and making sure the skin-check paperwork is current.

Quite simply, skin infections are easily avoided with the right precautions. So when the coach says, "hit the shower"—do it. Don't risk the wrestling team's season.

Step four: Leader on the mats—-leader moving the mats.

Everyone wants to wrestle in their home gym more often, except some coaches. If a coach is expected to do it all on his own, a home meet can be a ton of work. Those mats aren't going to move on their own, but many wrestlers approach mat moving like it is a game where they compete against the coach. How long can we make it take? Or, how can I sneak out of here?

When setting up for a meet or when the competition is finished wrestlers that are truly leaders are the ones that dive into tearing down the mats with the intensity of an Airborne Ranger. If the coach has to stand over the team to get the mats back to the practice room then jobs like media promotion and interaction with alumni suffer.

Keep a smile on your coaches' face and take a leadership role in the setting up and tearing down of home meets.

Step five: Promote with Don King's Intensity.

It's not too exciting to wrestle in an empty high school gym. The coach feels the same way that the wrestlers do. He'd love to see more people in the seats to watch the matches, after working so hard to field a competitive team. Be a wrestler that finds ways that get people to turnout for home matches.

Be creative and be active in the effort. Make sure that everyone on the team is pulling together to jam the gym for those home duals and tournaments. If wrestlers attend basketball games then basketball players should go to wrestling meets. Always alert classmates to home matches. Type up a flier for the home meet. Make an announcement in each of your classes and ask the teacher to write it up on the chalkboard. Go out of your way to ask all of your teachers and classmates to be at the upcoming match. Be prepared to give detailed answers on what time it starts.

Once people attend a wrestling meet they can be hooked. So, push hard to help your coach promote the upcoming events.

Step six: On time with no whine.

As the season gets to rolling at some point the coach has to deliver the bad news. "Everyone needs to be here at 5:10 a.m. so we can make it to the weigh-ins on time." Of course the coach probably doesn't enjoy the early start to the day anymore than the wrestlers do. But, whining and complaining about it won't change it.

Additionally, wrestlers that decide to go out the night before and have a good time won't be effective on the mat the next day. Get your rest before the early start to these tournaments. Make sure that you make it to the bus in plenty of time, so the coach has one less person to worry about.

A little thing like being on time and not whining about it will help the coach enjoy the wrestling season as well.

Step seven: School is the priority—make sure you study.

With all of the things a wrestling coach has to take care of, probably the most frustrating thing that happens is a wrestler is not eligible to compete. Students who let their grades slip, put the team in jeopardy.

Then, when the coach calls the kid on the carpet about it the excuses start flying. Excuses like "I didn't know about the test" or "that teacher hates wrestlers" don't address the real problem. Dedication to class work is more important than the wrestling season.

Keep the priorities in line and don't fall into the trap of acting cool or sleeping through study halls. Most students have at least one study hall a day, that when used effectively can keep grades to acceptable levels. Too often high school wrestlers decide to blow off class work for a mid-day nap in study hall. Don't go down that path.

The coach and the team are counting on all athletes to get the work done in the classroom. So, help the coach and follow through from your end.

Step eight: Represent yourself and wrestling.

Making it through high school is a minefield full of choices. Of course everyone likes to have a good time. And, a mischievous nature is not confined solely in a wrestler's spirit. However, more than once a wrestling coach has been confronted by an administrator or fellow teacher with the phrase, "Did you hear what your wrestler did?"

The pride that a coach feels in his program can be shattered by the poor judgement of one of his athletes. The foolish, prank or disrespectful statement to a teacher, immediately gets attached to the wrestling team.

Be careful, think twice, your actions reflect on the sport that you represent. A coach would much rather hear from another teacher about how well mannered his team is. Save the tough guy image for the time on the mat and spend the rest of the day showing everyone, from the janitor—to the Spanish teacher—to the principal why wrestling makes a difference in people's lives.

When a coach makes it through the season he'll remember it as a successful year that he never wanted to see end, or a season he's glad is over. Primarily, the coach will judge the year on the ability of his team to represent the sport of wrestling with pride.

Step nine: Clean your own room.

Just because wrestling is a war on the mat, doesn't mean that the practice room has to look like a war-zone. A coach often becomes the team janitor as well. He spends much of his time picking up orange peals or the discarded sports drink bottle or the abandoned sweat-soaked clothes and wads of athletic tape. Is it his responsibility to clean the mats and empty the trash cans, and find whose head-gear is this?

Coaches want wrestlers to take ownership and pride in their own practice facility. Help him out and pick up your own messes. When people walk by the wrestling room, it shouldn't look like a mess, and wrestlers on the team can help assure that by taking care of their practice room.

Step ten: See the potential in every practice.

Involve yourself deeply in the wrestling season. And, don't rely on the coach to jack you up and beg you to practice each day. At the end of each practice ask yourself, "did I get as much out of that practice as I should have?"

Also, remember to see your commitment to wrestling through the coaches' eyes. At some point during the season the ho-hum of another practice starts to creep into the team's mindset. Wrestlers will walk up to the coach and say things like, "I'm not feeling well…..I don't think I should practice."

Of course the coach will tell you if you are sick or injured then you should sit out. But, the real question should be the one from yourself. "Am I really sick or injured or am I cheating myself out of valuable practice time?"

The wrestling season will challenge you at some point. A long day of school will leave you wanting to head home early. When the season gets tough on you, the coach is counting on you to make the right decision.

Don't just wrestle when it's convenient. Dig deep and challenge yourself daily. The rewards of a champion are earned through the day-to-day struggle to be the victor.

The coach has many responsibilities and can always use a helping hand. Wrestlers don't have to work overly hard to help in these ten simple ways. When the season is complete, wrestlers should want to know that the coach didn't want the journey to end. Each and every day wrestlers will be presented with the opportunity to help the coach in the simplest of ways. He's counting on you to make the right decisions.

more positions with the attitude of "delegate or die." Meaning that one person cannot do it all themselves. Some other positions that you might think of adding are: head pairer, head referee, elementary, middle, and high school representatives, statistician, and membership director.

Who Will Coach the Team?

This can be a tricky question. The goal of this book, along with the USAW Video Syllabus, is to give people with limited experience the guidance they need to run a successful wrestling club. If you need to find a coach, start by seeing if any parent has experience in wrestling. Look around the community for an ex-wrestler willing to accept the responsibilities involved in coaching youngsters. Even look at getting high school wrestlers to coach your elementary wrestlers. Just be sure to find an individual whose goals are consistent with those of the club. You must be careful of who you put in leadership roles, as coaches can have the biggest influence on the direction of your club, and the loyalty of the kids. Someone who understands the importance of emphasizing fun, fitness, and fundamentals.

Do not be afraid to ask for help, but do not underestimate the time and effort the coach will need to spend on the job. Depending on the number of youngsters, you might also need to find people, possibly parents, to serve as assistant coaches. You need to make arrangements for the club to pay the expenses that all too often wind up being paid by the volunteer coach. The younger the age of the kids the more help you need. At the high school level although it is hard, you should try to have 1 coach for every 6 kids. Kids in the 5th through 8th grades need a slightly larger number of supervisors, and in the youngest ages, especially kindergarten and 1st grade you cannot have too many helpers. Every practice, begin by encouraging the parents to get involved in practice. Tell them the practice, and the benefits their kids will receive from wrestling are much better if they take an active role. They need no experience, just to watch the coach, and help reinforce what they coach has instructed.

Who Will Pay the Expenses?

One of wrestling's great advantages is that it really does not cost much for a youngster to participate. And most clubs strive to keep it that way, by keeping individual member costs as low as possible and at times by arranging for the club or its financial supporters to pay membership costs for disadvantaged youngsters.

Naturally, travelling to events can start getting expensive, especially if and when a club wants to begin attending state or national tournaments. Clubs use a variety of means to raise money.

Sponsors

Many organizations and civic-minded clubs regularly make funds available for youth activities. Businesses certainly can create a lot of good will, while putting their name in front of the public, by sponsoring youth sports teams. Do not be shy about asking for financial help, but be prepared to answer any question from how the money will be used to how it will benefit the kids in the program. As clubs grow, their revenues and expenditures can climb rapidly.

You don't necessarily need the local business community to pick up all your expenses. Most clubs sell concessions, including food and drinks and even T-shirts, to raise money. Turning over the job of managing concessions to one individual who will work closely with the treasurer to account for the money spent and earned is a very efficient and professional method. The person in charge of concessions also gets volunteers to work different booths during matches or tournaments. Make sure that when you ask for money from a business that you create a win/win situation. Businesses and people in your community are more likely to pitch in if they see this as some sort of help to their endeavors. Place a team photo in their business, or publicly thank your sponsors in the newspaper, or by placing their name on the back of your shirts. Get creative! There are many ways you can thank these businesses, and the more creative you get, the more businesses will want to help.

Booster Clubs

After some clubs reach a certain size and level of popularity, they can turn over the entire fundraising effort to a booster club, which will organize in much the same way as the Wrestling Club itself.

With or without one, a Wrestling Club can generate funds with some traditional methods such as car washes and bake sales (see Chapter 6). These days you can also rely on some more high tech money makers by having a parent with a home video camera tape matches or events and then sell copies to parents, grandparents, and other fans.

Where Will the Club Practice?

Here you may need to enlist the help of local high school or junior high coaches. Again, do not be shy about asking for their help because junior and senior high school coaches certainly understand how kids wrestling can help their own programs.

If the high school or junior high gyms aren't available, look for a YMCA, community recreation center, or church with a gym or auditorium. You need to make certain that your facility has plenty of mats. Because of the additional safety they offer, try to buy mats designed specifically for wrestling.

If you can't afford a wrestling mat, use smaller and less expensive tumbling mats. You must be sure to fasten or tape them together so that the mats do not slide around, allowing a youngster to fall on a hard floor.

What Will They Wear?

Like mats, proper clothing enhances safety. Wrestlers can use gym shorts, tee shirts, and tennis shoes. The only special equipment used consists of elbow and knee pads and headgear.

Uniforms for your wrestlers are optional. You really don't need them in the beginning. If the kids want them, and if their parents or the club can afford them, uniforms are well worth the price. Wearing a team uniform is important to most youngsters; and it certainly helps your athletes think and act like a team when they're dressed as one.

What kids cannot wear

Because they greatly increase the risk of injury, no youngster should practice while wearing . . .

● Any jeans or slacks with zippers
● A leather belt with a buckle
● Rings, watches or other jewelry

LEGAL RESPONSIBILITIES

Anyone starting a wrestling club is going to have questions about their possible legal liability. This is an area where you can get an enormous amount of help when your club applies for a Charter under USA Wrestling. Despite the relative safety of kids wrestling, there's always some risk of injury.

Clubs need both medical and liability insurance, which is available at very low rates through USAW. The details about medical and liability insurance, club charters, and memberships can be obtained by contacting USA Wrestling at (719) 598-8181. The issues concerning legal responsibilities are covered in greater detail in Chapter 3 entitled *Effective Teaching*.

8
Women's Wrestling

Katie Downing

QUESTIONS TO CONSIDER

- How many girls were wrestling on boys high school teams by 1999?
- What style do women wrestle in college?
- What opportunities do women have in wrestling after high school?

The development of women's wrestling presents new opportunities for athletes and coaches around the world.

BACKGROUND

Women's wrestling may be a new chapter to this book, but it is not as new to the story of wrestling as it may seem. Although the International Olympic Committee (IOC) did not name women's wrestling as an Olympic event until 2004, FILA (the international governing body for amateur wrestling) began hosting women's world championships as early as 1987. American women have traveled to the world championships since 1989. Three US women have earned gold medals at the world championships. Trish Saunders, originally from Michigan, earned her titles in 1992, 1996, 1998, and 1999. Sandy Bacher of California earned her gold in 1999. Kristie Marano earned her title in 2000. All together, US women have earned over thirty world championship medals.

Female interest in the sport of wrestling has been a bit of a paradox. On one hand, a girl wrestling in high school may be the only female wrestler in her school, region, or state. On the other hand, female participation in wrestling has snowballed every year since the early 1990's. In 1990, there were around one hundred girls wrestling on boys' high school (folkstyle) teams. By 1999, over two thousand girls wrestled in high school. USA Wrestling (freestyle) membership for women and girls more than doubled between 1994 and 1996. At the collegiate level, the University of Minnesota-Morris opened its wrestling room to women back in 1994. Although additional programs like Cumberland College in Kentucky and Missouri Valley College established themselves as solid women's wrestling schools over the years, the US still struggles to host more than around a dozen collegiate women's wrestling programs nationwide.

The pioneering women in wrestling struggled throughout their entire careers on the mat. They fought for respect, for recognition as a legitimate sport, for access to wrestling rooms and training partners, for opportunities to compete against males or females, for media or promotional exposure within the wrestling community, and for the right to train and compete in the sport they loved and took as seriously as their male counterparts. Wrestlers like Trish Saunders grew up wrestling the likes of Zeke Jones, faced exclusion and resistance within the sport during her junior high and high school years, and then went on to dominate the lightest weight class in women's wrestling both nationally and internationally for many years. The women of Saunders' time in wrestling built the foundation for women's wrestling, setting a standard of excellence for US women at the international level in wrestling. Unfortunately, the women that so deserved Olympic medals never even got the chance to compete in the Olympics.

The next wave of women in wrestling became the first US Olympic Team in 2004. The first Olympians were bronze medalist Patricia Miranda of California, Tela O'Donnell of Alaska, silver medalist Sara McMann of Pennsylvania, and Toccara Montgomery of Ohio. By the time these women could make the Olympics their ultimate goal, they had icons and role models like Saunders. Most of the women who are the same age as the first four Olympians came up through high school as the only girl on their team. This age group had a few more options for training and competing in wrestling, but still had to really work to create sufficient training conditions for themselves after high school. The resources finally came all together in 2002 when the resident program opened at the Olympic Training Center (OTC) in Colorado Springs, and USA Wrestling hired Terry Steiner as the full time women's national coach. Two years later, the US Olympic Education Center opened up at Northern Michigan University for student athletes who are emerging at the senior level.

Women's wrestling changes drastically from year to year. New opportunities constantly open up around the country. Some women have become well known names and faces in our sport, but there have been a number of new young women climb to the top of the ranks from out of nowhere each year. The incentive for athletes and coaches to get involved in women's wrestling grows in our sport because women's wrestling is now an Olympic level sport and because opportunities for athletes and coaches continue to materialize, develop, and evolve.

THE NUTS AND BOLTS AND THE GRAY AREAS

At the elite level, women train and compete with other women, and coaches deal with adults. When men and women train together it is voluntary for both people involved. For the rest of women's wrestling, coaches are working with girls and dealing with the issues surrounding boys and girls training and competing together. This is where coaches may feel nervous about girls wrestling on their boys' teams, and this is where the gray areas appear. Coaches have many questions about physical contact, strength differences that cause injuries, public opinion, and emotional differences or needs, to name a few. The best and simplest policy for coaches in uncertain situation is to do what is best for the boys and girls as wrestlers and teammates. Girls who stay in the sport are there to wrestle for all of the same reasons that the boys are. The sport of wrestling and the demands of a season on the mat will weed out any boys or girls who are not ready to take their wrestling seriously.

PHYSICAL CONTACT

Wrestling is a full contact, combative sport. The combative contact is exactly what draws many people into the sport, but it is also a gray area for coaches with boys and girls on their teams. Coaches and athletes certainly have to acknowledge that close contact between boys and girls can be an issue, but it should never be a big enough issue to hinder practice or obstruct any boy or girl from training. It may sound too simple, but the best way to avoid feeling uncomfortable is to purposefully think about and treat a female athlete as a wrestler-not a girl wrestler-just a wrestler. A lot of tension and apprehension about a girl wrestling boys dissipates when the wrestlers and coaches look at the girls on their teams and see wrestlers and teammates. Coaches can set the attitude for having a girl in the room and the program. Coaches can be careful and mindful of how it will look when they wrestle or shows moves on their female athletes, but should not exclude her entirely. How the coach treats girls in the room says a lot to the wrestlers about how they should act toward the female on the team.

STRENGTH DIFFERENCES AND INJURIES

Some parents and coaches worry about girls getting hurt wrestling boys. Girls certainly go into wrestling boys with disadvantages in speed and strength. Fortunately, wrestling cultivates perseverance and the ability to overcome obstacles and adversity. Girls often make up for strength disparities with mental toughness to even out the playing field for themselves. Regardless of how tough a girl may be, no one wants to see her get hurt wrestling someone much too big or strong for her. Parents would be worried about their 103 pound son training with the heavyweight every day, but what coaches and parents need to understand about girls wrestling boys is that the discrepancy is not as extreme as the difference between a 103 pounder and a heavyweight. The discrepancy between a girl and a boy in the same weight class is enough to make it hard for the girl to win, but it is not enough to put the girl in danger of getting hurt by wrestling a boy. A lot of times the best training partner for a girl may be the boys a weight class or two below her. The best girls in wrestling will be able to beat stronger opponents in their weight classes with better technique or conditioning. The best drilling and live wrestling situations will be with the boys who are as skilled as her at the lower weights. Then the match ups are more equal.

PUBLIC OPINION

Coaches at any level know that plenty of people in the community have opinions they are not afraid to convey about the way a wrestling program is run. Plenty of people also have opinions about women's wrestling. As the sport continues to grow, more and more coaches will have to step up to the challenge of dealing with public opinion on women's wrestling and on girls wrestling boys. Women's wrestling is in the Olympics just like men's freestyle and Greco-roman wrestling. Competitors and coaches involved in women's wrestling are working within a pool of competitors that is much smaller than that of men's wrestling. It is important for coaches to look at training a girl in local wrestling programs as a chance to train a future Olympian.

Coaches with girls on their teams will face some resistance or derogatory attitudes, but they can not allow themselves or their programs to be impaired by negative influences. Coaches can alleviate tensions with the public over girls wrestling by simply pointing out that girls have the right to wrestle, and letting people see what women's wrestling is all about for themselves. When coaches are big enough to give girls the opportunity to wrestle on their teams, everyone involved learns over time that wrestling is wrestling and that the girl on the team is a wrestler like her teammates. When people see a girl training hard or putting her heart out on her sleeve during a wrestling match, it does more to change minds about women's wrestling than arguing for hours does.

Any girl or woman in wrestling is a natural underdog. Having a girl on a boys' team can be great for team morale and attitude, and it can be a way to promote the team in the community. Boys may pick up the intensity if they do not want to loose to a girl, or they may learn something about heart when they see how hard the girl has to work in practices to stay competitive with her male opponents. It is easy for parents, boosters, and wrestling fans of all types to support an underdog and her team.

OPPORTUNITIES FOR ATHLETES AND COACHES IN WOMEN'S WRESTLING

Just as the numbers of participants in women's wrestling have snowballed, so have the opportunities to train and compete. Boys in wrestling can find training and competition with other boys in most towns or schools across the nation, but coaches of girls in wrestling have to seek out information about the opportunities for their female athletes to train and compete against other girls. There is no reason for a coach not to encourage female wrestlers who love the sport to continue their careers

after high school. For girls, the future of their careers will rely on freestyle wrestling. Everything outside of the training girls do within the boys' high school wrestling season will be in freestyle wrestling. That is the style that all of the colleges wrestle, the style of all of the nation's top women wrestlers, and the style that gives women the opportunity to go to the Olympics. The sooner coaches encourage their girls to learn freestyle wrestling, the better. Coaches can refer to USA Wrestling's web site at www.themat.com for information about girl's and women's camps, competitions, colleges, and general information. The national team coach for women's wrestling is Terry Steiner. He sends out a newsletter about everything going on within the sport to state leaders and directors of women's wrestling in each state. Coaches and athletes can contact USA Wrestling (USAW) and Terry Steiner at 1-800-999-8531.

Since the sport of women's wrestling is growing rapidly, the need for more coaches to get involved in the sport also grows. There are a lot of untapped resources for women's wrestling at the collegiate level. Coaches who want to get involved in women's wrestling at the collegiate level can approach coaches and administrators at schools with existing men's programs with the idea of starting a women's team in conjunction with the men's, or to approach schools (especially schools that are enrollment driven) with the idea of starting a women's program. It does not cost much to add women's wrestling to a school that already has a men's team because the facilities are already there. Adding a women's team can help struggling men's programs foster support and promotion as it develops as a new team. There is also a growing interest among coaches of men's collegiate teams to add girls' camps to their summer camp programs, and they need coaches to help.

USA Wrestling also provides a lot of opportunities for coaches to get involved in camps and both national and international competitions. Each year USAW hosts training camps to get the top ranked women ready for major competitions like the world championships, and developmental camps to help junior and cadets in women's wrestling reach the next level. USAW also sends a team of top ranked women, coaches, trainers, and officials on winter tours for international competitions. Coaches can contact USAW to ask about the possibility of being added to the coaches pool that the national coaches draw from to staff these camps and competition trips.

Finally, because women's wrestling is an Olympic sport, the Olympic Training Center in Colorado and the Olympic Education Center in Michigan both have women's resident athlete programs that are funded by both USAW and the IOC. The ultimate goal for a coach of a girl in wrestling should be to prepare her to qualify for these programs. Through an application process the top ranked women at the senior level can gain admittance into the OTC in Colorado, and the top prospects at the university level can gain admittance into the OEC in Michigan. The IOC also provides grant money to help America's top athletes to pay for school while they are training to reach their Olympic goals in the future.

9
USA Wrestling, Your National Organization

Gary Abbott

Members of the 2004 Women's Olympic Team, Patricia Miranda and Toccara Montgomery, ring the opening bell at the New York Stock Exchange.

This textbook is an important resource of USA Wrestling's National Coaches Education Program (NCEP), a valuable system of educational training for America's wrestling coaches on all levels.

Behind this program is USA Wrestling, the national governing body for amateur wrestling in the United States. Coach members of USA Wrestling are a valuable part of the largest and most active wrestling organization in the nation. Those who have chosen to join USA Wrestling and participate in the NCEP are seeking to improve themselves as coaches and leaders, and have made an investment in their wrestling future.

USA Wrestling means a lot of things to many people, mainly because it is involved in the sport at all levels. The organization offers opportunities for wrestlers, coaches, referees, tournament directors, club leaders and fans to actively pursue their interest in the sport.

WHAT IS A NATIONAL GOVERNING BODY?

USA Wrestling is a member organization of the U.S. Olympic Committee (USOC). Every sport in the Olympic movement has one organization which manages the sport on a national level within the United States. They are called National Governing Bodies (NGB).

Although USA Wrestling is a member of the USOC, it is an independent, non-profit organization completely dedicated to working within wrestling. Within the Olympic family, USA Wrestling is responsible for the selection and training of U.S. teams that compete at the Olympic Games, the Pan American Games, the World University Games and other such international events. USA Wrestling receives some of its funding from USOC grants, which are used for Olympic-level programs, as well as for other specific purposes. USA Wrestling represents wrestling in all Olympic-related activities.

USA Wrestling is also a member of FILA, the international wrestling federation. FILA recognizes USA Wrestling as the organization that represents international wrestling in our nation. USA Wrestling must be involved in all wrestling activities that occurs in other nations,

or when an international team comes to our country for competition.

In addition to its activities on the international level, USA Wrestling has a complete developmental program of wrestling on all levels. This is facilitated by the sanctioning of tournaments and the chartering of wrestling clubs. National and regional competitions are held for numerous age-groups, from Kids wrestlers through the Veterans age group.

HOW IS USA WRESTLING STRUCTURED?

USA Wrestling is a non-profit organization, overseen by a Board of Directors of wrestling volunteers. This Board sets policies for the organization, and provides direction and vision for those who participate in USA Wrestling. The leaders include officers who are elected to the positions from their peers, as well as representatives from a large variety of wrestling organizations and interests. The president when this book was produced was Stan Dziedzic of Georgia, who was a World Champion and Olympic medalist for the United States in the 1970s and became a world-class coach and a successful business leader following his competitive career.

The organization employs a national staff of professionals who carry out the day-to-day operations of the organization. USA Wrestling's headquarters are housed in Colorado Springs, Colo., in a building a few minutes away from the U.S. Olympic Committee. The chief executive is the Executive Director, who manages the activity of the staff and reports to the Board of Directors. The Executive Director at the time of this printing was Rich Bender, a career professional within USA Wrestling who served many years directing events for the organization prior to his promotion.

According to the USA Wrestling constitution, there are numerous standing committees of volunteer leaders who handle specific responsibilities within the organization. At times, the USA Wrestling president will create ad-hoc committees to handle special programs and activities for the sport when needed.

USA Wrestling has an affiliate relationship with 50 state associations, who conduct events and programs within their state and region. The state organizations are comprised of volunteers, coaches, officials, athletes and parents. The state leadership conduct tournaments, develop clubs, organize trips and coach athletes.

The mission of USA Wrestling is simple and powerful. **"USA Wrestling, as the National Governing Body for wrestling in the United States, shall responsibly advocate, promote, coordinate and provide opportunities for amateur wrestlers to achieve their full human and athletic potential."**

USA Wrestling is based upon democratic principles, where the people involved in wrestling have a voice in who their leaders are and what is the direction of the programs and activities for the organization. There is a place within USA Wrestling for anybody who has an interest in the sport and wants to be involved.

WHERE DOES USA WRESTLING FIT WITHIN WRESTLING?

USA Wrestling has a specific role within wrestling as its National Governing Body, the one national organization that has activities encompassing the entire sport. USA Wrestling is the most prominent organization within the sport, but certainly not the only one in the nation.

The aspect of wrestling that USA Wrestling is not directly responsible for is the competition within academic institutions, including college, high school and junior high school programs. High School wrestling is managed on the state level, and is coordinated through the National Federation of State High School Associations. Varsity college wrestling competition is run through the major organizations which include the National Collegiate Athletic Association (NCAA), the National Association of Intercollegiate Athletics (NAIA) and the National Junior College Athletic Association. USA Wrestling has cooperative activity with these organizations, and all of these groups have representation on the USA Wrestling Board of Directors. There is also an organization which

runs college club competitions for schools without varsity wrestling called the National Collegiate Wrestling Association (NCWA).

For wrestling outside of the school systems, USA Wrestling has the largest and most comprehensive schedule of national events. National and Regional tournaments in freestyle, Greco-Roman and folkstyle wrestling are organized for men and women from youth through adults, and include the following age divisions.

- Kids (9–14 years)
- Cadets (15–16 years)
- FILA Cadets (15–17 years)
- Junior (Grades 9–12)
- FILA Junior (17–20 years)
- University (18–24 years, class must have graduated high school)
- Senior (17 years and older)
- Veterans (35 years and older)

As a coach, especially if you run a club program, you have many options for competitions, especially on the youth levels. There are a number of organizations, some which are multi-sport non-profit organizations, and some which are for-profit private corporations. Wrestling is an active and thriving sport, and there are organizations which are regional in nature, and others that have more of a national scope to their programs.

USA Wrestling encourages coaches to stay involved with the sport, and bring their athletes to competitions on a regular basis. As a coach, you will have to spend the time to research what is available to your athletes and team and make decisions about where to go and what to attend.

When you participate in USA Wrestling events, you are part of the national system for wrestling development in the nation. An athlete has a **clear ladder of success within USA Wrestling**. Each year, wrestlers compete in local, state and regional competitions, with a national tournament set as the climax of the season. As an athlete gets older, he or she can move up through the age-group divisions, continuing to be tested as their skill improves and their level of competition progresses. National champion wrestlers receive the coveted USA Wrestling "stop sign" award, a tradition of excellence within the sport.

In addition to the regular program, on the USA Wrestling Kids and Cadet levels, there are a number of special programs for youth athletes. Created in 2004, the Ultimate Challenge Series is a series of quality youth events in which points are accumulated by each athlete, ending with the awarding of the Dominator Belts for the winners. For extremely talented athletes, there is the USA Wrestling Kids and Cadet Triple Crown, which is awarded to athletes who win national titles in folkstyle, freestyle and Greco-Roman during the same year.

Participating in USA Wrestling events provides your athletes with quality competition, professional event management and an organized system of progression. In addition, proceeds from these competitions go right back into the sport of wrestling through USA Wrestling, helping to strengthen the sport for all wrestlers.

WHAT DOES USA WRESTLING DO FOR COACHES?

USA Wrestling has more than 20,000 member coaches involved in its programs at all levels. This large and growing segment of the organization scans the entire breadth of the sport, from youth coaches, to junior high and high school coaches, to college coaches and elite international style coaches. These coaches work with hundreds of thousands of athletes at their clubs and institutions, building the sport of wrestling in communities across the nation.

A cornerstone for USA Wrestling's coaching program is the respected National Coaches Education Program (NCEP), which was created in the early years of the organization and has grown and expanded. Coaches have an opportunity to receive professional certification, starting at the basic Copper level for beginning coaches, and moving up through the educational system to the Bronze, Silver and Gold levels.

USA Wrestling is dedicated to providing first-rate professional training for its coach members. At Regional and National events, coaches are required to have a basic level of education, which ensures a high quality competition with safety and respect for the athletes. There are some events on the national schedule which USA Wrestling coach members receive free admission to attend and participate as part of their membership.

As a coach member, the membership publication USA Wrestler is sent to each coach six times a year. Numerous coaching resources are available online at TheMat.com (www.the-mat.com), including articles, technique demonstrations and videos.

USA Wrestling also produces a series of video tapes and DVDs designed to assist coaches and wrestlers in their quest for success. Some of these videos are strictly technical, while others are highlight tapes of competition, and others are complete productions of important national and international tournaments. These videos are professionally produced and allow coaches to learn more about wrestling while enjoying the excitement of the sport at its best.

Coaches are able to get involved with USA Wrestling by developing a club program. All of the athletes in a USA Wrestling club must become members, and then receive the benefits of membership. Included is an opportunity to participate in all USA Wrestling events, comprehensive insurance coverage, club organizing materials and many other benefits.

WHAT IS USA WRESTLING'S HISTORY?

USA Wrestling was not always the National Governing Body for the sport in this nation. Its roots come from an organization called the U.S. Wrestling Federation (USWF), which was formed in the late 1960s by leaders who were not satisfied by the direction of the NGB at the time, which was the Amateur Athletic Union.

A number of early pioneers came together and created the USWF, and began to hold tournaments and develop programs. Olympian Myron Roderick was hired as the first Executive Director of the organization, which was based in Stillwater, Okla. at the time. The membership of the USWF grew rapidly, and its activities were expanded.

The USWF became involved in a long legal process with the goal of becoming the NGB for wrestling, which took a decade to complete. The Executive Director for the USWF during that time was Olympian Steve Combs, who had a strong record of success in grassroots activities. In 1983, the NGB status was changed for wrestling, and a new organization emerged from the USWF which was called USA Wrestling. The first Olympic Games in which USA Wrestling was responsible was the successful 1984 Olympics in Los Angeles, Calif. Combs left the organization in the mid-1980s, and interim Executive Directors included Frank Rader and Jim Scott.

In 1988, USA Wrestling, then managed by Executive Director Gary Kurdelmeier, moved its corporate headquarters to Colorado Springs, Colo. Dave Miller served a few years as the Executive Director after the move to Colorado. For a decade in the 1990s, Olympian Jim Scherr was the Executive Director for the organization, a period which saw the United States win three World Team titles, two in men's freestyle and one in women's freestyle wrestling. After Scherr moved on to become an executive for the U.S. Olympic Committee, the new Executive Director became longtime staff professional Rich Bender.

Throughout the years, numerous wrestling leaders participated in the organization, serving as officers or members of the Board of Directors. In addition, other wrestling leaders were involved in expanding and improving the state associations, a process that continues today.

What are some of the highlights of USA Wrestling history?

Since becoming the National Governing Body (NGB) in 1983, USA Wrestling has had some impressive highlights and achievements including:

1984—Steve Fraser is the first U.S. Greco-Roman wrestler to win an Olympic gold medal in Los Angeles.

1985—Mike Houck is the first U.S. Greco-Roman wrestler to win a World gold medal, in Kolbatn, Norway.

1988—USA Wrestling creates a National Team program to support its elite international athletes.

1990—John Smith becomes the first wrestler to win the USOC SportsMan of the Year and the AAU Sullivan Award.

1992—John Smith wins his second Olympic gold medal, a record sixth straight World-level gold (87-92).

1992—Tricia Saunders is the first U.S. Women's wrestler to win a World gold medal in Villerbanne, France.

1993—USA Wrestling helps develop the USOTC resident athlete program in Greco-Roman. In later years, a USOTC resident programs are developed in men's freestyle and women's freestyle.

1993—The United States wins the World Team Title in freestyle in Toronto, Canada, its first ever Senior Level team title.

1995—USA Wrestling hosts the Freestyle World Championships in Atlanta, and the U.S. wins the title.

1996—Bruce Baumgartner elected by his peers to carry the U.S. flag in the Opening Ceremonies at the Atlanta Olympic Games. He claims an Olympic bronze medal, a record fourth Olympic medal. It is also his 13th career World level medal.

1996—USA Wrestling combines its Junior National and Cadet National Championships, creating the world's largest wrestling event with more than 3,600 competitors.

1999—The United States wins the World Team Title in women's wrestling, its first women's team title.

1999—USA Wrestling helps develop the USOEC University Greco-Roman resident program. In 2004, a USOEC program is developed for women's wrestling.

2000—TheMat.com is launched, with a goal to become "The Ultimate Source for Real Wrestling".

2000—Rulon Gardner upsets three-time Olympic champion and previously unbeaten Alexander Kareline for the Olympic gold in Sydney, Australia.

2001—The U.S. placed third in the Greco-Roman World Championships in Patras, Greece, its highest finish ever. Rulon Gardner won the World gold medal, the first U.S. Greco-Roman athlete to win World and Olympic titles.

2002—Wrestling for the Next Millennium capital campaign successfully completes.

2002—USA Wrestling adds weight classes to the Cadet and Junior National Championships in Fargo, N.D. and shatters the records for entries in the world's largest wrestling meet. A women's division is held at the Junior Nationals for the first time.

2003—World Freestyle Championships (men and women) were held in New York City, Sept. 12-14, The International Federation declared it the best World Championships in history. U.S. men and women place second in the team standings.

2004—USA Wrestling set its all-time membership record of 135,519 athlete members

2004—Cael Sanderson wins the men's freestyle Olympic gold medal in Athens, Greece at 84 kgs one of six U.S. Olympic medalists. Women's wrestling is contested for the first time, and the U.S. wins two medals.

These are just a few of the highlights from over 20 years of activity as the NGB for wrestling. USA Wrestling has set high goals for its athletes and for the sport, and new achievements will be reached every year. Member coaches play an important part in raising the bar for wrestling in the future.

HOW DO I GET MORE INFORMATION ABOUT USA WRESTLING?

USA Wrestling has its national headquarters in Colorado Springs, Colo. You can write to the organization at USA Wrestling, 6155 Lehman Dr., Colorado Springs, CO 80918. The office switchboard number is 719-598-8181, and the FAX machine is 719-598-9440.

The official web site of USA Wrestling is TheMat.com (www.themat.com). There is information on all of USA Wrestling's activities on the web site, including schedules, results, rankings, feature stories and much more. There is a capability for joining USA Wrestling online, as well. All USA Wrestling members have access to the special "Members-Only" web site, which has cutting edge features including special videos and technical advice.

Every state has a USA Wrestling organization, where coaches and athletes can join and participate in the programs there. A list of the state chairpersons and state leaders can be found at TheMat.com, or by contacting the USA Wrestling national office.

USA Wrestling offers an extensive program, where coaches and their athletes can thrive, improve and grow. Coaches education is a small part of an entire package of benefits and activities for USA Wrestling members. Join USA Wrestling and be part of the national organization dedicated to improving and expanding the sport at all levels.

10
Positive Coaching

Ted Witulski

QUESTIONS TO CONSIDER

- What approaches are there to coaching?
- What are the benefits of using the positive approach?
- What problems can occur when using the negative approach?
- How do I develop a positive approach?
- How do I cope with losing when using the positive approach?

Positive coaching can make the difference in whether a young athlete remains in wrestling or not.

INTRODUCTION

Any time sport psychologists are asked to discuss motivation and positive reinforcement, one gets the feeling that coaches are looking for a "quick fix" for a specific athlete. Motivation is one of those elusive concepts that coaches learn about through experience, through what our coaches did, or through the media. Because a college coach gave a blistering intermission speech to a team that went on to win the match, other coaches assume that the speech changed the motivation level and performance of the team. Should coaches deliver similar speeches to their athletes when they need to be motivated? This approach may work once during a season or a career. However, to be effective in motivating athletes, coaches must not adopt techniques blindly.

The essence of motivation knowing your athletes and understanding what they want from sport. In other words, do you know why your athletes are participating in this sport? Youth compete in sports for a variety of reasons that may include: 1) to improve skills and learn new ones, 2) for thrills and excitement, 3) to have fun, 4) to be with friends and make new ones, and 5) to succeed or win.

Because kids enter the sport of wrestling at differing points in their lives, it is often important to note how long they have competed in the sport to understand their motivation. Usually athletes that have stayed with the sport for a longer period of time will have a stronger motivation based on winning. However, it is important to note that even an experienced competitor will still place an emphasis on skills development and fun, outside of winning.

Coaches must come to the realization that the culture of wrestling in the U.S. places a heavy emphasis on competition and winning. It is not uncommon for a child as young as five or six to join a wrestling team and within a few weeks to be entered into a competitive tournament. Almost immediately in this wrestlers "career" winning will be added to the wrestlers motivation, where initially the participant wanted to join wrestling for the socialization, fun, and skills development.

While most youth club coaches would take great pride in building a wrestling team that is known for their success in tournaments. It is also important to recognize the coaches that are known for building a large team that retains wrestlers in the sport and whose participants develop a lifelong affinity for wrestling.

The age of 12–14 years old should become a target age that coaches concern themselves with. This group of students, at the middle school age, is very ready to shed past behaviors and activities in a quest for individuality. Students in this age group are exposed to many different activities and new groups of potential friends—many of which can have a negative influence.

Club coaches must pay particular attention to these kids noting that competition and winning might not be their primary source of motivation. Instead, these wrestlers look for opportunities to socialize and fit in with the group. So, organized trips to watch a collegiate or international tournament and cross-training activities like a canoe trip can go a long ways into retaining kids in the sport of wrestling.

Recently, the National Federation of High School Athletics began to discuss reducing the number of weight classes at the high school level. The Federation noted that across the country many schools were having difficulty filling out a lineup that included fourteen weight classes. Pennsylvania's squad size was used as an example. Despite Pennsylvania being one of the most prestigious wrestling states the Federation's surveys of squad size revealed that the average high school team in Pennsylvania was only 18 wrestlers—just four more than the total varsity slots.

Positive coaching plays a primary role in the development of the sport of wrestling. While an authoritarian model of coaching may motivate young wrestlers, it is important to note not all ages of kids are readily motivated by the militaristic approach. Clubs and coaches must come to recognize the need to retain more kids in the sport of wrestling particularly at the middle school age.

The key to motivation knowing your athletes and understanding what they want from your sport.

Although striving to win is important, winning is not the most important reason why athletes participate in sports.

The purpose of this chapter is to focus on how coaches can be more effective in meeting the participation motives of athletes. We will discuss how to create a good learning environment in which athletes can acquire the technical skills needed to be successful in sport. A related purpose is the creation of a social environment in which athletes can experience positive interactions with each other.

THE POSITIVE AND NEGATIVE APPROACHES TO COACHING

When working with athletes, young or old, it is important to remember that we are dealing with people. The number 1 rule to keep in mind is that we should treat athletes as we would want to be treated. Most of us respond better to a person who is empathetic with our shortcomings and who is patient with us while we learn.

There are two basic approaches to coaching: the positive approach and the negative approach. Each approach is capable of influencing the behavior of athletes. Both approaches are based on the assumption that an individual's behavior is influenced by the consequences each behavior produces.

The positive approach focuses on *desired* behaviors or consequences by asking athletes to behave or perform in a specific manner and by reinforcing the athlete when the desired behaviors occur. For example, if you ask an athlete to compete at a higher weight class for the benefit of the team and the athlete does so (desired behavior), then you reward or reinforce the athlete for attempting or executing successfully the desired behavior. With young athletes or beginning athletes, you reinforce attempts to produce the desired behavior.

A positive coach concentrates on desired behaviors and rewards wrestlers who display the desired behaviors.

The negative approach to coaching involves eliminating **undesirable** behavior through

Effectively communicating a positive approach to overcoming match situations separates the best coaches from the rest.

physical and verbal punishment and criticism. This negative approach is based on fear. Although we do not advocate this approach, there is evidence that this approach can eliminate poor performance in certain athletes. There is also evidence that this approach can eliminate athletes as well!

Often we hear coaches tell athletes, "The team that makes the fewest errors will win." Obviously, there is much truth to the saying. Because errors are often easier to see than steady, unspectacular performance, coaches tend to focus on eliminating errors. To eliminate errors, coaches simply punish athletes who make them. These coaches assume that if wrestlers are scared enough of making errors, they will be more likely to perform better.

It is not hard to find examples of coaches who use the negative approach. Many highly successful coaches scream at their athletes for every mistake, grab athletes by their uniforms during timeouts and publicly humiliate them, and may actually hit athletes who are not meeting expectations. For inexperienced coaches, these successful negative coaches serve as role models. Negative behaviors are imitated, with the naive coach thinking this abusive behavior causes athletes to perform correctly. These inexperienced coaches do not realize that the negative coaches' success may be due to their effective teaching techniques.

While punishment and verbal abuse may change the behavior of some individuals, there are some undesirable side effects. Perhaps the most serious is the fear of failure that results when athletes are criticized or punished excessively for making mistakes. Closely associated with a fear of failure are decreased enjoyment of a task and increased likelihood of more errors. This cycle of fear, leading to more errors and less enjoyment, may cause wrestlers to become hesitant and uncertain, experience high anxiety about performing in critical situations, or be more vulnerable to injury during competition.

A negative coach focuses on errors and punishment for athletes who make errors.

A negative approach often results in an unpleasant teaching situation. Athletes who are exposed to verbal criticism, punishment for errors, or sarcastic comments about their performances will often withdraw socially and emotionally. When this happens, the group becomes very quiet during practices and matches. In addition, there is a sense of resentment or hatred by the team members for the coach. With older athletes, these negative emotions may draw the team together and actually strengthen team cohesion. For younger athletes, the negative environment may cause them to drop out.

The environment created by negative coaching may cause young athletes to drop out of sports.

One of the questions frequently asked by coaches is whether they should avoid criticiz-

ing or punishing athletes. The answer is no, because these techniques may be useful in maintaining discipline. However, in order for these techniques to remain effective they must be used sparingly. Unfortunately, we often see coaches who are very successful using the negative approach. This may result because these coaches have very good athletes and/or they are exceptional teachers and strategists.

The technique employed by most coaches is a combination of the positive and negative approaches. There is evidence that a mixture of both positive and negative reinforcement is likely to produce the best results. Athletes know when they have made mistakes, and your credibility rests on your honesty in evaluating their performances. However, a coach can be honest and help athletes learn from their experiences or a coach can punish athletes who make errors and create athletes who "fear failure! The key is your intention. The effectiveness of a coach's reinforcement may depend on the coach's intention in giving the praise or punishment. There is little doubt that most athletes, and adults, respond best to the positive approach.

STRIVE FOR THE POSITIVE APPROACH

The positive approach aims at strengthening the desired behaviors through the use of encouragement, positive reinforcement, and technical instruction. Young athletes are generally highly motivated to learn a sport, and the use of positive reinforcement strengthens their enjoyment.

All of us spent hours practicing sport skills and, even though we try to repress the memories, many of our early attempts were failures. However, friends provided us with positive support, plenty of encouragement, and the reassurance that we'd "get it" soon. Our persistence may have been directly related to our friends' support. When friends stopped giving us support and encouragement or ridiculed our attempts, we often withdrew from the activity. A coach's feedback works the same way.

The positive approach fosters a positive learning environment for youth sport participants. In this positive environment mistakes become "stepping stones to achievement." Athletes learn from their mistakes. They know that positive coaches will provide them with the technical information to change their performances plus the encouragement and support to try again.

Most coaches of sport teams want to be respected and liked by their teams. This mutual respect results in improved communication and fosters a willingness to work together to resolve individual and team problems. This result was reported in a study of Little League coaches. One group of coaches was taught to be positive and encouraging by increasing the frequency of positive reinforcement by 25 percent. A second group of "untrained" coaches continued to coach as they normally had. At the end of the season, the athletes who played for the trained coaches reported that 1) they liked the coach more, 2) they thought the coach was a better teacher, 3) they were more attracted to the team, and 4) they had better self-concepts. This latter finding was especially true for athletes who had low self-concepts.

Athletes with low self-esteem are likely to benefit most from a positive approach.

Low self-concepts are often the result of being told directly or indirectly how bad we are at a task. If told often enough that they are not very good, athletes begin to believe that they are not very good. Athletes with low self-concepts are particularly vulnerable to failure because they interpret failure as "proof" that they are not very good. To turn this negative thinking around, coaches must be positive and help these athletes see errors as temporary states that can be corrected. The fact that coaches can be effective in improving self-concepts by increasing their positive reinforcement to athletes by 25 percent is powerful evidence of the effectiveness of the positive approach.

In addition to helping kids feel better about themselves, the positive approach increases the athletes' learning of skills. Part of this learning may be a result of viewing a positive coach as a better teacher. Additionally, the

positive approach creates an atmosphere whereby athletes are willing to try new and different skills. There is no fear of failing. Thus, young athletes will ask more questions and practice more.

DEVELOPING THE POSITIVE APPROACH

Implementing the positive approach begins with the coach's awareness of effective reinforcers, how often to use these reinforcers, and what behaviors should be reinforced. Each of these aspects of the positive approach will be discussed below.

Choosing Effective Reinforcers

When working with athletes, it is important to know what rewards are effective in changing behavior. In other words, what are athletes willing to work for? Surprisingly, research has shown that the best rewards are free. For example, a pat on the back, smile, friendly nod, and verbal praise are all effective, free reinforcers. In this respect, young athletes react to these reinforcers in much the same way as adults do. All of us appreciate this simple acknowledgement of a job well done.

These free rewards are effective with athletes of all ages. Specifically, research has shown that verbal praise and the coaches' attention are particularly effective with athletes 13 to 15 years of age compared to 9- to 12-year-old athletes. The effectiveness of coaches' attention was compared to giving candy and money to 9- to 15-year-old swimmers and was found to be comparable in terms of the number of laps the athletes were motivated to swim. One drawback that should be noted with regard to using food or money to reward performance is the decline in intrinsic motivation. Practically, coaches may not be able to afford the use of food or money as rewards. Certainly it is not necessary because free rewards are as effective.

The most potent rewards that coaches can use are free—a smile, a word of encouragement, a pat on the back.

The use of free reinforcers should be combined with an instruction or instructional reminder to improve their effectiveness. For example, as you pat the wrestler on the back for winning a match, you can tell him that he did a good job of executing the single leg takedown that won it. This instructional reminder provides a cue for the athlete that will help him be successful in the future.

Select and Reinforce Specific Behaviors

In addition to choosing effective reinforcers, coaches must identify the specific behaviors they want to reinforce. In other words, what must the athlete do to earn a reward from the coach? For starters, use your reward power to strengthen skills that a athlete is learning. For example, a wrestling coach tells his team that the team that scores the most takedowns will win the upcoming tournament. Therefore, the focus of the day's practice would be on singles and doubles. Unfortunately, the coach chose to teach takedowns by having the top wrestler in the referee's position try to hold the bottom wrestler down. If the bottom wrestler escaped, he/she could then try to execute a single or double leg takedown. Although this drill resulted in many takedowns, the coach never commented on how well the takedowns were executed but instead focused on the top man holding his opponent down. This behavior resulted in a mixed message for the young athletes: coach says it is important to get takedowns but only talks about the top man's riding ability. Thus, the wrestlers conclude that riding is more important than takedowns.

Along the same lines, coaches should break down complex skills into component sub skills and concentrate on one sub skill at a time. Most wrestling skills are complex in that many body parts are involved to execute a skill. The coordination of the body parts is critical as is the ability to integrate another person into the skill.

Positive coaches reduce complex skills to sub skills, then reward the parts that were performed correctly.

For example, executing a single leg involves starting in a good stance, moving your opponent out of position, lowering your elevation, penetrating, and lifting to finish. Each of these actions could be defined and practiced as a sub skill (basic) of a single leg.

Using this approach provides the athlete a chance to experience success doing smaller parts of the skill. In addition, the coach has the opportunity to positively reinforce sub skills performed correctly while providing pointers on how to improve the next sub skill. For example, after you have been working with your wrestlers on executing a single leg, your lightweight has a chance to demonstrate the skill in a match. He maintains a good stance, moves his opponent out of position, lowers his level, and then takes a terrible penetration shot. As a coach, you have choices: reject the entire attempt based on the bad penetration, or acknowledge and reinforce the sub skills performed very well. The final sub skill can be practiced more during the next practice.

If a coach chooses to reject the entire performance, the young athletes are led to believe that nothing was done right, rather than to understand that they performed sections of the skill correctly. By selecting and reinforcing specific behaviors, athletes gain confidence that they will improve with more practice. This outcome alone should result in your feeling successful as a coach.

When, and How Often, Should Reinforcement Be Given?

The answer to this question depends on how proficient the athlete is at performing the skill. When athletes are learning a skill, coaches should reinforce every desired response. Until inexperienced athletes have had a lot of practice, they cannot always tell whether they performed a skill correctly. When first learning a knee-over-toe penetration step, most wrestlers have difficulty forcing their lead leg knee down. Therefore, to determine whether the penetration was good or not, athletes look at the result. If they shoot incorrectly and score a takedown, they assume the technique was correct. The emphasis in the early stages of learning a wrestling skill should be on technique and correct decision making, not just outcome.

As athletes become more proficient, coaches should reinforce the correct behavior intermittently. Research has shown that continuous feedback following a learned skill is not as effective as intermittent feedback. As athletes come to know the difference between correct and incorrect technique, the coach's feedback is redundant, and athletes tend to ignore it. However, intermittent feedback either supports or refutes the athlete's own perceptions. Differing perceptions provide the coach with the opportunity to discuss the finer points of the skill which gives athletes new information to use. Environments must be conducive for athletes to accept and incorporate information that results in performance changes. The positive approach creates this type of environment.

Coaches should reinforce a desired behavior as soon as it occurs.

The question of when reinforcement should be given is an easy one to answer. Specifically, coaches should reinforce a desired behavior as soon as it occurs. This is equally true during contests as it is during practices. Waiting to tell athletes their faults at the conclusion of a drill often results in athletes not remembering what they did initially. The feedback is neutralized by time.

Reinforce Effort and Other Desirable Behaviors

Coaches, parents, and even athletes tend to focus most of their attention on outcome: scoring a takedown, getting an escape, pinning your opponent. This focus may be fine for elite athletes who are relatively consistent. For young athletes, and for most of us, who are not consistent in the performance of a skill, coaches should reinforce effort, or the attempt to perform a skill correctly. Thus, when we ask a wrestler to pin his opponent and the wrestler tries, using good technique, we should acknowledge the effort. This positive reinforcement tells the wrestler that his or her technique is basically correct and that the effort is appreciated.

Young athletes must be reinforced for their efforts as well as the outcome of those efforts.

The only thing that athletes have control over is the amount of effort they make. As mentioned earlier, the negative approach often results in athletes attempting to protect their self-esteem. One way to protect self-esteem is to give only "token" effort. Thus, when they fail, they can save face by acknowledging that they could have gotten a takedown if they had tried harder. We do not want to cause athletes to lose the motivation to try because we, as coaches, have challenged their self-esteem.

We have all experienced situations where we gave our very best effort, only to be denied a job, a promotion, or a victory in sport. Effort is the key to success in sport, and coaches must be ready to reinforce that effort. We must help young athletes understand that they control effort; the outcome is out of their control.

A coach can control the interpersonal relationships on a team merely by choosing the kinds of behaviors that are reinforced.

Finally, coaches can effectively change the behavior of athletes toward their teammates and opponents by reinforcing exemplary conduct. Reinforce young athletes who help pick up the equipment after practice. Acknowledge instances of good teamwork and athletes encouraging one another. The relationships among the athletes are a direct result of what the coach chooses to reinforce. If athletes are not discouraged from blaming one another for losses, this behavior will escalate to the point that athletes are afraid to try. Athletes will learn quickly to make excuses. To change this environment, or to prevent it from occurring, coaches must state the desired behaviors of athletes to each other and reinforce the occurrences of desired behaviors.

POSITIVE LOSING: A HEALTHY ATTITUDE

The goal for most athletes and coaches is to be successful. Success has generally been defined as winning. While this is a goal for par-

SIDEBAR: Focus!—You hear it yelled—Do you teach what it means?

Ted Witulski

Chances are you hear it yelled to a wrestler at tournaments all the time. Often, after a tough scramble, a controversial call, or a big move, listen closely, you'll hear coaches yell that one word to their athlete. That one word is meant to be both insight and comfort. Every coach yells it but not every coach teaches what that one word means.

"FOCUS", the coach yells! "FOCUS, you can win this match." "FOCUS, you're still in it. FOCUS!"

When coaches revert back to this one distinct command, the hope is that the coaching staff has taken time to teach the athlete a process of gathering focus. The wrestler that has "it" is often the one that can achieve that championship status; whereas, the wrestler who is still seeking focus is still trying to climb to the top.

Wrestling coaches know that their wrestlers at some point during the season in the heat of a match will only have a couple of fleeting seconds to return to FOCUS. The difficult thing is to teach wrestlers what focus is and how to achieve it, when the wrestler has that short break in a match.

As a wrestling coach yells to focus, the coach is engaging the wrestler to return back to only the moment of the match that is right in front of them. The coach is urging them to recognize the situation at hand, leave the referee's calls, the adrenaline rush, and the past scored points aside. Focus is a powerful tool for a wrestler to have at their command. So, as a coach do not neglect to teach what it means to wrestlers.

F-O-C-U-S can be better understood by wrestlers, if it is viewed as a five-letter acronym instead of just an often hurled word in the heat of match. Teach wrestlers to view each letter as a distinct action that must be undertaken to achieve focus.

First of all, the "F" of focus stands for forget. Forget anything negative that has occurred. Forget the referees call. Forget the locked-hands call that tied the match. Forget the cheap shot that you received out of bounds from your opponent. The coach is yelling at the wrestler to focus, but to achieve this, the wrestler must forget anything negative.

Second, if the wrestler is to be focused, then they must organize themselves. To organize, the wrestler must recognize the moment of the match. What is the exact situation that must be wrestled? A successful wrestler first forgets the negative and then organizes for the precise situation that they are in. For example, a wrestler has just given up a reversal on the edge and went out of bounds. Much has happened in this change of control. There might be only a few seconds left, the wrestler might have just went down by a point, the match might be slipping away. Hopefully, the wrestler, in the few moments he/she has to get set on bottom, will know how to organize for that situation.

A wrestler organizing for the moment in the match must recognize the score, the time left in the period, the position to be wrestled, and the attacks to be wary of that his/her opponent will initiate. There is a great deal of information to process in a short time for a wrestler to be organized and focused. It is up to the wrestler's coach to help to teach a wrestler the skill of organizing for the moment of the match during a whistle break.

Forget the negative. Organize for the precise situation. Now the wrestler must "Concentrate" on the action that must be taken to win in that moment. A good and focused wrestler will know if they are on bottom and there are only 12 seconds left in the third period and they are down by one, that it is important to be organized for that precise moment. Most coaches would probably be hoping their wrestler realizes that with the limited time on the clock, their more advanced scoring maneuvers, such as a granby roll, would take too long to score. A wrestler who is concentrating must pick the best and precise move to win.

When Brock Lesnar had the down position in sudden-victory overtime in the NCAA finals concentration played an important role in his win. After trying to escape with stand-ups unsuccessfully Lesnar switched tactics. He focused on the situation, did a half stand-up followed with a perfectly executed hip-heist. To the unobservant eye this might have been a chance maneuver, but if you watched the Minnesota staff, they helped Lesnar achieve the focus, by concentrating on this precise movement and it won him a national title. Instead of relying on a stand-up and the scramble for hand-control the change to a hip-heist was the perfect tactic to win the title. That small change was achieved by focusing in on the situation, due in large part to the Minnesota staff urging this tactical shift.

In the seconds before the whistle initiates a re-start of action in the match, the wrestler must unwind. Unwinding is really a simple process. It is a matter of the wrestler taking control of the moment. When a wrestler is at a critical point in the match you would hate to see him/her rush back to the center without being focused on the moment. Once a wrestler forgets, organizes and concentrates, encourage wrestlers to unwind.

The process of unwinding is that reassuring deep breath that can give that wrestler a moment of pause. In a way, to see a wrestler pause and unwind is also reassuring to the coach in the corner. Teach wrestlers to draw in a deep breath on a three-count, hold it, and exhale on a three count. When Brandon Slay won the Olympic Trials in 2000 he initiated this process of unwinding every time he started in parterre position. Before he would set himself on bottom or top you could visually see him focus on the moment of the match. He would check the score to organize himself, he would scan his mind to think of the movement he would attempt, and just before placing his hands to re-start wrestling you could watch him unwind by drawing in and controlling a deep breath. This process of unwinding, while focusing on the moment of the match, surely helped him gain the Olympic team spot.

Finally, the last part of focus is step. The acronym of F-O-C-U-S walks a wrestler through forgetting the negative, organizing for the moment, concentrating on the movement, unwinding to take control of the rush of adrenaline, and the step to be taken at the sound of the whistle. Now it is not enough to say to a wrestler hit the inside stand-up. Rather, the process of focus should help coaches teach the speed, and the force that needs to go into the precise step to be taken at the initial whistle. In the practice room, coaches can teach focus by going through a match situation and as the coach talks to the wrestlers about unwinding and getting set the coach should reinforce what kind of maximum speed and power they are looking for in that step.

Too often coaches see wrestlers go through the motions. They might be repeating that standup for fiftieth time in practice. Their feet and hands are moving to the right points. Their head position is fine. But something is lacking there is not the right speed to that step. F-O-C-U-S, specifically STEP is what those wrestlers are missing. Every coach wants to see his/her wrestlers hit that step in a higher gear. By breaking down the word focus coaches can renew wrestlers' attention and achieve higher focus for the speed, and force of any particular step.

Focus! Coaches will yell this to their wrestlers often during a season. If the wrestlers are truly going to understand what focus means, then they need to learn a process that can be done quickly in the heat of a match, which will actually help them achieve focus. Forget, organize, concentrate, unwind, and step.......when you a hear coach yell focus that's what they expect their wrestler to do. Make sure you take the time to go beyond the moves and teach the tactic of focus to all of your wrestlers.

ticipants, it should not be the only goal. The fact remains that in every match only 50 percent of the participants will be winners. If we use winning as the only criteria for success, then we must conclude that the non-winners were losers. There is a problem with this approach to defining success. The problem revolves around the attitude that results from this definition. Specifically, this approach suggests that winning, regardless of how poorly the athlete or team competed, is good. Likewise, losing, regardless of how well or poorly the athlete or team competed, is bad. This definitional approach to success and failure fosters an unhealthy attitude in athletes.

This attitude promotes the notion that athletes, and coaches, cannot learn from their mistakes. As most of us have learned, we can learn a lot from our mistakes and our losses. Losing is not a lot of fun, but losing should be viewed as "water under the bridge' " In fact, the key to viewing losing as positive is to learn from the loss. Even in losing, certain skills or strategies were executed correctly or better than they had been in the past. Athletes should understand which of their performances were good.

In addition, athletes should learn which of their performances needed improvement. Perhaps the loss was due to the other team's superior size and speed. This is particularly evident in youth sport and high school sports, where athletes must compete with older and bigger athletes. While learning and growing, athletes must know that losing is often the result of mismatches in size and experience, and not the result of them being unskilled at their sport. This latter conclusion can result in young athletes dropping out of sport before they develop fully the skills necessary to compete with older athletes. However, if the athletes did miss-perform skills or known strategies, they need to learn what the mistake was. And what they must do to correct it.

The coach is the key in developing a healthy attitude toward losing. Your attitude will be mimicked by the athletes. Even though you may understand that your behavior is the result of disappointment or frustration, the athletes may not. They could view your behavior as the correct way to cope with loss. Rather than learning from the loss, they associate a negative affect and self-perception with losing.

To foster a healthy attitude toward losing, coaches and athletes should analyze the loss, determine what was done right and what was done wrong, and then forget the loss, but continue to work on improving performance.

The coach's behavior is a powerful example in helping athletes to know how to deal with losing a contest.

The positive view of losing does not lessen the disappointment. However, it does provide insight into one's performance. The value of a positive losing attitude may best be summed up in the following quote from a youth sport participant. "When I was a kid I had a great coach. He taught me how to bounce back when things were tough."

11
Maintaining Team Discipline

Ted Witulski

Even the best wrestlers in the world continue to learn by being good listeners. (Pictured from l-r, Olympic and World Champions, Dave Shultz and Mark Schultz).

Similarly to the teaching profession, coaches often leave coaching to others because of the challenges they face in dealing with team discipline. Most coaches join the coaching ranks because of a love for the sport of wrestling; so, when dealing with discipline takes the joy out of coaching then usually coaches choose to leave.

Coaches must prepare to deal with discipline effectively according to the age group that they work with. It is important to note that clubs or teams who have too wide of an age range may more readily experience problems with team discipline. It is a natural by-product of an ineffective developmental system. If, for example, junior high aged kids are group with young first and second grade wrestlers, then the dynamic for bad discipline exists. The older kids may feel ignored, having to learn entry-level techniques; whereas, the young kids can be exposed to bullying. Programs that have a wide range of age divisions are encouraged to divide the group and carry on separate practices. This allows the coaches the maximum chance for success by focusing in on the needs of a single age group.

A second concern that coaches must constantly self-evaluate on is the consideration of the needs and motivation of the team. It is understandable that at an older age level a higher emphasis will be placed on winning. However, if the coach chooses to use an authoritarian team discipline model it is essential for success that the coach share the reasoning and motivation for running practices in this manner. Kids that are older enough to practice under an authoritarian model are also old enough to understand and analyze the essential nature of this dynamic.

Regardless of the age level or coaching style that is employed by the staff, the starting point for effective discipline is clearly defining expectations for the participants. Instead of relying on a cumbersome set of team rules with correlating disciplinary actions; coaches are encouraged to clearly communicate and outline the proper behavior for upcoming and ongoing occurrences.

For example, it is necessary for coaches to outline the expectations that participants should follow for team practices. Coaches may note starting times, appropriate dress, proper respect of teammates and other necessities.

As the season approaches a competition date the coaching staff will need to outline the essential expectations for the team in both home meet and travel situations. At home meets the coach may emphasize the need for athletes to help as a team to present wrestling in a positive light. As an example, a coach may outline the need for the team to work together to set up and tear down the tournament. On the road the coach may focus on respecting the opposing school's property and may use as an example that prank theft and petty vandalism results in developing a poor reputation of the

school or club as well as a black-eye for the sport of wrestling. Also, a coach may choose to clearly outline what sportsmanship means to the program, paying particular attention to the details of the match such as respecting an opponent with a proper hand shake.

Clearly defining the expectations for the team and the individual is a necessity that coaches must pay attention to. Coaches should go into team discussions with a clear picture in mind of the appropriate conduct of the team as a group and individually.

Although coaches may note their expectations early in the year, it is imperative that coaches view **defining expectations as an ongoing process, and not a one time commitment**. Coaches are in the business of molding and developing youth into people of character. Though a coach may expect participants to remember every expectation for the season, it is unlikely that developing youth will always do so. Follow up discussions give coaches the opportunity to further the team's understanding of the expectations as well as giving the members of the team compliments and praise for demonstrating adherence to the expectations or developing leadership in encouraging the expectations to be followed.

While dealing with team expectations may seem like only a change of semantics from team rules, it is important to note that the use of expectations, especially when dealing with middle school to high school wrestlers, gives the participants a strong feeling of ownership.

Coaches that coach from the perspective of being an enforcer of rules, often put themselves in opposition to the team rather than being a part of the team. This can be a difficult position to teach from especially in a culture that has the phrase "rules are made to be broke" in its lexicon. However, a position where a coach is recognized by the participants that they are working together for the betterment of the team gives the coach a position of authority that reflects leadership without the drawbacks of being the jail warden. So, if the coach wants to develop a cohesive unit with the coaching staff as integral part of that unit, then coaches should try to develop expectations versus hard and fast rules.

Additionally, the development of expectations allows a coach the freedom to speak individually with their athletes and work on expectations for specific athletes. A coach can use this freedom to speak forthrightly with a participant that has a tendency towards bullying, noting that this type of conduct can weaken the team by discouraging participation of upcoming youth. Also, a coach can vary their expectations from the minimum standard to a higher standard for an individual that the coach expects to assume a leadership role. While a good wrestler may be following the "rules" of the team, sometimes a coach wants that good wrestler to develop further in the sport. Expectations allow a coach this freedom.

Inevitably a team member will fail to meet the reasonable expectations of the team and coaching staff. When these difficult situations occur, there may be examples where a concrete discipline is part of the corrective action taken with the wrestlers. Corrective actions might include holding the participant out of practice, yet still requiring them to be in attendance, informing parents of the misbehavior, or losing a starting position.

A long held tradition that effective teachers and coaches have moved away from is the use of discipline associated with extra conditioning. While many coaches will debate this point, education studies have noted the ineffective nature of requiring a student to do push-ups or run stairs as a part of the correction to the behavior.

Studies show that participants find little association of the conditioning work to the inappropriate behavior, as well as the fact that the participants' penchant to repeat the misbehavior is not lessened. Again the coach assumes a heavy-handed role in which studies show return the coach to be in opposition to the athlete, as opposed to being a supporter of the youth's development. This type authority to participant confrontation often leads to a false-dilemma in the participant's mind. The participant may feel lingering hard feelings and resentment toward the coach, and may choose to quit the team as opposed to recognizing the deficiency of their behavior.

Instead of trying to punish a wrestler into submitting to the will of the staff, coaches should look to use the expectations as a part of an individual discussion with the participant that returns focus to the nature of the team. Again, coaches and athletes are involved in the sport to develop not only individually but also as a team. Coaches can elude to the importance of good members of the team to develop wrestlers individually—the comments that mimic "a good training partner will make you a better wrestler" statement. But, coaches should go further in describing why that individual is important to the coaches and to the team. A coach that says "we need you to be a part of our team because you are going to help us build a great program," directly encourages the athlete to look at their role as not just small part, but something that has a much bigger purpose.

Coaches may go on to say things like:

"Your actions were a let down that did not reflect your best performance or reflect positively on the team."

"We had a bump in the road, but together we can overcome this and get back to helping you become a better wrestler, and helping us have a better team."

"We know that sometimes we make mistakes, but your actions are taking away from your development as a wrestler."

Statements such as these frame the inappropriate behavior, so the wrestler can see that they are part of wrestling for a reason that is important. After a wrestler knows that their behavior is disappointing to the coaches and lets the team down they will often see the need to act appropriately and follow the outlined expectations of the coaches. Following this course of action does not negate the need to have penalties for some bad behavior all of the time. However, coaches may find out wrestlers having to endure a sit-down with the coaches, knowing that their behavior let the team down, may often be a punishment in itself. Coaches do not have to berate or demean kids in these meetings, nor do they have to follow a rigid set of rules that may not apply effectively to the situation. But, coaches will be teaching communicating with kids about the greater purpose of the wrestling team and program which will often lead to a positive resolution.

LIMITING THE POSSIBILITY OF DISCIPLINE PROBLEMS

Coaches that recognize effective teaching is a primary responsibility of successful coaching are more apt to run effective practices that hold the athletes interest and lead to a greater enjoyment of the sport. These effective practices also translate over to better behavior as the team travels to and runs their own events.

Planning ahead is a cornerstone for any coach looking to succeed at a practice. A well planned practice has a steady flow that moves from activity to activity seamlessly, and focuses on pre-determined objectives.

Coaches have a more difficult time planning a practice these days considering the proven fact that attention spans for youth are shorter in today's culture. Ignoring the fact that kids can stay focused for only three to five minutes without the natural tendency to become distracted cannot be an option for an effective coaching staff.

To keep wrestlers on task, a coach must be prepared to inter-mix technique evaluation, team discussion, drilling, and live situations together. A coach that stays "on the clock" will find that their athletes get more out of their practices and the team will experience less discipline problems.

As a part of planning ahead, a coach should choose their activities very carefully. At very young ages, coaches should remember that the primary motivations for a youth to wrestle include positive socialization, mastery and enjoyment of the sport, and social interaction with adults outside of their family as well as learning to win. Coaches should prepare practices that suit the age division appropriately.

Boring drills or drills that are not tied to an understood purpose lose their effectiveness and may encourage discipline problems. Coaches using drills in practice should recognize that drilling must be timed in short intervals to be effective. Also, the participants must clearly understand the objective of the drill and how it relates to the purpose of that part of practice. Further, drills that use competition keep kids more motivated, as do drills that keep athletes engaged and in motion.

Also, coaches at younger age levels should be prepared to involve the parents. The parents must understand what the reasonable expectations of the staff are. By enlisting their support, coaches will find that many behavior problems can be eliminated. Coaches should also be on the lookout of active parents who may be suited to help the coaching staff in a supervisory role with proper training. With many young participants in the practice, another adult helping the process of the practice can be an excellent ally.

Recognizing the difference between open acts of defiance and childish irresponsibility is also an important thing for coaches to remember. Open defiance of the expectations for the team is a much more severe problem then the occasional mistake of irresponsible behavior. Open defiance should be dealt with immediately and effectively but coaches should be wary of being drawn into a confrontation with team member. Athletes on occasion may attempt to challenge a coach's position and leadership. Taking the bait and reacting with anger will only hurt the coach in the future. Coaches should attempt to lessen the hostility and get back to focusing on the expectations for the team.

Coaches that understand the flow of a good practice and the enjoyment that comes from being involved in a fun wrestling setting will always go back and place themselves in the athletes' shoes. Team discipline does not have to be an over-arching concern for a coach provided that they effectively deal with teaching proper expectations to the athletes, making all members of the team feel valued.

12
Leadership, Image and Respect

Gary Abbott, Eileen Bowker

Rulon Gardner gained new respect for the sport of wrestling in the United States following his historic upset of the unbeaten legend Alexander Kareline at the 2000 Sydney Olympics.

When it comes to leadership, wrestling coaches are the center of the universe for a wrestling team. What a coach does and how he does it plays the most important role in how the team will perform and act in competition.

Ask any former athlete who the role models were who helped them to achieve their goals and taught them how to succeed, and most will name one or more of their coaches. Certainly, parents and family play an important role in the development of wrestlers at all ages. However, the athletes and their family look to the coach for leadership and as an example for the entire team and for each individual athlete on the squad.

Coaches will say that one of the most rewarding parts of being in the profession is making a difference in the lives of the young people who they coach. The impact that a coach can have on a wrestler can be significant and lifelong. And the lessons that are learned can be both positive and negative.

A coach teaches much more than techniques, training and conditioning programs and match strategy. Coaches teach life skills and values, things beyond wrestling that carry over into life. It is very important for a coach to think about what he is teaching his athletes, not only in what they say, but what they do and how they do it.

It all comes down to leadership, public image and respect.

SETTING THE EXAMPLE

As a leader and role model, a coach sets an example for his team and each individual athlete on a daily basis. Little details are very important. Attitude is also something that makes a big difference in setting a good example for the team.

Think of a team in wrestling, or in any sport for that matter, that you respect. Certainly success is important to that respect. But those teams that really stand out are the ones that act like champions, win or lose. They know how to act when the pressure is on. They receive respect for how they compete, not just what the result is.

Think of a team or an athlete that you don't respect. In most cases, you feel this way not based whether the athlete or team wins or loses, but the way that they do it.

When you are coaching, all eyes are on you. In practice, it is your team that is looking towards you. At competitions, the referees, the parents, the fans and the media are looking at you. Like it or not, the coach is often the focus. You have an opportunity to take that focus and use it in a very positive way.

Each day, people notice what a coach does. Knowing that provides each coach with a chance to think about things and to do the right thing. Just like the rest of life, there are no set rules for this. It comes down to common sense and showing respect for those you deal with. And always remember, the athletes expect the coach to be the leader.

You can set an example so many ways, such as always being on time and being prepared for each workout and competition. A coach can set an example by making sure to communicate well with his or her athletes, along with their families.

At competitions, it is more than just your team that will notice how you act and what you do. A coach can influence that by how he looks and dresses, what he says and how he says it, and how he treats other people.

For instance, coaches that wear suit and ties, or appropriate team apparel, for their competitions are sending a message to the public as well as to their athletes. They are showing that this competition is important and that they care. Also, how a coach deals with referees and opposing coaches makes a powerful statement. Using foul language or angry speech should be avoided. These are things that a coach can control and influence.

People who believe all that matters is winning or losing, and neglect these other vital things, do not understand the power of image and have lost sight of what is truly important in sports and in life.

TELLING ATHLETES WHAT IS EXPECTED

Once a coach decides to set a good example for the athletes, there must still be clear, well-defined and well-communicated expectations given to the team. If a coach wants his team to act with sportsmanship and class, win or lose, setting a personal example is not enough. The coach must tell the team what is expected, and must remind them on a regular basis.

One of the keys to making this work is to also communicate what the consequence will be if an athlete does not live up to the expectations set for the team. If the coach has chosen to ask the athletes to exhibit a certain behavior, when a team member does not meet these expectations, there must be a consistent and fair disciplinary action.

It is not just what you say, it is what you do. If the athlete can get away with falling short of the team's standard of behavior, that standard has no meaning. The coach must live by that standard and must enforce the rules when they are not met.

WHY IMAGE IS IMPORTANT

There is a cliché that goes like this: Image is everything. There is a lot of truth to that saying. As a coach, you must pay constant attention to the image that you represent and that your team expresses to other people.

It is important that coaches and their athletes realize that they represent much more than themselves. How a coach and the team behaves in public will be what people remember and think of them, not just that day but well into the future. Certainly, people can and will make mistakes, especially under the pressure of competition. If this continues to be repeated, it is no longer just a mistake but is a learned behavior. This should be unacceptable to the coach. There is never a chance for a new first impression.

Initially, they are representing the school or club they compete for, as well as their entire community. The athletes are also representing their family and their personal convictions. It is all about self-respect, as well as respect for others. And the coach sets the tone for this for the entire team.

For athletes who compete around the nation, such as the ASICS Cadet and Junior Na-

tionals, they are representing their entire state. And for those athletes who have a special opportunity to compete overseas at an international competition, they are representing their entire nation.

Ultimately, however, athletes and coaches represent wrestling. Those who love wrestling realize that the sport does not get the kind of recognition and special treatment from society that perhaps it deserves. In order for wrestling to grow and to achieve greater things in the world, the behavior of the participants makes a big difference. How people outside of wrestling perceive the sport can be influenced greatly by the behavior that the athletes and coaches display in public.

HOW TO ACT WHEN YOU LOSE

For some reason, wrestlers often forget that in every wrestling match or competition, half of the participants do not win. In the course of a tournament, only one athlete in the entire weight class becomes the champion. Losing is a part of wrestling, but the desire to win often causes motivated athletes and coaches to forget this fact and set unrealistic expectations.

The greatest wrestlers of all time hated to lose. It is a physical, emotional and psychological core to their being. Because wrestling is an individual sport, and the spotlight is always on the athlete on the mat, wrestlers truly understand how painful losing can be. The sport has such high demands of sacrifice and effort to succeed, and the personal satisfaction of achieving high goals can be tremendously rewarding.

That does not excuse a wrestler (as well as the coaching staff) for bad behavior after a loss. Everyone in wrestling has seen it happen when an athlete loses; he refuses to shake hands, yells at the referee, throws his headgear, cries uncontrollably, knocks over water coolers, runs out of the stadium and acts improperly. We have witnessed this at all levels, and nobody feels good about it when it happens.

Losing with class is difficult during the emotional time when a person falls short of his or her goals. Nobody likes losing, but it is a part of the sport. A person is often remembered more for how they handled a loss than a win. Once again, coaches must remind their wrestlers that all eyes are on them, and to act accordingly.

A truly important aspect of wrestling is the post-match tradition of shaking hands and showing respect for the opponent and the officials. The protocol for wrestling requires that the athlete must shake the hand of the opponent, win or lose. When an athlete refuses to do that, or does it with disrespect, that athlete has violated a core value of the sport. This must be talked about with the athletes, even practiced if necessary, so when the heat of the competition is at its peak, the wrestler knows how to react to adversity. It really comes down to maintaining personal dignity and showing respect for others.

Believe it or not, every wrestler loses. Even the great Alexander Kareline of Russia, who won three Olympic gold medals, nine World gold medals and every other tournament in his Senior-level career, ultimately was beaten. When Rulon Gardner pulled his shocking upset over Kareline in Sydney, Australia, the world was reminded that even the best can be beaten. Kareline was able to handle an unimaginable disappointment with class and dignity, and his legacy will reflect that behavior for the rest of his life.

Athletes who have misbehaved after losses sometimes are not aware of how that is perceived until later, and then regret it for the rest of their lives. This is especially true at major events, such as the Olympic Games, the NCAA Championships or the high school state championships. People will remember this behavior in the future because it happens on such a big stage. However, this is a learned behavior, and is equally important at small, unattended competitions, and on the youngest levels of youth wrestling.

Athletes and coaches are role models for younger people, and respectful behavior sends a message to the next generation of wrestlers. It's not just Olympians and college stars who set this example. High school wrestlers are often heroes to the kid wrestlers in their communities, for example. It really does matter what you do when you lose.

HOW TO ACT WHEN YOU WIN

Thinking in advance about how you act and what you do when you win a match is just as important as being prepared for a loss. Certainly, every wrestler will have their own way of expressing their joy and satisfaction when they win. However, there are ways to do that which can be positive, and other ways that take away from the value of the victory because they are negative.

Winning with dignity and respect is not something that just happens. It is a behavior which can be practiced, and should be thought about in advance. How you present yourself after a victory will tell other people about the kind of person you are and about your values.

Young athletes learn about how to express themselves in victory by watching other athletes. Often it comes from other sports that are on television more than wrestling. Football is perhaps one of the sports that has the most public opportunities for post-success celebrations and personal expressions.

On any given Sunday, football fans will see a variety of reactions when an athlete scores a touchdown. Some players have wild and creative touchdown rituals after they score. Others just drop the ball in the endzone, hand it to the referee, or give it to a fan. Every time a football player scores, they have a choice on how to behave. Likewise, every time a wrestler wins a match, they have that same opportunity.

Some of the greatest football players of all time never put on a single endzone celebration. As football coaches are known to say, these athletes "acted like they had been there before." They knew how to win with dignity.

Celebrations can be exciting when done with respect. Everybody remembers Rulon Gardner's two celebrations, his gold medal cartwheel at the 2000 Olympics and his leaving the shoes on the mat after his bronze medal at the 2004 Olympics. Others will remember how John Smith ran completely around the mat area when he won his gold medal at the 1988 Olympics. There are many wrestling people who remember how Jeff Blatnick in the 1984 Olympics and Kurt Angle in the 1996 Olympics broke down in tears after their Olympic gold-medal victories. Bobby Weaver carried his small child with him on the mat after winning the 1984 Olympic gold medal. Mark Schultz, a World and Olympic champion, was known to do complete backflips after major victories. Cael Sanderson leaping into the arms of coaches Bobby Douglas and Kevin Jackson at the 2004 Olympics will be an image many remember for a long time.

Sometimes these expressions were spontaneous, and other times the athlete had planned them in advance. These celebrations are memorable, but they were done with respect for the opponent. They were also saved for the most important events of these athletes' careers. Rulon Gardner does not do cartwheels after every win, and Mark Schultz saved his back flips for when it really mattered. Throughout their careers, these athletes won their matches with humility and pride, and chose to express their emotions at the proper times, not every time.

There are some antics after a victory that are not well received, because they are done without respect for the opponent and for the sport. Many of these are actions that appear to mock the athlete who was defeated. They are similar to situations in other sports that are considered "smack talk" or "junk." Regardless of how an athlete feels about an opponent personally, or how heated the competition was during the match, once the final whistle blows, it is truly over. Disrespectful actions do not add to a victory, they take away from it.

Shaking hands while looking the opponent in the eye, having the hand raised properly by the referee, shaking the opposing coach's hand and the referee's hand all show respect, not only for yourself and your opponent, but for everybody in attendance at the event.

Athletes need leadership from their coaches on this issue. If the topic is not discussed, then there is no way to be sure that when the time occurs, athletes will display good behavior when they win. Leadership on this comes from the coach, through thoughtful discussion in advance. In addition, when an athlete's behavior is inappropriate, the coach needs to immediately address the issue and explain to the athlete why it is unacceptable.

Emotion is one of the reasons that people enjoy watching wrestling. It is a heated and emotional sport, and athletes should be encouraged to enjoy their moment of victory. Taking pride in how you act after a win is an important part of telling the world the kind of person you are.

MEDIA RELATIONS 101

It is not just fans and parents who watch athletes and coaches at events. At any given wrestling competition, there may be members of the working media covering an event. This happens all the time at the major national events at all age levels. However, often there are journalists at high school tournaments and even at youth wrestling events.

Wrestling coaches and athletes should understand that dealing with the media is a part of being a wrestler. It is not an add-on or something extra. It is as much a part of being an athlete as attending workouts, studying film, going to weigh-ins, warming up prior to matches and competing in a bout. Having good behavior is important because it is something that might end up being reported in the newspapers or shown on television.

Some athletes and coaches enjoy speaking to the press, while others are either uncomfortable or nervous about it. In either case, when an athlete is in a competition they may be asked to talk to a reporter. This is an opportunity for the athlete to tell their story and give their viewpoint, not only on the competition at hand but also on what is meaningful to them.

A media interview is a chance for an athlete to recognize their coaches and their parents and those who have helped them. It allows a coach to thank the booster club or administrators or sponsors and get them some well-deserved recognition. It is a chance to make positive statements about the sport and about people within wrestling.

The athletes and coaches who make U.S. World and Olympic Teams have assistance dealing with the media from USA Wrestling's Communications staff. Many colleges have sports information staff that assists the wrestlers with their media activity. However, on the youth and high school levels, it is the athlete along with the coach that will have to manage things when the media seeks an interview.

Athletes need to learn that the media is doing a job. They have been assigned to cover the competition, and in some cases, to file reports on a specific athlete. At major events, their media outlet may have spent hundreds of dollars on plane fare, hotel rooms, rental cars and food for that reporter to be there.

When an athlete or coach refuses to give an interview, the journalist is not able to complete the assignment that they have been given. In many cases, this will also affect whether that athlete or team will get media coverage in the future. Some journalists enjoy covering wrestling, while others are just there because it has been assigned. If the journalist is unable to complete the assignment, or has a bad experience when trying to do their job, it is possible they may choose not to attend wrestling events in the future. Giving an interview, win or lose, is important if wrestling is to receive more attention and publicity in your community.

Especially at tournaments, athletes must understand that the press will want to interview them shortly after a match. There are reasons for this. Certainly, the athlete often has the best quotes immediately afterwards, when the emotion is still fresh. Also, many journalists are on tight deadlines, and can't wait for very long to get the interview in. In addition, the journalist may also be assigned to write about other athletes and topics later in the session, and only have a limited time frame for that specific athlete or coach.

There are times when an athlete is not able to speak right away after a match, because of their emotional state, because of an injury or for other reasons. It is OK for an athlete to ask for a short cooling down period. However, if that is the case, the athlete needs to keep his word and return for the interview in a timely fashion. This is a matter of integrity and respect, making sure to live up to a commitment.

When speaking to the press, a coach and their athletes need to be careful about exactly what they say. Taking a breath and slowing things down to collect your thoughts is a good practice for any coach and athlete being interviewed. Trying to be relaxed and thinking about what is said will help ensure that you are not misquoted and that you come across at your best.

Working with the media is a learned skill, and is something that can be practiced. Coaches can take a leadership role in this, by discussing the issue with the team in advance and providing advice and support for the athletes.

Everybody wants to see more wrestling coverage in the media. However, there is a responsibility for coaches and athletes to be accessible when the media does come. As with public behavior, wrestlers and coaches need to consider their image, reputation and character when dealing with the press.

13
Performance Enhancement: Mental Skills Development

Ted Witulski, Beasey Hendrix, Tyler Brandt

Major events such as the Junior National Championships can tremendously heighten competitive stress in a wrestler.

During the wrestling season the need for mental skills development is constantly at hand for wrestlers and their coaches. One wrestler during a match can be visibly seen berating themselves after making a bad move. Another wrestler looks at his draw and loses the match before it is even contested. Still another loses control in a match and begins arguing a call with an official.

Mental skills can make or break a wrestler's performance. While many coaches believe teaching skills such as positive self talk, stress management and imagery are aspects of coaching for the elite level the opposite is true. Mental skills should be used at all levels of wrestling. Wrestler that are taught mental performance enhancement at a young age are more likely to gain positive breakthroughs at a young age and move forward in their training.

The coach who works with their athletes on mental skills aims to positively effect the core beliefs of their athletes. Studies have consistently shown that an individual's core beliefs will determine the reality they draw into their life, whether it is positive or negative. The determined coach draws on this knowledge and develops a plan to assist their athletes to succeed through mental skills.

Throughout the day people have an active dialogue with themselves, between 150 and 300 words a minute. This translates to between 45,000 and 51,000 thoughts per day. For wrestlers the dangerous self talk occurs in a variety of ways. "There is no way that guy can be in my weight class; he is just too big." "I can win this match if the ref does not screw me." "I have not been feeling well, so I hope I can do alright."

Beliefs, such as these are literally etched into our brains. The neural pathways that carry thoughts to the brain for interpretation hold these beliefs while incoming information is passed over them. A wrestler's mind assesses information and attempts to square it with their pre-conceived self talk that has been processed in the past. Negative or limiting thoughts like the ones expressed earlier can be rewritten. However, to do this a wrestler must rewire the neurological pathways that hold these self-defeating thoughts.

To achieve desired changes in negative thinking there are four elements that a wrestler and coach must know—Relaxation, Realism, Regularity and Reinforcement.

Relaxation is a key component for wrestlers to include as they practice positive mental imagery. Development of relaxation prior to use of mental imagery allows the mind to focus on the message at hand; instead of being distracted by competing thoughts and external situations.

The goal of realism in imagery is to create a situation that is so realistic the mind actually believes the image is the real thing. Coaches and athletes should focus on clarity with vivid images that include color. Vividness in the image encourages the incorporation of as many of the minds' senses as possible. This includes putting emotion into the image, allowing the participant to connect the feelings of the situation to the positive outcomes being visualized. Control keeps the participant focused on the differing components of the skill or situation being visualized. Finally, the realistic image must include the desired positive outcome. Realism of imagery is necessary so that the participant believes in the ability of imagery to improve their performance.

Regular practices of imagery are required in order for an athlete to improve their performance. The most effective use of imagery is to break the session down into three to five minute chunks. In total, an athlete should practice imagery ten to fifteen minutes a day.

The final "R" is reinforcement. Reinforcement means the athlete should look to develop ways that will return their thinking back to their image training, further developing the skills and thoughts they have worked on. Script writing is a very effective tool at reinforcing the desired thoughts and outcomes of an athlete.

A participant that is motivated to gain the positive results from mental skills training should be invested enough in the process to reinforce their training by developing their own script for mental skills development.

Written scripts should be in the first person and include all parts of the skill or execution. Participants should pay particular attention to the many traits of realism as previously outlined. The script for the athlete must be a piece that is in constant flux, as the participant writes and rewrites it. Descriptors such as adjectives should be added to develop the color and detail of the work. Context should be created to make the work even more vivid, such as discussing the speed of shots or the opponent's inability to handle the athlete's attacking pressure. As the script is refined the athlete should read it to themselves trying to remember the event in all of its sensory action and emotional detail. The athlete should be willing to tape the script for self-playback as well as sharing the script with coaches and teammates so that they develop a stronger understanding of the individuals thinking and motivation.

Imagery is a wide topic that covers a variety of mental skills terms commonly used in the sport like visualization, stress management, relaxation training and positive self talk. By understanding the five types of image training athletes can enhance performance in a variety of different situations.

IMAGERY CATEGORIES

The five main categories of imagery have been identified as follows:

1. Motivational-Specific (MS)—This involves seeing yourself winning an event, receiving a trophy or medal and being congratulated by other athletes. MS imagery may boost motivation and effort during training and facilitate goal-setting, but is unlikely on its own to lead directly to performance benefits.

2. Motivational General-Mastery (MG-M)—This is based on seeing yourself coping in difficult circumstances and mastering challenging situations. It may include maintaining a positive focus while behind and then coming back to win. MG-M imagery appears to be important in developing expectations of success and self-confidence.

3. Motivational General-Arousal (MG-A)—This is imagery that reflects feelings of relaxation stress, anxiety or arousal in relation to sports competitions. There is good evidence to suggest that MC-A imagery can influence hear rate—on index of arousal—and can be employed as a 'psych-up' strategy.

4. Cognitive Specific (CS)—This involves seeing yourself perform specific skills, such as a finishing with a turk off of a double leg, or executing a granby roll for a reversal. If learning and performance are the desired outcomes, evidence suggests that CS imagery will be the most effective choice.

5. Cognitive General (CG)—This involves images of strategy and match plans related to a competitive event. Examples could include developing a strategy to ride-out an opponent with short time left in a period or countering an opponent's best takedown like the short-carry.

SIDEBAR: Applying Sport Psychology To The Real World of Athletes: A Model of Offensive And Defensive Mental Skills

By Sean McCann, Ph.D.
USOC Coaching and Sport Sciences

All great coaches and athletes know that mental skills are critical to sport success, but how exactly? Sport psychology as a profession has not done a great job of explaining why athletes need to develop mental skills. The way sport psychologists usually talk about mental skills is to organize skills into a teaching plan rather than show how and why these skills impact athletes in the real world of sport.

Without a clear answer to the why and how, we still have many athletes resisting coaches' efforts to introduce mental skills training. Have you ever heard a football lineman say that you don't need to be physically strong in football? Of course not, the reason is obvious. An opponent will push a weak football lineman all over the field. The lineman may deny it, but coaches can show him a game video and prove it beyond dispute. The benefits of physical strength in sport are visible. One of the problems with sport psychology is that it is invisible. Coaches and athletes need a model of sport psychology that explains why athletes need mental skills and how they work in various sport situations.

Recently, I started using a model of sport psychology mental skills that organizes my thinking about sport psychology. In addition, this model helps coaches and athletes understand what happens during competition when athletes are strong in some mental skills and weak in others. The model aids in making invisible mental skills become more visible. It starts by organizing all mental skills into two major categories: offensive skills and defense skills.

OFFENSIVE MENTAL SKILLS

Offensive skills let an athlete dominate a competition. Offensive physical skills might include the terrific top-end speed of 400-meter runner Michael Johnson or the high VO2 Max of Lance Armstrong that allows him to pass other cyclists in the Alps. Unusual strength and quickness are offensive physical skills in a majority of Olympic sports. When these offensive skills are well developed in an athlete, other athletes know that athlete is a contender. Offensive skills are absolutely necessary to be a truly exceptional athlete.

Offensive mental skills also allow an athlete to dominate an event. Tremendous **competitive desire** causes athletes to put in time learning new skills to take their game or sport to a higher level (think Tiger Woods). Athletes' competitive desire helps them rise to match and surpass great efforts by competitors.

A **drive to set and achieve goals** keeps athletes striving for improvement, identifying and eliminating weaknesses and keeping training intense and focused.

The **ability to visualize success** lets athletes practice for excellence and keep thoughts simple and practical. For athletes under pressure, **self-talk skills** help them think in a positive and useful way.

The **ability to develop effective competition plans** is a critical mental skill for athletes who compete in complex, dynamic sports with frequent decision making. A willingness and ability to **commit** to a plan of training and competition is an offensive skill that allows athletes to give 100 percent in competition and get the most out of new and innovative training methods.

Comfort with risk is an essential offensive skill for competitive situations where too much caution can be the difference between a medal and tenth place. The **ability to maintain a relaxed "athletic" approach** is a related skill that allows athletes to act without hesitation and avoid the danger of cautious over-thinking.

Finally, **confidence in skills and the competition plan** allows athletes to stay on the offensive in important competitions.

Offensive Mental Skills	Impact on Performance
Competitive desire	Helps motivate athletes to improve skills and "battle" for the win in a tight contest.
Drive to set and achieve goals	Helps athletes achieve personal bests, keeps intensity high and constantly improves the process of training and competing.
Visualization skills	Allows athletes to see a path to success and keeps their thoughts simple during competition.
Self-talk skills	Athletes skilled in self-talk are aware of the language in their heads and actively adjust it to stay positive and action oriented.
Competition planning	Helps athletes make decisions before competition, so that during the event they simply can execute rather than decide.
Ability to commit	Allows athletes to give 100 percent during competition and lets them stay with new approaches long enough to see a benefit in training (such as changing technique).
Comfort with risk	Athletes with this skill understand that taking risks at some events reaps rewards, and that a winning approach sometimes requires a willingness to lose (fear of losing may prevent risk taking).
Relaxed athletic approach	When athletes are athletic, they are relaxed, mainly visual, looking for opportunities rather than danger and avoid hesitation. They do not over-think their situation.
Confidence	Confidence is the offensive skill that makes it easier to set high goals, see and believe success and execute good competition plans.

The word that may best describe athletes with extremely strong offensive mental skills is predator. These athletes are focused, intense, athletic, looking to win and ready to take advantage of the opportunity for success that competition provides. Without these offensive mental skills, athletes may be good, but they will never be great.

DEFENSIVE MENTAL SKILLS

Defensive skills help athletes succeed consistently and in all conditions. Defensive physical skills might include Nordic skier Bjorn Dahlie's ability to handle tremendous training loads, Speed skater Eric Heiden's ability to quickly recover from the effort of the last race, Olympic champion Haile Gebrselasie's capacity to adapt and respond to surges in the race by other runners, and Edwin Moses' tremendous technique that stood up to the test of a decade-long winning streak. When athletes' defensive skills are strong they are consistent performers, winning big events as well as small. They are resilient and easily adapt to changes in their environment.

If offensive mental skills are necessary for excellence, athletes need defensive skills to maintain excellence, handle adversity and allow them to be at their best at the big events like the Olympic Games. Defensive mental skills also help athletes be resilient and consistent in any condition. Athletes' **desire for excellence in training** results in practicing the way they should compete in an organized, efficient and useful manner.

Controlling competitive anxiety becomes more important as the significance of the competition increases. The ability to control anger and frustration before and during competitions allows athletes to quickly gain balance and recover from errors or problems in the environment.

Control of energy levels falls into three different defensive mental skills: 1) ability to raise intensity level, 2) ability to recover emotional energy between efforts, and 3) ability to adjust energy up or down depending on the competitive situation.

The skill of quickly recovering from performance setbacks is a defensive mental skill that pays dividends in lengthy competitions or competitions with repeated efforts. Flexible response to changes in the environment may be most important at big events (Olympic Games, World Championships, etc.) where environment changes the most.

The ability to focus, despite distractions is also critical at events where distractions increase in proportion to the size and importance of the event.

Finally, mental maintenance skills or the ability to maintain simple, effective thoughts under pressure is often the difference between having a great plan and executing it.

The key words that describe defensive mental skills include: balance, resilience, and invulnerability. Athletes with strong defensive mental skills are individuals coaches count on for consistent performance at competition after competition, big event or small.

Defensive Mental Skills	Impact on Performance
Desire for excellence in training	Athletes should train as they compete, practically and efficiently, avoiding the problems of over-training and under-recovery.
Controlling competitive anxiety	Allows athletes to stay in control, which is especially critical as the events get bigger and athletes become vulnerable to anxiety.
Controlling anger and frustration	Allows athletes to save energy for competition, control thoughts and stay on task, even when real problems exist.
Energy management (raising intensity)	Allows athletes to "ramp up" energy when the situation calls for it.
Energy management (recovery between efforts)	Allows athletes to use the recovery time available so they have needed energy at the finish.
Energy management (adjusting energy)	Allows athletes to be aware of the correct energy level needed for a given situation and to make quick adjustments, up or down, for physical and mental readiness..
Recovery from performance setbacks	Allows athletes to quickly "bounce back" from mistakes, defeats or bad luck and yet retain positive and useful thoughts.
Flexible when environment changes	Allows athletes to quickly adapt to change, tolerate disruptions to routine and see all changes as opportunities.
Focus despite distractions	Allows athletes to stay on task, keeping all five senses oriented only towards useful signals, even when all five senses could get pulled away from the task.
Mental maintenance skills	Allows athletes to be self-aware, noting changes and variations, making adjustments needed to keep thoughts simple and effective.

What does the Offense-Defense Model add to the usual list of mental skills needed for sport? An important item is the way to explain the behavior coaches see in athletes. Here are a few brief examples:

1. An athlete with a strong desire to dominate expects and plans to win and is dominant at the national level, but he/she always makes big errors in international competition. This athlete may have excellent offensive mental skills, but his/her defensive mental skills probably need some work. He/she may lack control of competitive anxiety, in part because of the overwhelming desire to win or because the energy level gets so high at big events that thinking suffers, and he/she makes basic errors. This athlete may be resistant to working with a sport psychologist because the strong offensive mind perceives discussing anxiety as a weakness. He/she needs to understand that anxiety is normal, and unwillingness to deal with it is a weakness.

2. An athlete gets in a rut. His/her times or scores have not improved, and he/she always loses to the same competitors. This athlete is never terrible, but coaches know he/she has more potential than is shown. This may be an athlete with good defensive mental skills but he/she may be missing offensive mental skills such as confidence, comfort with risk or drive to set and achieve goals.

3. An athlete is unbeatable when on a roll, but he/she can also go into the tank for months at a time. He/she may have deficits in defensive mental skills, making him/her vulnerable to distracting thoughts and unable to do mental maintenance. The athlete also probably is lacking offensive mental skills and needs to improve in the areas of competition mental planning, self-talk and confidence.

Offensive mental skills allow athletes to achieve greatness. Defensive mental skills gives them consistency and resiliency. Combine the two, and you have dominant athletes. Athletes missing one or the other of these skills are tremendously frustrating to coaches, because you know they can perform so much better than they do. If this model of mental skills is useful to you, talk about it with your athletes. By tying these invisible mental skills to visible results and using the simple Offense-Defense Model, you may find that fewer athletes resist the idea of developing mental strength

Coaches should encourage athletes to understand these five general categories and work on helping athletes develop the beginning use of these training concepts. As coaches work with specific athletes they will narrow their focus and encourage individuals to focus on traits that are specific to them.

Working with the athletes on a group and individual level, coaches should look to move athletes into the "achievement zone", the feeling where everything comes clear and focused. Nothing bothers the athlete and everything becomes instinctively clear. The wrestler will always handle any difficult situation with the right reaction, knowing that nothing can bother them, in their quest for athletic excellence. Coaches pushing athletes towards the achievement zone should actively work with individuals to key on either mind/body skills for success.

THE EIGHT MIND/BODY SKILLS FOR SUCCESS

These are the eight skills that will help you reach your Achievement Zone:

Action Focus: This is the skill of knowing how to successfully reach your long-term goals. It requires focusing on the task you need to accomplish, rather than on the desired result. It means setting achievable goals as a stepping stone to ultimate success.

Creative Thinking: This is the skill of using your imagination to achieve your goals and solve problems.

Productive Analysis: We all have an inner voice. If we talk to ourselves negatively we perform poorly. Productive thinking helps us stay confident. It also helps us identify weaknesses and find ways to improve.

Keeping Cool: The keeping cool skill allows you to deal with anxiety and to prevent panic. Top athletes recognize that they will be nervous before big competition. They practice skills such as deep breathing and muscle relaxation so they can calm down when the pressure is on.

Concentration: The ability to enjoy the present is critical for competitive success. Elite athletes learn to focus their concentration so that they pay attention only to the things which will help them succeed. As a result, their performance flows smoothly.

Emotional Power: Strong emotions are a natural part of sports and business. The best performers use their emotions constructively. They learn to deal with the inevitable negative emotions such as disappointment, frustration and sadness. It is important to be able to refocus after getting upset if you wish to be successful.

Energizing: Doing your best on a consistent basis takes lots of energy. The skill of energizing enables you to keep going when you feel like quitting. You need energy if you frequently feel tired and worn out.

Consistency: Sport psychologists have found that the best athletes prepare very carefully for every performance. They often have a set routine that they follow exactly.

Mental skills development is not something that athletes should wait to learn late in their careers. Rather, athletes should be encouraged to focus on these skills early in their career by the complete coach. Coaches should organize a plan that will start with simple mental skills such as sportsmanship and move to more active imagery skills such as positive self talk until athletes are fully engaged with the process of consistently developing the mental skills to succeed in wrestling.

14
Basic Skills, Strategy, and Technique for Successful Coaching

Isaac Ramaswamy, Ted Witulski, Tyler Brandt

QUESTIONS TO CONSIDER

- What are the seven basic skills?
- What factor discourages many coaches from learning the international styles?
- What is the importance of mastering the basics?
- What two basic skills are often overlooked by coaches?

High level technique and strategy must be developed at the youth level for athletes to be successful.

For many coaches one of the largest frustrations with wrestling is the seemingly ever-changing rules, especially in the styles of free-style and Greco-Roman. Over the last twenty-five years FILA (the international governing body for wrestling) has chosen to adopt new rules and interpretations much to the consternation of the general wrestling public.

Many people have wrestled under vastly different rules than those that are employed today. When the likes of Stan Dziedzic and Ben Peterson represented the United States internationally three three-minute periods were commonplace. Later in the 80's and 90's a one five minute period was utilized and by the late 90's two three-minute periods were standard.

Additionally, the use of par-terre or mat wrestling has been emphasized at different times then others. FILA has made nearly continual adjustments to the number of gut-wrenches and ankle laces that could be scored, making requirements that have varied from multiple turns in succession to scoring two turns to one side to only scoring one turn per gut-wrench or lace. Further, interpretations about the aggressors' arch and the defenders hand-to-hand turn across their back have also played a role in the ever-evolving rules. The most obvious point of emphasis was the inclusion of the clinch rule in '99 that eventually played a role in Rulon Gardner's defeat of the wrestling legend Alexander Kareline.

As recent as the fall of 2004, FILA radically altered the rules searching for a balance of a speedy competition, exciting scoring, and a marketable sport. The member countries of the world all have a voice in what rules the international styles will be contested under. Unfortunately, there is no guarantee that the rest of the world's wrestling associations will support the United States' (USA Wrestling) position.

Coaches are encouraged to check their understanding of the rules constantly. Amendments and addendums come in almost a steady flow. But, please do not let this discouraging part of the sport deter you as a coach from making a difference in the lives of the youth that look to you.

BASIC SKILLS: THE KEYS TO MASTERING WRESTLING

The sport of wrestling involves a myriad of moves and counter moves, all intended to break an opponent's position, to score points, and to eventually pin a competitor. The successful execution of any of these moves is dependant upon the athlete having mastered a series of very specific, yet basic skills.

The wrestler must first and foremost develop control and movement of their own body. Too often coaches and wrestlers concentrate first on various holds and maneuvers that are executed against an opponent. Before such maneuvers can be successfully executed, however, a wrestler must have disciplined himself to know where their own body is in space and the relationship of certain key body parts to each other.

There are seven (7) basic skills that emphasize the discipline to move in space relative to an opponent. When combined effectively they provide the wrestler with both mobility and power.

1. Stance—the ability to keep the head, neck, back, hips, elbows, and legs in a prescribed position to each other.
2. Motion—the ability to move the body from one position on the mat to another in a lateral or circular direction and remain in a good position.
3. Changing Levels—the ability of a wrestler to move his/her hips up and down in relationship to their opponent while remaining in a strong position.
4. Penetration—the ability of a wrestler to move his/her hips directly into, under and through their opponent while remaining in a strong position.
5. Lifting—the ability of a wrestler to move his/her opponent's body mass in an upward direction, up and/or off the mat.
6. Back Step—the ability of a wrestler to move his/her hips into and under an opponent while twisting backwards into his/her body.
7. Back Arch—the ability of a wrestler to control body parts and remain in balance while

There might be many reasons that cause people to think that it should be easy to just start up coaching a sport that they once were adept at. However, the truth is quite different. Coaches that have been away from the sport soon find out that wrestling is an ever-evolving sport where the technique, tactics, and rule changes force coaches to constantly change what they thought could be set patterns.

Watch a hard fought college matches these days and chances are one or both of the wrestlers will inevitably choose bottom. But, go back in time to the epic match when Dan Gable faced Larry Owings the story was quite different. With all the pressure of what is still arguably the most famous collegiate match in the history of the NCAA tournament the tactics were far different. When Gable and Owings squared off in what was ultimately Gable's only collegiate loss both wrestlers chose top—a rarity in today's tough collegiate matches. Back then, wrestlers wrestled more for the pin, and both wrestlers were determined enough to take top.

We are part of an ever changing sport and it is important that coaches study the changes that have been made over the years.

Technically there have been a number of changes in wrestling. Many people are familiar with the mastery of the low-single that John Smith demonstrated in his career that included two Olympic Championships and four World Titles. Smith's low single was revolutionary compared to the standard high-level singles that most wrestlers utilized.

Another change in wrestling has come from countering an opponent's shot. Back in the day a good ol' cross-face was the bread and butter of a defender. Now wrestlers know two types of front headlocks as well as a number of ways to re-shoot from an opponent's shot.

Another area that has changed comes from the top position. Years ago, a leg-rider from the top position would deeply grapevine a leg. Now, the more common method used by wrestlers using the legs is a heal-in-ride, that extends the body and head forward of the down man—a technique that once would have been criticized because the top man was riding too high.

Techniques, tactics and rules have all changed dramatically over the years. A coach that wants to jump back into the sport that he once competed in should take the time to learn what has changed. It is often easy to rely on past knowledge, but it is definitely more exciting to gain exposure to the new way that wrestling works in the twenty-first century.

---

driving his/her hips into and under their opponent as they go from their feet into a high arching back bridge.

The ultimate result of mastering each skill and executing it in the proper sequence is the wrestler's ability to lift an opponent. Because the back step and the back arch are special forms of lifting, the basic skills back step (6) and back arch (7) are interchangeable with the basic skill lifting (5).

A well-executed sequence in a technique follows the basic skills.

POSITION → MOTION → LEVEL CHANGE → PENETRATION → LIFTING

ALL OF THE BASIC SKILLS ARE IMPORTANT TO ALL WRESTLERS

USA Wrestling's National Teams and the National Coaches Education Program encourage coaches to reinforce all of the basic skills in their wrestlers on a daily basis. Very often, coaches see basic skills one through five as more useable or adaptable to their style of wrestling, forgoing the teaching and reinforcement of the basic skills of the back step and the back arch.

Coaches that opt out of teaching the back step and the back arch are limiting their wrestlers' ability to fully master the sport of wrestling. It is hard to imagine that a coach in scholastic wrestling would decide to omit teaching a basic switch to his/her wrestlers. The switch is universal in our sport nationally. Even the youngest wrestlers learn the switch early in their wrestling career. An important point to emphasize to any coach or wrestler who would overlook the importance of all of the basic skills is to note that even an entry level move like the switch contains the movement of a back step as the need to.

The same can be said for the basic skill of a back-arch. While most coaches view a back-arch as a high level throw, when coaches take a detailed look at the ability of a wrestler to bridge and turn from their back or to hip-heist away from an opponent they will quickly see the relevance of the basic skill of back-arching and turning.

All of the basic skills are relevant to all ages and all styles of wrestling. Coaches must readily look for ways to incorporate the basic skills into all practices so that wrestlers maximize their abilities and constantly access new and better skills against their opponents.

USING THE BASIC SKILLS IN PRACTICE

As noted previously the basic skills practice the essential skills necessary for athletes to excel in the sport of wrestling. Coaches should look to constantly reinforce the importance of these seven essential skills in their practices by actively working on them in warm-ups and conditioning as well as referencing the basic skill movements when analyzing techniques.

Drills to reinforce the Basic Skills:

Stance

Scramble to a Stance Drill (Stagger or Square): A wrestler flat on their stomach scrambles to their feet coming to a solid stagger stance.

Done first with no resistance, and then with a wrestler pushing or weighing down the defender from various angles.

Scramble to a Base Drill: Done in a similar fashion to the stance drill starting the defender on their stomach or back first without an opponent's pressure, and then with an opponent's pressure.

Scramble to Control Drill: Done with an opponent who bridges off of his/her back while the top wrestler maintains contact and shuffles behind the defender then comes to a top position of elbow and tight-waist control. The drill can be advanced to give the top wrestler a command to go to a specific breakdown for scholastic wrestling.

Motion

Circular Motion Drill: Done by an individual wrestler who concentrates on footwork moving in a circular motion using both a staggered and square stance.

Lateral Motion Drill: Done by an individual wrestler who concentrates on footwork moving left to right and backward and forward.

Mirror Drill: Two partners mirror each others' movements in their stances.

Changing Levels

Limbo Level Changes: Done by using a broomstick or stretched out jump rope held by in-active assistants. Wrestlers shuffle to the raised stick and level change under it using proper form and technique.

Up & Through Drill: Done by starting a wrestler from a position on one knee. A defender shuffles into the wrestler, when he/she reaches the wrestler the attacker on one knee lifts the opponent using a double, high-c, or single leg.

Push & Drop Drill: Done by using a partner who aggressively tries to put hands on his opponent while pushing. The drilling wrestler enacts a level change against the pressure causing the opposing wrester's pressure to force him/her into contact with the wrestler who hits a level change. Wrestlers will begin to see the use of the level change against pressuring opponents.

Penetration

Under the Sheet: Done by using a folded sheet held by assistants. Wrestlers penetrate under the sheet using various penetration steps. The sheet can be adjusted in size so that wrestlers have varying distances that they have to travel as they practice the penetration step.

Jolt Drill: Done by popping an opponent's outstretched arms and penetrating into their torso using a step-in penetration. The jolt drill is very useful for single and double leg steps, teaching wrestlers the importance of strong physical contact as they penetrate.

Run Down the Legs Drill: Done by starting an opponent in a bear crawl position. The attacking wrestler starts in a front headlock position, sidesteps and penetrates into the opponents' lowered and open hips.

Lifting

Up & Through: Done by having a partner walking into a kneeling shooter. When the opponent makes contact the shooter lifts up and through their opponent using a double, single, or high-c.

Stand-up Returns: Done by having a partner repeatedly standing up. Each time the partner stands up the top person returns them to the mat using a lift.

Buddy Carry Lunges: Done by balancing a partner on the back or shoulders. The wrestler uses a lunge step, touching their knee to the mat. This drill emphasizes building strength.

Back Step

Back Step on the Wall: Individually a wrestler builds timing by executing a back step with their hands placed on a wall. The wrestler jumps into the back step to both sides building speed.

Back Step Carries: The wrestler uses a partner and executes a back step lifting his opponent across his back and hips. The wrestler carries the partner for a set short distance.

Back Step Summersaults: Individually a wrestler executes a back step twisting and lowering their level facing the opposite direction. The wrestler should execute and an explosive roll bringing them back to their feet.

Back Arch & Turn

Back Arch Explosion: Individually a wrestler kneels on the mat, grasping their palms together in a tight grip. The wrestler should explode upward into an arch and catch themselves with head and hands coming to rest in a high bridge on their head.

Back Arch Partner Catch: A partner stands behind the executing wrestler and starts their arch. The assisting wrestler catches the arching wrestler with hands behind their neck. When the wrestler feels the catch he explosively turns his/her chest to the mat to complete the throwing motion.

Back Arch Kickovers: A partner is in the down position, the drilling wrestlers uses their back as a sort of pommel horse to arch over. The arching wrestler executes the arch and kicks their legs over the head taking them to the other side of the down wrestler.

For wrestlers to truly succeed in absolute mastery of the sport, the seven basic skills are essential. Coaches must work to constantly integrate the active movements of the seven basic skills into their practices. The focus should not just be on the next move or "trick" to win a match; rather, the coaches should look to reinforce the basic skills that supply a strong foundation for future success.

Beyond the Basic Skills: Contacts

Beyond the Basic Skills a coach must decide what techniques and strategies he will employ to improve his wrestlers' chances when they step on the mat. As noted before, the basic skills should be emphasized repeatedly throughout any season. From there coaches can then move to working on the varying techniques that are a necessity for competing successfully in the sport.

The initial area that wrestlers will need to master before they can attack an opponent is the area of contacts. Contact, when used effectively, places a wrestler in a position to control their opponent even before a shot or attack is unleashed.

The Contacts that coaches should focus on are:

1. Head Tie (Collar Tie)
2. Head and Bicep Tie
3. Biceps Tie (one or two)
4. Elbow Tie (one or two)
5. Two on One (Russian)
6. Underhook (one or two)
7. Wrist Tie (one or two)
8. Forearm Hook
9. Over Tie
10. Over Under

Each contact opens up differing attacks that can be used with relative success. In order for the use of the contacts to succeed by a wrestler, the wrestler must "dominate" or control the position. Coaches must teach their athletes to be physically commanding and move from one contact to another with skill and authority. An important part of learning these contacts is teaching the athletes to "hand fight". Often young wrestlers attack an opponent by shooting quickly without establishing any type of strong positioning with strong contact through hand-fighting. With new rule changes dominating tie-ups is even more important in matches. Coaches must focus on developing drills and activities that help wrestlers to internalize the principles of controlling tie-ups.

Set-ups

After wrestlers establish control through contact they should look for opportunities to attack their opponent using the set-up motions individually or in combination. Set-ups give the wrestler the ability to move out of a contact into a strong attacking position.

The essential set-ups that coaches should teach their athletes are:

1. Pop—quick, short upward movements against an opponent's arms or elbows

2. Chop—quick, short downward movements against an opponent's arms (wrist, elbows)
3. Shuck—pushing a control point such as an elbow or head from the outside across the attacker's stance or position
4. Drag—pulling a control point such as a tricep from the outside across the attacker's stance or position
5. Snap—an extended pulling, downward motion on a control point such as an opponent's head or shoulder
6. Pummel—rolling or digging arms inside an opponent's arm for control of an inside position commonly seen from an over-under position
7. Fake or Feint—any action or movement attempted to draw attention to an area of an opponent's defense to open an attack.
8. Post—securing an opponent's control point such as hand or head to the mat so that the attacker can move past it. *(Note the difference between pop and post—wrestler cannot post a control point into the air.)
9. Block—securing an opponent's control point such as an elbow and holding it in place so that the attacker can move past it or secure a lift

Attacks

Following the ability to control and set-up an opponent a wrestler must master a variety of attacks. The main set of attacks greatly varies between freestyle and Greco-Roman wrestling.

Freestyle wrestling challenges a coach because of the wider variety of techniques that can be utilized by wrestlers and their opponents; whereas, Greco-Roman wrestling minimizes the attack zone forcing coaches and athletes to focus on fewer attacks seeking a much higher level of precision for success.

The common freestyle attacks that coaches should prioritize are:

1. Sweep Single
2. Double Legs
3. High-Crotch
4. Front Headlocks
5. Duckunders

6. Ankle & Knee Picks
7. Fireman's Carry
8. Low Singles
9. Throws
10. Trips, Props, Grapevines

Beyond formulating an attack coaches must develop in their wrestlers the ability to finish shots successfully. The multitude of finishes to attacks makes it difficult to categorize finishes into primary areas of concern. A few important finishes to shots may include: lifting or flairing an opponent, running the pipe, elevating under an opponent, as well as various trips and blocks. Successful finishes focus not only on gaining control but also maneuver the attacker into better position for turns and falls.

The common attacks in the Greco-Roman style that coaches should prioritize are:

1. Arm Drags
2. Slide-bys
3. Duckunders
4. High Dives
5. Reach Arounds
6. Hiplocks, Pivots
7. Front Headlocks
8. Back-arch Throws
9. Sag Throws
10. Back Step Throws

Since Greco-Roman wrestling is much more of a style based on precise attacks finishes to maneuvers though varied usually do not take as much time to master. For example, a strong duckunder usually leads an opponent to fall flat to the mat, or if the attacker ducks behind an opponent and captures an opponent's torso with him still on the feet the dramatic finish is an arch and lift. However, a skilled wrestler knows when their position has been broken and they will usually "bail" to avoid giving up major points.

Par-Terre

With differing rules and interpretations par-terre wrestling can become more or less important. Coaches should balance the need to teach par-terre considering the use of par-terre with the current rules being applied.

Standard freestyle par-terre techniques include:

1. Gut Wrench
2. Ankle Lace
3. High Gut Wrench
4. Leg-in turns
5. Trapped Arm Gut Wrench
6. Arm Turns
7. Crotch Lift
8. Cross Knee, leg and arm turks
9. Side Headlocks
10. Tilts

Standard Greco-Roman par-terre techniques include:

1. Gut Wrench
2. High Gut Wrench
3. Reverse Gut Wrench
4. Straddle & Straight Lifts
5. Reverse Lifts
6. Front & Side Headlocks

Tie-ups, Set-ups, Attacks, and par-terre offense should be primary areas of concern for coaches to organize technique and practices around. Beyond formulating an attack coaches must develop in their wrestlers the ability to finish successfully. As a part of par-terre teaching coaches also must prepare wrestlers to successfully defend mat attacks in these areas. It is wise that coaches while teaching the offensive skill also allude to the defense for the technique so that wrestlers can consider the needs of both the offensive and defensive side of the sport. Further, coaches should also include teaching on the mat of various pin holds and corresponding pin positions for techniques such as chicken wings and cradles.

Counter Offense

The more refined a wrestler becomes in their abilities the more opportunities they will see to utilize counter attacks, especially in freestyle. The beginning point that many coaches start from in this area is the sprawl drill. Eventually, coaches should progress and refine an athlete's technique by integrating the use of the down-block and cross-block techniques. The

SIDEBAR: Greco-Roman skills in folkstyle wrestling

Isaac Ramaswamy

It's pretty amazing to think that the oldest form of wrestling is the most misconceived and the least credited among coaches and athletes here in the United States. Successful college, high school, or club coaches avidly seek to learn and incorporate new and varying freestyle and folkstyle techniques into their programs, but the implementation of Greco-Roman skills remains a very distant third, if at all, in the picture as the season's practice plans are being drawn. So, the question is, "How can Greco-Roman fit in, or more importantly, WHY should Greco-Roman fit in?"

Many coaches may be intimidated by the initial frustrations that come with the idea of trying to teach Greco-Roman technique and strategies to their kids. Some may be concerned that Greco-Roman technique doesn't transfer to freestyle and folkstyle, and that its teaching engrains bad habits (i.e., standing up straight, going for bad throws, etc.). Others are probably insecure about their own knowledge and ability to successfully teach in this area. Either of these is a poor excuse. A shrewd coach realizes that ALL wrestling knowledge is useful to both coach and athlete, in ANY style of wrestling.

Wrestling Greco-Roman is like using chopsticks—it requires great patience and precision. It forces an athlete to concentrate, and narrow the focus of his wrestling. Look at it this way: How many moves do coaches teach during the course of a regular high school season? There are hundreds of techniques from the various positions, and more than likely, most coaches have a broad enough base knowledge of folkstyle to cover a large percentage, if not all of these even in a single season. Now, consider all the hours that go into teaching these techniques, and then, stop and think:

How many moves do you actually see executed by either wrestler in a regular match? Six? Eight? My guess is, in a common match on the high school level, you'd tend to see the same two or three techniques attempted over and over again. All that time spent teaching, and the best that most of the kids can put together is two or three moves. But then, there's the standout - that kid who's operating at a completely different level. He just flows through matches, even the tough ones. What separates him from the others?

Knowledge? No, he's been in the same room with all the others as you've been teaching. Talent? Maybe, but I'm sure there are at least five other kids in the room that could out throw, out run, or out power him. Experience? That's most likely it. Chances are, this kid has put his time in, and he has a true "feel" for wrestling. He understands the total concept of it, from every position, not because he's been taught, but because he's been there, over and over and over again, and he is now completely comfortable on that mat, even if you start him out in a back bridge. How many of your wrestlers can you say that about?

"Feel" is not an easy thing to teach; as previously stated, it most likely comes from the experience of being exposed to and becoming comfortable with all positions in wrestling. Once a wrestler has feel, he's on a different plateau in regards to skill level. He understands not only the techniques, but the nuances that allow him to successfully execute:

How to position, Where to focus. When to attack, and, if necessary. How to adjust.

Exposure to Greco-Roman technique can help a wrestler achieve this feel at an incredibly accelerated rate. Most kids are so limited in their understanding of upper body wrestling concepts, that they rarely ever gain the real confidence to become totally comfortable on the mat, and such misgiving can prevent an athlete's realization of his true potential. So, as a coach, exposing yourself to Greco-Roman technique, and then giving that exposure back to your athletes can help you to maximize the overall success of your program.

Five fundamental Greco-Roman skills, which not only transfer to, but enhance freestyle and folkstyle wrestling are handfighting, pummeling, level changes, hip pop, and the back arch and bridge.

Hand fighting is a commonly overlooked skill in folkstyle wrestling, but it is a staple for success in Greco. A wrestler's ability to take control of and manipulate the hands and arms of his opponent can lead to a more effective offense, and certainly, a much stronger defense. Training and sparring in the Greco-Roman style helps to focus on and enhance skills such as double wrist ties, inside bicep control, outside elbow control, 2 on 1 positions, and arm drag attacks. Undoubtedly, when you have two evenly matched wrestlers going at it, hand fighting strategies can make all the difference in determining how the scoring goes on the feet, in any style of wrestling.

Another skill developed through Greco-Roman wrestling is the art of pummeling. Pummeling, when done correctly, is a fight to gain an advantage during upper body contact. What most coaches don't realize, however, is that a good pummeler also maintains great lower body position. Teach a wrestler how to pummel, and he'll learn to gain a feel for strong position. His balance will be better, his feet will be more agile; his overall stance will improve. A strong pummeler can take control over the pace of a match, regardless of his technical skill level in the other areas.

Level change is another concept that is enhanced (and in some cases, corrected) through practice in Greco-Roman technique. Right away, the misconception is that level change is a freestyle or folkstyle concept, and that Greco causes wrestlers to stand straight up, comes to question. In response to that, consider this: How many times have you as a coach had to correct "bad shots" meaning, that leaning, bent at the waist, head-down lunge for a leg or ankle that looks more accidental rather than a strategic attack? How many points have your wrestlers given up because they took those bad shots and got sprawled on and spun behind?

The problem is, as long as the wrestler has a hold of his opponent's leg, he thinks he is doing everything right - regardless of his own body position. In Greco-Roman, if a wrestler executes an incorrect level change, there is no failsafe of a leg to grab and hold on to, so the immediate result is a failed attempt with one or more points scored against him. Many Greco-Roman techniques require not only level change, but precise level change. Greco-Roman techniques teach not only proper execution (maintaining balance and control) but also varying degrees of level changes. A shrug requires only a slight level change, while a duck-under requires a bit more, and a slide-by or hi-dive requires the attacking wrestler's head to drop down to his opponent's hip, similar to a single or double leg attack. Teach an athlete a good slide-by or hi-dive, and you will see how his level change leg attacks also will improve.

There are a lot of studly-looking wrestlers out there, even on the high school level these days, with bulging biceps and tremendous chests. But on more than one occasion, we have all witnessed some wiry kid mop the mat with one of his more impressive looking opponents. Coaches usually share the same comment after seeing such a spectacle: "Boy, that kid didn't seem like much, but he sure had great hips." A good hip-pop is the great equalizer in wrestling. It is the central point from where all useful power for wrestling comes. A wrestler with a good hip-pop has great lifting power and maneuverability. Leg attack finishes, sprawling ability, and even riding skill are all greatly improved with stronger hip-pop skills. The throwing demands of Greco-Roman help to develop hip-pop skill in a faster, safer, and more efficient manner than any weight lifting exercises ever could. Teaching athletes how to execute proper back-step and back-arch techniques such as headlocks, armspins, and belly-to-belly throws will help them get to that next level on the ability scale.

Finally, the back arch and bridge are solid skills within the repertoire of wrestlers trained in Greco-Roman, while prevailing freestyle and folkstyle thought generally sees these as things you need to worry about only if you're already on your back and have nothing else to lose. The back-arch is a component of the hip-pop skill. A good back-arch allows a wrestler to be effective in any situation where his own back is moving in a downward direction toward the mat. Back-arching out of this situation results in a switching of positions between the wrestlers, bringing the executing wrestler out on top by the end of the action. A good back-arch, combined with a strong hip-pop, can turn any average wrestler into that guy in the line up that no one wants to face.

The bridge is also a resulting component of the hip-pop and back-arch. Offensively, a strong bridge skill aids the wrestler in safely completing any rolling maneuver on the mat, and defensively to work out of compromising positions such as pinning holds applied by his opponent or improperly executed techniques on his own part. Since popular Greco-Roman techniques such as the gutwrench and front headlock turns require bridging as an offensive skill, it becomes more developed in Greco-Roman wrestlers.

However, the skill becomes invaluable in any style of wrestling when recognized for its most common use, which is the defensive wrestler's fight in the attempt to prevent a fall.

So, what's the point? Learn the skills of Greco-Roman wrestling. Teach your kids Greco-Roman wrestling. Their overall abilities, confidence, and success will improve—in any style, on any occasion; even if you start them out in a back bridge.

SIDEBAR: Protocol with Officials
Isaac Ramaswamy

Mat officials in freestyle & Greco-Roman wrestling:

There is a 3-person crew designated to officiate bouts in freestyle & Greco-Roman wrestling, with responsibilities as follows:

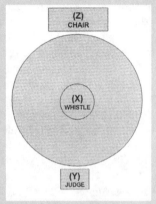

X – "The Whistle" or center mat official. He/she is directly responsible for controlling the action on the mat, and assigning any resulting points.

Y – "The Judge" or matside official. He/she observes the action form the outside vantage point and is responsible mainly for confirming calls made by the mat official.

Z – "The Chair" or mat controller. He/she is responsible for observing the whistle and the judge, and, if necessary settling points of disagreement between the two by siding with one or the other. The Chair CANNOT overrule or initiate new discussion pertaining to a call. However, when appropriate, he/she may call the officials together to conference about the consistency of a call. The Chair also is the vehicle of communication between the mat officials and the coach in addressing questions or offering explanation when necessary.

Your role as the coach:

As a corner coach, it is your duty to take full responsibility in assuring that all protocol is properly followed as it applies to your wrestler and official staff. KNOW the rules and procedures as outlined in your yearly FILA rulebook.
    Here are some basic guidelines to follow:

1. Have your wrestler ready BEHIND the correct corner, wearing the correct color singlet IMMEDIATELY when he/she is called to the chairman's table for pre-bout check in.
2. DO NOT take the mat or enter your designated corner area until the previous wrestler's party has exited. This will prevent your incidental involvement in any matters that pertain to the previous bout.
3. Upon entering your corner, have your wrestler report in FULL MATCH ATTIRE (singlet correctly worn, headgear, knee guards, shoestrings, and other equipment securely fastened) to the center of the mat. The coach(es) should take a seat in the chair(s) provided. If there is no seating made available, then kneeling in the corner area is acceptable, so as to not obstruct the view of spectators or table officials.

In the event of a disagreement with or uncertainty about a confirmed call, the proper protocol for address of such is as follows:

- Approach the chairman's table and signal him/her; then, wait to be acknowledged.
- When there is a break in the match action, the chair will motion for you to approach with your question.
- The chair will then either respond immediately to you with an explanation, or, if necessary, will call the mat official and judge together for a review of the call. (If the officials do confer in such manner, you will be asked to step back and neither interject into nor interfere with their discussion)
- Once the final decision is reached, you will be motioned back to the chairman and be offered an explanation. Once the explanation has been given, the center mat official will officially signal the call, and the points will be recorded on the scorer's sheet.
- Once the call is officially signaled and recorded, the coach should neither initiate nor engage in any further verbal disputes with any of the mat officials in regard to the call in question. If the coach remains dissatisfied in regard to the officiating team's proper application of the rules in the given situation, an official protest may then be filed with the tournament director's table (refer to the FILA rulebook for protest procedure).

Please keep in mind: Mat officials are an important facet of and contributing factor in the arena of international wrestling. Often, they themselves are or have been competitors, coaches, and/or parents involved with the sport; certainly, they are fans in their own right. That being noted, the assumption should be made in situations where differences arise, that all personal feelings and previous relationships are set aside and immaterial in the 3-way interaction between the wrestler, coach, and official when it comes to preserving the integrity of competition and sportsmanship.

down-block and cross-block are refined motions that allow a wrestler to defend an attack without leaving their feet and defending on the mat. Coaches furthering the wrestlers' discipline to counter attack should couple a strong understanding of shot defense.

Shot defense requires that a wrestler understand the essential positioning of their stance in order to move into position to counter-attack. Shot defense has four primary parts. The first is head position. When attacked a wrestler must develop the ability to stop or redirect an attack by using the center of their forehead. If a wrestler fails to defend using their head, then the hands become the next area of defense. The skills of down-block and cross-block directly relate to this area as well as the next. A wrestler that is able to defend against a shot using only their head or hands in combination have a greater likelihood of effectively re-shooting or running down an opponent's legs. Forearms movements like the forearm shiver or shuck as well as punching

underhooks and looking for whip-overs must be utilized to develop an attack defense. Punching hip motions are the last area of defense for wrestlers in their stance. A wrestler naturally uses their forearms as they counterattack with proper hip motions like whizzers, or ground sprawls, or the offensive minded counterattacks of laterals and whipovers.

Counterattacking requires an athlete to readily recognize the position they are defending. A common maxim in counter-offense is for a wrestler to "re-direct the opponent's head". Wrestlers that attack in a single should have their shot re-positioned by re-directing the opponent's head to the outside of the defenders body. Conversely a wrestler that shoots into a high-crotch would have their head re-directed into a single leg position.

Clearing Ties

Dominating the center of the mat has become increasingly important for wrestlers with new rules interpretations. When an opponent loses position to their opponent by giving up control of their own arms or head it is imperative that a wrestler know how to effectively react and clear the tie-up.

Suggested teaching for clearing a tie-up includes the following:

1. Collar tie
   A. Pass the elbow-grab above the elbow, shrug your shoulders, step and circle to he outside to get the angle, pull her elbow down and across her body as you drive into her
   B. Duck-try to pass the elbow first, if she's really grabbing tight, push her elbow then outside step, lower your level, throw her elbow behind you, and shoot
   C. Throw by-collar tie her, step to the outside, put back of your hand above her elbow, keep your elbow high, throw her elbow along the side of your face and past you, keep the collar tie, drive her forward and go behind

2. Two-on-one
   A. Get head position, sweep single to leg opposite of the arm they have, pull your elbow to your ribs hard as you swing around
   B. Chop her hand at your wrist, swing other arm into an underhook
   C. Pull the elbow of her arm that has your wrist until her hand pops off, UH (underhook)
   D. chop wrist or pull elbow into a drag

3. Under-hooks
   A. She has UH on your control arm-get head position, circle away from UH, and bring your elbow to your ribs until you slide down past her elbow, sweep single to leg opposite of UH
   B. She has UH on your attack arm-get head position, circle away, bring your elbow in until her UH slides down past her elbow, hi-c or double same leg as UH
   C. windmill arm back into inside tie

4. Straight arms
   A. Pop her arms up, above the elbows and shoot
   B. Snap her arms down, start above the elbows and slide down to wrists, front headlock or shoot after she bounces back up
   C. Pop one side and Snap the other-single or hi-c
   D. Pop-take a small step to the outside to get the angle, pop above her elbow, drive her bicep into her face, lower your level and shoot hi-c or single

5. Wrist ties
   A. She has your control arm with 1 hand-drag to hi-c; She has control arm with 2 hands-sweep single
   B. She has your attack arm with one hand-drag to single; She has attack arm with 2 hands-hi-c

6. Front head Locks
   A. Grab her elbow with your same side hand-shrug shoulders, circle to the arm you've grabbed until you get the angle, slide your head across her chest, drive up and pass her elbow by
   B. Reach across to grab her elbow with your other hand, drag (sucker drag) her elbow across, cut the corner with your hips, pop your head out and bump her hip with yours

A wrestler needs to have a few different ways in which to clear a tie, and expect a fight, it won't always be easy to clear a tie you may have to put two, three, four motions together to get it done.

SIDEBAR: Better drilling by controlling the tempo

Ted Witulski

At the start of every tournament the teams take the mats, and begin the process of warming up. After the jogging and stretching the wrestlers pair off and begin going through the familiar tasks of drilling the techniques, which will be used in their matches. Even before the matches are wrestled coaches and fans in the stands can probably conjecture as to which wrestlers are the studs in the tournament, just by viewing their drilling habits.

Some wrestlers have it together firing off shots and counters with speed and finesse. Other less advanced wrestlers appear cumbersome as they try to imitate the techniques they'll need to win.

Drilling is a means to an end—the goal, of course, is to be a champion. Coaching wrestlers on how to drill successfully is as important as showing a sprawl or a single-leg. Beyond the moves, successfully drilling will help wrestlers better learn the basic skills associated with the techniques of wrestling. Wrestlers and coaches should concentrate on outstanding drilling to take strides forward in their wrestling skills.

The purpose of drilling is varied. In some instances drilling serves as practice for a brand new move. At other times, drilling is part of a cardiovascular workout associated with conditioning. And, in other cases coaches are looking to perfect basic skills such as a precise level change or a speedier penetration step.

To be able to coach wrestling successfully coaches need to teach their athletes how to drill at different speeds. USA Wrestling's National Coaches Education Program notes that wrestlers should be able to establish three different speeds of drilling. Each speed acts as another gear for wrestlers to move in when focusing on the varied areas that drilling involves.

Coaches may choose to name the drill speeds differently, but the establishment of these varied gears in drilling is important to help wrestlers learn the art of drilling. Three suggested speeds of drilling for wrestlers on the youth and high school level are "ICE" drilling, "Working Pace" drilling, and "Match Realistic" drilling.

ICE drilling acts as the slowest speed for wrestlers to drill. ICE stands as an acronym for Intense—Controlled—Energy. When coaches want kids drilling slowly the message to the wrestlers shouldn't be take a breather. Instead, coaches are looking for focused intensity, controlled movements, and energy spent on deep concentration for learning.

Generally, in moves drilled, a coach should be able to see the setup, the attack or penetration, and the precise finish. ICE drilling should get the wrestlers to focus on all three parts for a slow count of one—two. When wrestlers use the ICE method all parts should be readily apparent to the coach.

In a typical double leg takedown, a wrestler might head shuck, penetrate, and then finish with a turk step. If a coach asks his team to drill this move at ICE speed, then the wrestlers should slow down immensely.

The wrestlers footwork as he moves to the head shuck should be slower. While grasping the head the wrestler pulls it tightly to his chest and then push it across his stance. Think of a slow thousand one—thousand two count. As the second count is reached for the setup, the wrestler should have preset his feet to penetrate after the setup.

(Visualize a shuck of the head with the right hand pushing the opponent's head across the stance to the left. The attacking wrestler to ready for an inside step double would have placed his left leg in a lead leg stance.)

With the head shucked into place and lead leg set, the opponent is open for attack. Still in a slow one—two count, the offensive wrestler will deeply change levels, count one. At count two, wrestlers should penetrate in a clean continuous but slow motion.

Don't get wrestlers to pound their knee to the center of the opponent's stance and stop. Successful penetration is not viewed as reaching an opponent's stance, but rather penetrating through it. On the second when a wrestler's knee hits the mat his trail leg should be moving to cut the angle, so that the attacker can come off of his planted knee.

Having slowly moved the level change step and trail leg movement of penetration, then wrestlers should enact a slow finish. In this case wrestlers on the slow count would change levels up and through their opponent. On the second count wrestlers would hit a slow controlled lift and turk step through the split legs of the opposition.

Drilling a move at such a slow speed serves the purpose of teaching wrestlers the importance of each part of a move. It is hard to say what is most important the setup, the attack, or the finish. But the ICE drilling procedure gives the coach ample opportunity to check over the wrestlers hand position, footwork, level change and other aspects of the takedown, by not allowing the wrestlers to hide flaws with speed.

If a coach has noticed that his wrestlers are not looking across the back on their double leg lift, then he can cue his athletes into this simply by saying, "lets drill ICE—Doubles and I'm looking to see that your eyes are looking up and across your opponent's back." By mentioning the precision of looking across the back wrestlers will have a mental cue and plenty of time to focus correctly on the cue while they hit the technique.

Coaches will find many uses for ICE drilling once their athletes learn the procedure. The goal should not be for the coach to count one—two as the wrestlers work through the setup, attack and finish. Rather, wrestlers should feel the power to control the speed and slowly advance through the technique. Again, precision is the key. Every movement should be intense, controlled, energy easily viewed and evaluated by the coach.

Once wrestlers have learned ICE drilling, then they should be comfortable in drilling at a working pace. Working pace drilling does not require athletes to slow the speed of a technique to a large degree as opposed to the ICE drilling method. Rather, the focus should be on a smooth speed with one focused explosion after the level change.

Wrestlers will not be going all out in the working pace, accept in one part of the setup-penetrate-finish model. When wrestlers go at a faster pace they need to learn to be explosive with their attack. In the working pace model wrestlers will level change loading their hips into a strong attack position. Once they have level changed precisely, they should flip the switch and explosively penetrate through the opponent.

Instead of focusing on a slow methodical penetration athletes should tune in on quick movement into the attack. The contact from attacker to the opponent should be solid. An attacker's head or shoulder, depending on the shot, should strike powerfully into the defender.

Some coaches indicate to wrestlers in this form of drilling that a good "shot" can be heard as well as seen. After coiling up tightly and loading his hips into a striking position, the attacker's knee pads and shoes will make a sweeping sound across the mat. But the real sound that a coach should hear is the hard contact of the attacker into the torso of the opponent. A little forced exhale from the defender is a good sign the attacker is penetrating solidly into the opposing wrestler.

Once the wrestler has penetrated as quickly through his opponent as possible, then he should perfect the finish. The pace of the drill does not need to slow dramatically. Instead, the momentum from the explosion into the defender should be used to carry the attacker through the finish.

The "working pace" should tell wrestlers to get reset quickly. Wrestlers should build speed, and power in their attack by consistently practicing loading their hips.

Another way that working pace drilling can be enhanced is to require the attacker to repeat his setup before changing levels and exploding through the attack. If a wrestler is working on hitting single legs with a "Russian" (two-on-one) setup, then the wrestler will be required to hit a Russian release it and as the defender reaches again he will control the same Russian. After controlling the Russian on the second time the wrestler will then lower his level and attack at a working pace.

The final gear that wrestlers can build in drilling is "Match Realistic" drilling. Whereas ICE drilling, and Working Pace drilling slows the wrestler to produce the concentration needed to build basic skills to perfect technique, match realistic drilling should be all out speed.

Once wrestlers know the techniques and feel comfortable with their footwork and level change, coaches should encourage them to build speed and force in their drilling. Coaches should instill in their wrestlers that match realistic drilling gives them the opportunity to build faster setups, penetration, and finishes. Additionally, wrestlers need to build more power in these parts of their moves.

Coaches in match realistic drilling can look for a variety of things to encourage wrestlers. For example, a wrestler's footwork should not be repetitive. And, when a wrestler's feet move his hands should be moving. Another mental cue to focus athletes on when drilling match realism, is the distance a wrestler reaches when making contact with an opponent. An extended reach opens up counter-attacks.

While these mental cues will help wrestlers stay focused even when going all-out with their techniques, it is best to constantly reinforce the idea of speed and power. A coach that consistently relies on the aspects of speed and power will get wrestlers' attention to really go hard in match realistic drilling.

Match Realistic drilling is far removed from the precision of the ICE drilling concept. The second gear for wrestlers, working pace drilling, focuses less on precision and allows wrestlers to explode into their drilling partner after a deep and controlled level change.

Match realistic drilling should really get the team's adrenaline flowing. They shouldn't be in a confined area. Wrestler's should be encourage to run through their shots, while going all out with the most speed and power that they can muster for their techniques.

Drilling technique in wrestling is an important part of developing wrestlers. By giving wrestlers three speeds to drill at, a coach will find that he can further direct the team. The wrestlers will have clearer expectations drawn for them when the coach asks them to "drill it". With the tempo set by the coach direction, he can evaluate for anything from precision, to speed and explosion. Better drilling will eventually lead to more success for any wrestling team.

SIDEBAR: Chain Wrestling from Bottom

Ted Witulski/USA Wrestling

6/4/2004

Wrestlers continually work to improve technique by drilling. One wrestler shoots two takedowns and then the other takes his best two shots. Back and forth they will go, exchanging takedowns from November to March. Drilling in wrestling can sometimes focus only on takedowns, while omitting ways of improving bottom wrestling.

To accomplish a solid drill of chain wrestling from the bottom, wrestlers will need to know the following moves.

1. Switch
2. Stepover
3. Granby or Shrug
4. Short Sit to a Gazonie
5. Short Sit to a Hip-Heist

SWITCH: The switch is one of the more universal terms in scholastic wrestling. Coaches and wrestlers know the goal is to gain a reversal using an opponent's arm as a lever while scooting their hips into a position of control.

When wrestlers work on switches to often they perform them from a stationary almost stagnate position. Commonly, these wrestlers will hit a switch from only the top-bottom starting position—step one clear the arm—step two sit to your hips.

This switch situation while good at introducing kids to the move when they first learn the sport does little for wrestlers when they have to perform the technique under match conditions when their opponent is no longer static.

To further improve wrestlers switches teach the kids to perform their switches out of motion.

Five good motion set-ups for switches:

A. Tripod
B. Camel Crawl
C. Leaper
D. Head Post Shrug/Sit-out Turn-in
E. Standup

Each of these motions can be very effective in clearing hips or forcing the top-man out of position.

Tripod: The wrestler on bottom rises to the four-point stance often referred to as a bear-crawl position or a tripod. The bottom wrestler's only contact with the mat is his two hands and his two feet dug into the mat. This position elevates the bottom wrestlers hips usually forcing the top man out of position.

A coach-able phrase that comes from this setup for a switch is to get wrestlers' "far hip to hit the mat first". Commonly wrestlers mistakenly believe an effective switch comes from the power of the arms. Instead, a strong switch comes from the power of a strong side hip-heist. When wrestlers practice a tripod switch they should really focus on getting their far hip to hit the mat first.

Camel Crawl: Wrestlers may feel embarrassed at first, but an effective way to setup a switch is to use a simple crawling motion. The camel crawl is really just a quick scamper across the mat that forces the top wrestler to clutch and chase their opponent.

Out of this motion wrestlers can clear their arm and switch. The teachable phrase from this setup comes out of the top man tendency to grasp the near arm or to chop it. Here wrestlers should be taught to "limp arm and switch". The limp arm motion is very useful in many match situations and the camel crawl setup consistently forces wrestlers to practice this motion.

Leaper: A less common bottom motion for wrestlers to learn is the diving motion known as a leaper. A leaper is a hard springing motion forward. The wrestlers load their hips back over their ankles while their toes curl under their feet. The wrestler dives forward using an extended leaping motion. The leaper when performed correctly forces the top wrestler back down the opponent's torso and towards his ankles.

Essentially the top wrestler slides down the bottom man's body taking him out of position. Once the top person is out of position if their hand is not around the bottom man in a tight waist they will quickly attempt to return to this position. As the top man tries to regain a tight waist the bottom man can hit his switch.

Head Post/Shrug: Wrestlers spend much of their career following the axiom "head up". However, one effective way to set up a switch is to teach the bottom man how to move his hips with his head posted to the mat. There are a variety of ways that a wrestler can get into a head post. Wrestlers that are well versed in the Granby School of bottom offense know this position as a shrug. Being able to smash back into the top man and shrug your head to the mat while getting off of your knees is an excellent position to set up motion for a switch.

Essentially the head post is a pivot point. Once in proper head post or shrug position the bottom wrestler should get off of his knees and on his toes. From this true tripod position the wrestler should begin to circle his hips away from the top man. As the wrestler clears his hips he forces the top man to follow his movement. The wrestler can then hit his switch by pushing out of the head post.

Standup: The standup to a switch is probably one of the most practiced ways to drill a switch out of motion. The half standup can be a powerful way to catch an opponent off guard. If a wrestler can get to his feet an escape may not be their only option. The bottom man that can control the lever arm of their opponent should also consider the possibility of a switch instead of the simple escape.

While wrestlers may be used to hitting a standing switch with their feet on the ground, another unique way to practice this switch is to have the top man lift the bottom wrestler. Switching out of a lift can help wrestlers learn movement even when their feet are not in contact with the mat. To switch out of a lift, wrestlers should practice moving their hips while they are elevated, basically falling to the mat in good switching position.

STEPOVER: The stepover is one of the earliest moves that wrestlers learn from the bottom. The key component of the stepover is to get the bottom man to bring his inside leg over first so that he doesn't get rolled through.

The stepover can be successfully accomplished to either side in scholastic wrestling. Wrestlers should be able to develop hand control and force the top man into a bad position. Once hand elbow or arm control on the top man is gained, then the wrestler can "wing" the top man down to the mat effectively posting his arm and shoulder down giving the bottom man the stepover opportunity.

GRANBY OR SHRUG: The granby and shrug series are very complex rolling maneuvers that can become a whole practice in and of itself. The easier to teach of the two is probably the shrug, where the bottom man posts his head to the mat using his forehead as a turning axis he then walks his hips in a circle away from the top man. With wrist control off of the stomach a shrug can lead to a simple reversal or even a three point nearfall, using the granby cradle.

GAZONIE: The gazonie is a less universal term for scholastic wrestling, so a description of the move may help coaches understand its intent. The bottom wrestler gets to a short sit position, with top man riding directly behind him. The gazonie also called a head wrap, in some parts of the country requires the bottom man to catch the top man's head hanging over either of his shoulders.

When the top man gets out of position his head might slip on to the right man's shoulder. If this happens, then the bottom man would use his right arm to wrap around the head while "turning in" to his left shoulder. The bottom wrestler would gain a reversal by shrugging out the back door perfecting the gazonie reversal.

HIP HEIST: The last fundamental move that wrestlers need to know from bottom is a hip heist. The hip heist can be done from a number of positions on bottom, but for simplicity teach wrestlers to get to a short sit position. When a bottom wrestler can stay solid in a short sit position, then the top wrestler's offense can often be frustrated.

Once in a short sit the bottom wrestler will battle for hand control. This is a very important position for wrestlers to wrestle well in. As they clear wrists, or backside underhooks, the bottom wrestler will perform a hip heist. The hip heist when done correctly will get the bottom man in a face off position, earning an escape.

Chain Wrestling from Bottom: The objective of the bottom wrestling drill chain is to have the wrestlers performing all five of the base bottom moves correctly in a series. To be clear to the wrestlers, expect them to perform the move in the following series.

Switch, stepover, granby or shrug, short sit to a gazonie, short-sit to a hip heist.

Let the wrestlers know that you want them to follow these simple rules:

*Every move performed is a reversal in which the top man when reversed does not go to their back.

(The one exception will be the last hip heist, which actually will get the bottom man an escape. Be clear that you want the top wrestler to give the opponent a good look by not falling to their back, inhibiting the flow of the drill.)

*The movement in this drill should be continuous, with the top wrestler applying little resistance, giving a feel of constant flow.

(The top man is not trying to block the bottom man; rather, the two wrestlers working together will develop muscle-memory and speed from the bottom position.)

*Follow the series precisely: switch, stepover, granby or shrug, short sit to a gazonie, short sit to a hip heist.

The wrestlers as they go through the drill will start in the down position. The first wrestler on bottom hits a switch, then the second wrestler hits a switch. The first wrestler on bottom will hit a

stepover, then the second wrestler now on bottom will do the same.

The granby or shrug will then be executed by the first wrestler. Again, make sure the top man doesn't fall to his back it will interrupt the flow of the drill. Once the first wrestler reverses with a granby or shrug, then the second wrestler will do the same.

The same pattern is then followed with a short sit gazonie. The last position is the short sit to a hip heist. In this case the first wrestler will perform the hip heist by successfully facing off against the second wrestler. Once the first wrestler faces off then the second wrestler will turn the opposite direction and assume the bottom starting position. The first wrestler will get set on top, and the whole series will be started again. The second time through the second wrestler will hit the hip heist.

Once the wrestlers know these very basic bottom moves putting them into an easy to follow chain will narrow the wrestlers focus. The goal is to develop movement in the wrestlers and perfect the fundamentals of each move. When done correctly the hand, leg, arm, hip, and head position should be very precise.

The bottom drill chain also once taught to the team will give the coach a simple drill that he can call out and expect the wrestlers to get into immediately. The drill chain can be a consistent part of a team's workouts and warm-ups throughout the season.

While wrestlers tend to drill takedowns because of the heavy emphasis of neutral wrestling these days, it is still important to excel in from the bottom position. Teaching wrestlers a simple drill chain from bottom will help wrestlers learn the intricacies of each move as they develop speed and power.

15
A Scientific Basis For Resistance Training Programs in Wrestling

William J. Kraemer, Dave Curby

QUESTIONS TO CONSIDER

- What common characteristic does wrestling share at the high school and collegiate levels, according to Horswill?
- How many times more is lactic acid present in a wrestler following a match?
- Why are non-linear programs being utilized more?

Many factors go into success in wrestling as one of the most demanding sports. Resistance training prepares the neuromuscular system to meet the demands of each match.

INTRODUCTION

Conditioning has proven to be a key element for success in wrestling over the years. From the fabled conditioning drills used by Dan Gable to push his body to the upper limits of collegiate and Olympic performances to the conditioning level achieved by Cael Sanderson in his undefeated collegiate and Olympic careers. The sport of wrestling is one of the most physiological demanding sports in the world.

As a former wrestler as well as junior high school and college wrestling coach I saw first hand how demanding the sport can be. Now as a practicing exercise and sport scientist our studies have proven wrestling to be the most physically demanding scholastic sport (Kraemer et al., 2001 and Yankanich et al., 1998). A wrestler must be able to sustain repetitive high intensity efforts over the entire length of a match. A wrestler must be able to exhibit great muscular power under dramatically fatiguing conditions in order to finish off a move or hold an opponent down in over time. In addition, they must have the strength to maintain holds. Thus, a resistance training program must address a host of different physical capabilities in order to develop the wrestler's physical potential for competition.

Many factors go into success in wrestling and many of the great wrestlers have used many combinations of technical skills, quickness, high levels of physical conditioning, strength and power to achieve success. No doubt inherent mental toughness and competitive spirit are also vital to competitive success in wrestling due to the "Spartan nature" of the sport itself. The purpose of this chapter will be to examine some of the important physiological mechanisms which provide the underlying basis for conditioning in wrestling and the development of strength and conditioning program. Furthermore, some examples of conditioning programs are given along with some guidelines for younger wrestlers with regards to resistance training.

It is important to understand that as wrestling is an individual sport so to is the need for individualization in a wrestler's conditioning program. However, certain over all scientific principles must be observed in order to optimize one's physical development and conditioning level.

BASIC TERMS AND PRINCIPLES OF RESISTANCE TRAINING

Before discussing the basic principles of resistance training it is necessary to define some basic terms commonly used when describing resistance training programs or principles.

Repetition: A repetition is one complete movement of an exercise. It normally consists of two phases: the concentric phase or lifting of the resistance and the eccentric phase or lowering of the resistance.

Set: This is a group of repetitions performed continuously before stopping performance of an exercise. While a set can be made up of any number of repetitions, sets typically range from 1 to 15 repetitions.

Breathing: A Valsalva maneuver (holding your breath with a closed glottis) during performance of resistance training is not recommended. Blood pressure does rise substantially during the performance of resistance training exercises. Normally, it is recommended to exhale during the lifting of the resistance and inhale during the lowering of the resistance during each repetition. During performance of an exercise at 1 RM or during the last few repetitions of a set performed to momentary voluntary fatigue some breath holding will occur. However, excessive breath holding should be discouraged.

Proper Technique: Proper technique of various resistance training exercises is partially determined by the desire to train specific muscle groups with specific exercises. Altering the proper form of an exercise allows the utilization of other muscle groups to help perform the exercise movement (Kraemer and Fleck, 2005). This decreases the training stimulus on the muscles normally associated with a particular exercise. Proper technique is also necessary as an injury prevention measure. This is especially true in exercises such as squats, deadlifts, and power cleans. Breaking of proper form in these types of exercises normally places undue stress on the lower back region. Improper technique in these types of exercises should be avoided and is normally associated with performing the exercise with resistances presently greater than the lifter's strength capabilities.

Full Range of Motion: Normally exercises are performed through the full range of motion allowed by the body position and the joints involved. Although no definitive studies are available, it is assumed that to develop strength throughout a joint's full range of motion, training must be performed through the full range of motion. Studies involving isometric training's joint angle specificity indicate that if training is only performed at a specific joint angle, strength gains will be realized in a narrow range around that specific joint angle and not throughout the joint's full range of motion (see Fleck and Kraemer, 2004). Thus, the need to perform exercises through a full range of motion to ensure strength gains throughout the full range of motion seems founded.

Repetition Maximum (RM) and RM Zones: This is a resistance that allows performance of only x number of repetitions per set but not x plus 1 repetitions per set with proper lifting technique. Thus, a 1 RM is the heaviest resistance that can be used for one complete repetition of an exercise. A 10 RM is a lighter resistance that allows completion of 10 but not 11 repetitions with proper exercise technique. An RM zone is a range of repetitions that only allow one to perform the number of repetitions in that zone, e.g., 3–5 RM or 8–10 RM. Repetition training zones are used as while it is important in many exercises to know where your resistance is for a given set, one just wants to fall into a RM zone so as not to under train for a given set (Fleck and Kraemer, 2004). Going to complete failure on every set can lead to compression soreness in joints in some athletes. Most of the time the lifter knows if they could do more then the number of repetitions for a given resistance if a target RM zone is 3–5 and the lifter can do 6 or 7 reps then the resistance is increased for the next set.

Rest Period Lengths: Rest is important when weights get heavier as the amount of time needed to rest will increase. As a general rule of thumb, rest period lengths under 1 minute are considered very short rest period lengths and are used for heavy anaerobic training of the lactic acid system. 2–3 minutes are considered moderate rest periods and are the most common and 5 minutes or longer are considered long rest periods and are used when very heavy lifting attempts are being made (e.g., 5 RM and lower). In wrestling it is important that the athlete can perform under fatigued conditions and therefore rest periods are varied to train different levels of fatigue.

Power: Power is the rate of performing work. Power during a repetition is defined as the weight lifted times the vertical distance the weight is lifted divided by the time to complete the repetition. If 100 pounds is lifted vertically three feet in one second, the power is 300 foot-pounds/second (100 pounds x three feet divided by one second). The highest power in a lift is achieved at about 30–45% of the 1 RM maximizing both force and velocity of the movement. Not all exercises can be done effectively for power development and the Olympic lifts, medicine ball, and other plyometric drills allow one to develop power without the deceleration that can occur with some movements where the mass of the weight cannot be released.

Strength: Is the maximal amount of force a muscle or muscle group can generate in a specified movement pattern at a specified or determined velocity of movement (Knuttgen & Kraemer, 1987). In an exercise such as a bench press a 1 RM is a measure of strength.

Training Volume: This is a measure of the total amount of work performed in a training session, week of training, month of training or any other time period. Frequency (number of training sessions per week, month, or year) and duration (length of each training session) have a direct bearing on the volume of training. The simplest method to estimate volume is by summing the number of repetitions performed in a specific time period, such as week or month of training. Volume can also be estimated by the total amount of weight lifted. As an example if 100 pounds is used to perform 10 repetitions the volume of training in 1000 pounds (10 repetitions x 100 pounds).

Program Variation: Variation in the volume and intensity of training or periodization of training is extremely important for optimal gains in strength (Fleck and Kraemer, 2004). A periodized program will use different resistance intensities and volume of exercise over the year based on the training goals of the wrestler (Kraemer and Häkkinen, 2002). Periodized programs allow the wrestler to prioritize the type of training they are doing during the year while allowing for planned rest periods. Rest and recovery are vital for an optimal resistance training program.

Progressive Resistance Exercise: Progressive resistance exercise or progressive overload refers to the need to continually increase the stress placed on the muscle as it becomes capable of producing greater force or has more endurance. At the start of a training program the 5 RM for arm curls might be 50 lb, and is a sufficient stimulus to produce an increase in strength. Later on in the training program 5 repetitions at 50 lb would not be a sufficient stimulus to produce further gains. The muscles involved can easily perform 5 repetitions with 50 lb and consequently 5 repetitions with 50 lb is no longer a 5 RM or a sufficient stimulus to increase strength. If the training stimulus is not increased at this point, no further gains in strength will occur. Progressive resistance training is needed within the context of a periodized training program.

Specificity of Training: The training program and exercises used must be specific to the characteristic being developed. If one want to develop total body power during a training cycle then the exercises must have such characteristics within them e.g., power cleans, hang pulls and/or hang cleans with 30–45% of 1 RM loading for maximal mechanical power development.

Spotting: Proper spotting is necessary to ensure the safety of the participants in a resistance training program. Spotters serve two major functions to assist the trainee with the exercise and to summon help if an accident does occur. Understanding the spotting technique for each exercise is vital to ensuring safety in the weight room (Kraemer and Fleck, 2005).

PHYSICAL DEMANDS OF THE SPORT

For further reading on the physical demands of the sport of wrestling, the reader is referred to an important article on wrestling by Horswill (2000) which provides a comprehensive view of the sport. Wrestling remains the most physiologically demanding sport in scholastic athletics today. Wrestling remains the most physiologically demanding sport in college athletics today. As a former junior high school and college wrestling coach, I have had a keen interest in the sport over the years as how to better train wrestlers to meet the rigorous demands of the sport. The conditioning program must be individualized but then must be matched up against the sports profile of being a sport which challenges the anaerobic metabolism (especially the lactic acid system and dramatically disrupts the acid base status of the body), the need for power and power endurance under dramatic conditions of fatigue, isometric strength, flexibility, and tissue strength of the joints to help prevent injury. This chapter will start to examine some of the underlying physiological mechanisms that impact the resistance training programs used in wrestling.

The conditioning program must be individualized but then must be matched up against the sports profile. The major demands for the sport of wrestling are the following:

1. The ability to tolerate the dramatic anaerobic metabolic stress. During a wrestling match high levels of energy is needed (called ATP hydrolysis) which creates dramatic reductions in blood and muscle pH and the acid balance in the body. This contributes to the extreme feelings of fatigue that every wrestler has experienced. The body must be trained to buffer acid and adapt to such high acidic environments. This requires resistance training workouts using shorter rest periods lengths to be part of a total resistance training program.
2. The need for muscular power. Few wrestlers are able to succeed without the ability to produce high levels of muscular power in their various moves. This necessitates power training and also power training

Physical demands of wrestling are dramatic compared to other sports.

under fatigued conditions different from most other athletes' physical needs.

3. Strength is also needed as the ability to get out from under and opponent or hold on to an opponent's limb is a function of both dynamic and static strength. Training both types of strength is also vital to a wrestler's performance.

4. Flexibility is also vital and needed for both prevention of injury as well as allowing moves to be accomplished from dramatically difficult angles and positions.

5. Proper body weight management is vital to eliminate the drastic starvation weight loss programs used by wrestlers in the past.

WEIGHT MANAGEMENT AND PHYSIOLOGICAL STRESS

While well beyond the scope of this article, weight class identification and weight management plays a large role in the sport of wrestling. With the tragic deaths of three wrestlers several years ago, it is obvious that any mistakes in weight management confounded with extreme exercise capacities of young men can lead to fatal results. Unfortunately, this has gone against the culture of wrestling which has developed over decades. The origin of this lack of concern for 5% weight loss in wrestling can be traced to an early study out of the University of Iowa in the 1940s showing no decrements with a 5% weight loss. Yet no underlying biological measures of hydration were evaluated.

Over the past few years these tragedies have stimulated a closer examination of weigh-ins and weight class management. One might propose that "on the mat" weigh-ins may be the only way to limit weight loss practices used to cut that 5 to 10 pounds prior to the weigh in. This is due to the fact that with such weight loss prior to a match will exact a distinct physiological disadvantage but again it is the "culture" of the sport that uses the concept of eat and purge mentality that will be difficult to rid from the sport. Many states in scholastic wrestling have made some strides forward with weight management programs that assess both body fat and body mass. A recent program on ESPN tracking the Iowa wrestling team season dramatically reflected some of the eating and exercise purging behaviors during the season that have been established in the culture for years. Nevertheless a competitive disadvantage would be exacted if weight was not controlled up to the point of competition with "on mat weigh-ins". More research on this topic is needed but we are all left with the challenge of how to stabilize weight management in wrestling as it still remains one of the great threats to the sport and its popularity in the lay public today. For coaches, parents, and wrestlers but especially strength and conditioning professionals this must be a concern to be addressed with the sport at both the elementary, secondary and college levels of competition.

Again, more research may be needed to determine if this approach will work. Dehydration is a serious problem and we have in my laboratory groups over the years shown in college wrestlers as others had demonstrated in high school wrestlers earlier in the 1970s that wrestlers may not have a normal set point for what is called their "osmol" regulatory center in the brain (Yankanich et al., 1998, Kraemer et al. 2002). The normal values for a hydrated individual are on average about 289 mosmol/L. This is readjusted in many wrestlers who gain and lose weight and when the value increases toward 300 mosmol/L is more related to severe dehydration, but in many wrestlers this is just a new normal! Classic research out of the University of Iowa by Dr. Charles Tipton's group in the 1970's had shown that high school wrestlers had unusually high osmolality values representative of chronic dehydration (Zambraski et al., 1975). We have shown this as well in elite college wrestlers using direct blood measurements. We have demonstrated that fully hydrated wrestlers after a college season had on average had a measure of 302 mosmol/L for resting values. This did not change with the hydration changes due to weight loss and even more disturbing was the fact that how the wrestlers choose to lose 6% of body mass prior to a match did not matter (Yankanich et al., 1998). In other words this means that the hydration status was not affected whether the wrestler lost the weight over 7 days or over 24 hrs time period. So it appears that wrestlers who have been cultured in the weight cycling mentioned above and have a set water component that is acutely used to lose this 5–10% of body mass and then eat and drink to replace it after the weigh in and before the match. Thus, many wrestler's bodies have evolved to tolerate this higher dehydration level.

With a match wrestlers can push this value to an unreliable physiological level of over 320 mosmol/L. This remains both a dramatic physiological stress to produce and underlies the tragic circumstances that show that young men can exercise and starve themselves to death. This phenomenon has not been observed in heavy weights who do not lose such body mass prior to the match. With recent rules on upper limits of heavyweight wrestlers, some have had to revert back to the practices of the other weight class teammates. This is a phenomenon that must be monitored and even upper limits adjusted to eliminate this problem.

Physiologically, this suggests that elite high school and college wrestlers have over their careers have developed a "new normal" for their osmol-regulatory "set point" and have a water compartment which appears to be used just for this weigh loss practice. More research is needed on this point, but unless cycle of "loss-gain" practices of losing 5–10% body weight during the days or day prior to the match are removed from the culture of wrestling, the health impact of the weight management basis of the sport will never meet its intended goals. As we have seen such practices have also led to eating disorders such as bulimia in order to meet weigh class demands. Members of a sports performance team, strength and conditioning specialists along with athletic trainers, sports nutritionists, and sports medicine physicians need to make sure wrestlers are hydrated and have normal levels of plasma osmolality in order to quantify a healthy condition going into all conditioning and competitive cycles of the sport. Ultimately this practice was pushed by the desire for the lightest weight on the largest frame to gain leverage on an opponent. Another concept that has started to gain popularity is to limit weight loss and go into the match physiologically stronger and have more vigor than an opponent who suffers from such dehydration stress and is physiologically at a disadvantage.

The American Medical Association, the American Academy of Pediatrics and the American College of Sports Medicine (ACSM) have published position statements regarding weight control in wrestling starting more than 25 years ago. A guideline to weight loss and hypohydration has been in the NCAA Sports Medicine Handbook since 1985.

WRESTLING SKILLS

One can speak about conditioning but unless the skills and strategies of the match are mastered with high levels of technique and on the mat smarts, you will have only highly conditioned athletes but performance will not be enhanced when matched against a technically superior opponent. This can be observed from junior high school to collegiate competition. Nevertheless, proper conditioning is vital for safe and effective performances at every level of competition as it is the fatigued athlete who is more susceptible to injury. A combination of genetic talents combined with extraordinary skills and mental toughness are the prerequisites for success. Optimal conditioning can then augment this to produce the best performance results for the athlete.

THE METABOLIC STRESS OF COMPETITION

It is obvious as one of the combative sports that wrestling presents a dramatic stress to the body beyond the discipline of weight management and the physical nature of the one on one competition. From a metabolic perspective it is one of the highest lactate producing sports in which the acid-base balance is severely disrupted. Lactate does not cause fatigue but has been a good marker of dramatic anaerobic fatigue where ATP hydrolysis and acid base disruptions are high (Robergs et al., 2004). With a college match or a freestyle match ranging from 5 to 9 minutes blood concentrations of lactate can range from 18–20 mmol/L much higher than a typical maximal treadmill test which may go just beyond 10 mmol/L. The ability to tolerate increases in the acidity of the muscle and blood is related to buffering systems from the lactate itself to the body's inherent intra (bicarbonate)-and inter (phosphate)-cellular buffering systems is a trainable phenomenon which can be accomplished with short rest weight training or interval training (Fleck and Kraemer, 2004). This process has been shown to take about 8 weeks to achieve and demonstrates the need for such pre-season conditioning program durations to eliminate the nausea and vomiting associated with wrestling practices when such anaerobic pre-season conditioning has not been prescribed or completed. On the high school level this is most evident in the season transitions of football players who do not have the time to properly prepare themselves for the sport of wrestling due to extended seasons and playoff schedules seen today.

Early season injuries are many times caused by the dramatic fatigue caused by practice itself and coaches need to understand that if the wrestler has not been participating in a sport or conditioning program that stimulates the body's buffering system time is needed to adapt to the metabolic demands.

IMPACT OF A SINGLE MATCH

With a single match a dramatic stress can be observed. The high lactate concentrations observed after a match had been presented by Kraemer in 1982. This has been replicated by several other investigators showing that blood concentrations can reach close to 20 mmol/L with the concomitant muscle concentrations even higher due to a more direct biocompartment measure. The match responses go well over 15 mmol/L in the blood and as previously discussed create dramatic disruption of the acid-base balance. (See below) The effect of this is that the wrestler must be able to buffer this high acid content and cope with it in order to express strength and power capabilities. Since lactate and hydrogen ions directly interfere with the contractile mechanisms, conditioning must be directed as achieving a trained state to limit symptomatology in both practice and competition. An important adjunct to this phenomenon is that dietary practices with reduced caloric intake can make this matter worse.

To achieve this effect of training the acid base balance one can use short rest resistance training program starting with a 2 minute rest period between sets and exercises and periodizing the rest periods down to 1 minute typically performing circuit style or set-circuit style training at least 2 times per week. In wrestling one is faced with the performance of whole body movements under great fatigue at the end of the match for example to compete a takedown or defensive move and therefore placing a whole body power movement at the end of the circuit will enhance the ability to perform under conditions of fatigue. Thus,

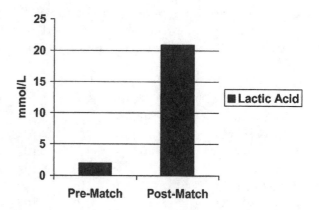

Serum lactate response to a single competition match (Kraemer, 1982)

typical exercise order of large muscle group exercises first in the workout is altered in this case to promote strength and power endurance.

In such a protocol you must periodize from 2 minutes rest to 1 minute the rest period over a 4 to 6 week period and maintain in the program for at least 8 weeks at the 1 minute rest level. The addition of each circuit or set which means greater total work must be added sequentially upon demonstration of toleration of the prior circuit. Loading is targeted at a 10 repetition maximum which in reality is an 8–10 RM training zone. Loading is increased or decreased to maintain this resistance range and care if taken not to lose exercise technique or necessarily go to failure due to technique disintegration. You can go down the exercise order or after attainment of all three circuits go in a set fashion for each exercise prior to moving to the next exercise. However, the most effective styles in going down the order leading to the whole body exercise movement at the end of the circuit. You will see that the resistance that can be used by the wrestler for a given set in the protocol will increase as the body starts to more successfully buffer the acid production. This is especially true for the whole body movement which is placed at the end of the circuit. Remember, symptoms of nausea, dizziness and overt vomiting must be carefully monitored. When they occur greater the protocol should be stopped. The athlete should be rested and recovered and then one must fall back to a longer rest period length for the protocol. Symptoms represent an in appropriate "overshoot" in the progression of rest period reductions in the protocol. As pointed out many times, the so called "puke index" is not a good index of the quality of the workout, it is representative of an inappropriate stress when it rises to the level of overt sickness and symptomatololgy.

THE NEED FOR ISOMETRIC STRENGTH AND TRAINING

Prior work has shown that the isometric strength is compromised with a wrestling match and over the course of a tournament (Kraemer et al., 2001) (See below). This was seen in the grip strength and a bear hug strength so important to many moves and positional holds in wrestling. Isometric force is much higher than concentric force production and therefore cannot be typically trained specifically using just weight training. For wrestlers a sports-specific program for isometric strength of the hand grip, upper body movement strength of the torso and arms needs to be included in a resistance training program.

It is generally believed and supported by the majority of research, although not fully substantiated, that maximal voluntary muscle actions (MVMA) are superior to sub-maximal voluntary isometric muscle actions in bringing about increases in strength (Fleck and Kraemer, 2004). The majority of sport scientists and practitioners now use 100 percent of maximal voluntary muscle action (MVMA) for training

EXAMPLE CIRCUIT RESISTANCE TRAINING
WORKOUT PROTOCOL

- Squats   10 10 10
- Bench Press   10 10 10
- Seated Rows   10 10 10
- Sit Ups   10 10 10
- Arm Curls   10 10 10
- Upright Rows 10 10 10
- Hang Cleans   5   5   5

1 minute rest period between each set.

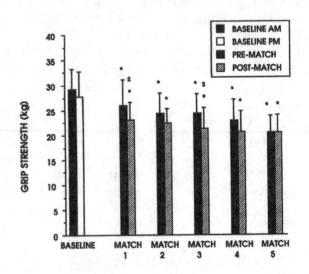

Responses of grip strength over a free style wrestling tournament (Kraemer et al., 2001)

purposes. The majority of research has utilized MVMAs of three to ten seconds in duration and a relatively small number of muscle actions per day and therefore the crucial isometric hold positions must be chosen to include in a wrestling workout. Grip strength is fundamental and upper body dual and single arm holds are also isometric in nature and can be trained. This is where the creative touch of the strength and conditioning specialist must come into play to create the part of the workout.

The duration of the muscle action and the number of training muscle actions per day individually show weaker correlations to increases in strength than muscle action duration and the number of muscle actions combined and this means that the length of time a muscle is activated is directly related to increased strength. It also indicates that optimal gains in strength are the result of either a small number of long duration muscle actions or a high number of short duration muscle actions. To increase maximal strength, the optimal isometric program should consist of MVMA performed on a daily basis. Furthermore, when isometric training is performed the gains in strength occur predominantly at the joint angle at which the isometric training is performed, this is joint angle specificity. The majority of research indicates static strength increases due to isometric training are joint angle specific. Many factors may affect the degree to which joint angle specificity occurs including the muscle(s) group trained, the joint angle at which the training is performed, and the intensity and duration of the isometric actions. Isometric training of the elbow flexors at four different joint angles does increase static strength at all four joint angles and significantly increases dynamic power of the elbow flexors (Kanehisa & Miyashita, 1983a).

Collectively this information indicates some practical guidelines if an increase in strength and power is desired throughout the entire range of motion. First, the training should be performed at joint angle increments of approximately ten to 20 degrees. Second, the total duration (duration of each muscle action x number of muscle actions) of the isometric training per training session should be long (three to five second actions and 15 to 20 ac-

tions per day). Third, if isometric actions can not be performed through out the entire range of motion, it is best to perform them when the muscle is in a lengthened position as opposed to a shortened position.

EXAMPLE PROTOCOL

- Straight Arm Grip 15 to 20 reps as at 100% of effort
- Bear Hug 15 to 20 reps as at 100% of effort
- Grip Strength Style Grips (finger cups and wrist grips) 15 to 20 reps as at 100% of effort

IMPACT OF A TOURNAMENT

In a unique study undertaken with a group of elite collegiate wrestlers at Penn State University (top 3 nationally ranked team) I resided for ten years as Director of Research for Sports Medicine some interesting results were discovered for the first time. This study needs to be carefully examined by strength and conditioning specialists who condition wrestlers as in that study, Kraemer et al. (2001) demonstrated for the first time the tournament demands are very different from a single match response and stress can be accumulate over several matches of a tournament. Even with the rebound in body mass due to the use of food and fluid intakes after weigh ins, isometric strength and physiological status (e.g., testosterone concentrations were continually reduced down to adolescent levels over the two day tournament). In fact it was apparent that by the time of the championship match on the evening of the second day, each wrestler was in a reduced and compromised physiological state. This gives some factual support to the concept that the mental toughness needed in the sport due to the dramatic and compromised physiological state that wrestlers must perform under in order to be successful. What strategies can be used to offset such effects remains speculative but the basal origin appears to reside in the food and fluid behaviors still used despite the attempts by regulatory bodies to effectively curve their use. Changing this culture and using weigh loss strategies that stabilize muscle mass and body mass with a requirement of less than 2%

body mass loss to prepare for a match appear to be the best strategies to eliminate physiological breakdown and stress and allow the wrestler to perform at a higher level of physiological readiness. This may be vital for all wrestlers starting at the beginning of their career which can be as young as 5 or 6 years of age.

STRENGTH AND POWER

It is obvious that the sport of wrestling requires high levels of strength and more importantly power to perform at the highest level. However this must be put into the context of different individual strategies of techniques which vary between wrestlers. One can easily see this by studying World and Olympic champions of which not all exhibit pure power techniques in their styles. First neurological reflexes and response times and sequential anticipation and touch reaction-response patterns cannot be underestimated as well as flexibility and joint configurations. Nevertheless, threshold levels of whole body strength and power are important factors that must be trained to give each wrestler a fundamental level of conditioning. The classic lack of whole body power can be seen when a wrestler cannot put a wrestler back down on the mat from a standing position after an attempted escape. As coaches say "walking around" with your opponent on the mat is not an optimal position to be in when preventing an escape. So in such case you need to be able to exhibit structural power to get one's hips under and explode up to lift an opponents struggling body into the air and back down to the matt. This requires the type of power that is exhibited when lifting your body mass augmented by movement. So structural lifts as well as core lifts must be included in the program at loads equal to the athletes body mass for power specificity and then at heavier loads to produce increases in the strength power equation within a periodized training program. The key here is the power output related to the handling your weight class body mass and under conditions of fatigue already addressed in a previous section of this article.

EXAMPLE CORE EXERCISES IN A STRENGTH AND POWER PROTOCOL

Core Resistance Exercises
- Squat
- Split squats
- Side squats
- Lunges
- Squat Jumps
- Power Cleans
- Hang Cleans from the Knees
- Hang Cleans from the Thighs

Supplemental Exercises
- Flex Band Power Exercises
- Vertimax Power Exercises

Loading for such exercises follow the classical periodized training programs which have been well documented and reviewed in a host of different publications in the literature (Kraemer and Häkkinen, 2002). It is important that the "strength" base is maintained especially when specialized power training is used with lighter loads which approach the maximal mechanical power outputs (i.e., 30–45% of 1 RM). Some insights into a wrestling specific program is the determination of how much associated hypertrophy and muscle growth is desired if a weight class limit is desired. However, normal muscle size gains that are muscle with age and training progression should be more readily accepted as a normal progression. Problems have been observed when diet and starvation are used to fight the positive impact of a resistance training program on muscle. To accomplish this muscle breakdown and not fat loss is the result. Thus, the sports medicine and performance team must carefully determine the ideal weight class each year for the young athlete rather than give in to the "rule of thumb" that a wrestler participates at the lowest possible weight class to gain limb-length leverage advantages in the match. Many organizations at the state and national levels have tried to implement weight class management but their success remains to be determined. However, be aware that this natural antagonism between the optimal height and limb length leverage advantages at a given weight class versus the classic muscle size increases seen with an optimally designed weight program in young and growing wrestlers.

In our recent work in our own laboratory here at the University of Connecticut and work we have done with our collaborators Dr. Robert Newton and Dr. Keijo Häkkinen it has become evident that one has the choice between "quality" power training or "endurance" strength/power conditioning. Sets should contain no more than 6 repetitions and our data shows that 3 may be more optimal. Based on the peak power, in a quality power workout we strive to achieve at least 90% of our best effort. In a set of three or even 6 this is accomplished only for one or two reps. If it is not achieved then one starts to condition the endurance of the lifting movements at much lower sub-maximal levels of neuromuscular recruitment. When you are using the mechanical power output loadings from 30–45% of the one repetition maximum (1 RM), lower power outputs are due to the inability to accelerate the mass. Interestingly one would think to perform just one repetition at a time and while successful for some, most individuals produce some type of warm-up phenomenon with the use of a multiple rep set. Rest between sets for optimal programming is still under study but 1 to 3 minutes seem to be one possible range to work with. Finally you need to understand the performance level and this can be difficult without an external measurement system as we have historically used our Plyometric Power System which allows us to gain rapid feedback and includes audio cues for successful or non-successful reps. Thus this is an emerging need for information on the performance of power training reps to determine the level of performance beyond the weight on the bar or end point failure of a number of reps. This concept will be further developed with more research but we all have learned that the athlete must be rested and ready to perform similar to what is needed in quality efforts in plyometrics. Here one must carefully monitor the status of the athlete prior to a workout and deal with the sport coach to make sure that they are not compromising the weight room workouts by loading athletes with practice stress prior to a "quality" power day in the weight room. Otherwise you are left to performing endurance protocols which will not affect the peak power capabilities of the wrestler. These protocols should be done before any other conditioning activities of the day. Our experience is that early morning protocols are not as effective with the attainment of peak power outputs as later in the day and this may be due to a host of physiological mechanisms related to the high level of power capabilities and other physiological adjustments in younger people's circadian rhythms (e.g., melatonin concentrations). This requires further research as untrained and recreationally trained individuals do not seem to reflect this time of day performance deficit.

Strength Training

Nowhere else in sports is the need for total body strength as evident as it is in wrestling. The ability to push, pull, and stabilize with the upper body and torso and to perform lifts with the body weight of a competitor by using the legs are movements occurring regularly during every 6-minute match. Therefore, strength development should include a variety of exercises that will improve those skills. It is also important to remember that both unilateral and bilateral exercises should be chosen for the program. Compared with circuit resistance training, the rest periods are longer (2–4 minutes) and require heavier loading (6RM and lower). Multi-joint exercises are necessary to develop the strength of the myriad movements integral to wrestling and should be performed with multi-planar actions. Not all the exercises listed below can tolerate 6RM loading and should be considered supplemental lifts to overall strength development. Example exercises would include the following:

● Chest: bench press, incline press, decline press.
● Upper back: lat pull-down, pull-ups, rows.
● Lower back: good morning exercise, deadlift, hyperextensions, thighs, squats, split squats, linear and lateral lunges.
● Hamstrings: stiff-leg deadlift, standing leg curls.
● Arms: arm curls, triceps extensions, wrist curls.

SIDEBAR: Strength Training as a Team

Ted Witulski/USA Wrestling

Every season you'll hear it from coaches, trying to make sense why their team isn't winning, "if only we were stronger as a team." Coaches see it all the time. Their kids have the technique, the conditioning, maybe even the mental toughness, but physically they just aren't there yet.

It's always a challenge for a coach to find a way to build strength training into a workout. Many coaches are reluctant to take the draconian step of having 6:00 a.m. lifting sessions. Other coaches just don't have the access to weight room facilities, and little or no budget to make strength training a priority.

If this sounds familiar then your team might need the leadership from the coach to take control and fix the strength gap that exists. With three simple solutions your team can avoid having to set the alarm clock for the wee hours, and you can probably avoid the coach's poor house as well.

Creativity in strength training is really the key. And, here are three easy to manage ideas that can get your team working together on the important area of strength during your regular wrestling practice.

Step one: load your team up with knuckle-pins. What's a knuckle-pin you might ask? And just a few years ago I was asking one of my wrestlers dad's what a knuckle-pin was. One of my wrestling-dads had come to me with the idea of outfitting the team with hand weights. The hand weights were a simple idea, the dad worked for the railroad, and all along the lines of tracks lay old knuckle-pins. These knuckle-pins were what held train cars together. Eventually, the pins broke off and fell to the tracks. The dad picked them up for us and our team was outfitted with hand weights. The weights were between 5–8 pounds. For the stronger wrestlers we branched beyond knuckle-pins to window well weights from old houses. These weights attached to rope secured to windows and acted as a counterbalance to open the window. With a team of 60 guys we had a vast array of hand weights of varying sizes. From the lightweight knuckle-pins of 5 pounds to heavier window weights that weighed 15 pounds.

Once we had hand-weights for the team we painted them and put them to use.

The possibilities were endless. But we used the hand-weights in two main ways. One was jogging with them. You'd be amazed what a difference in a workout jogging is when you throw in carrying hand-weights. On a normal 20 minute run, we usually only had the kids carry the weights for about 10 minutes. It truly adds a lot to jogging, and I'm sure it made a difference in our team strength.

Also, about 3 days a week we would gather into a large circle, everybody with a manageable set of hand-weights. This usually would come at the end of practice, since it was such a demanding workout. For about 9 minutes the wrestlers would put themselves through a series of different exercises that mainly concentrated on shoulder and back muscles. The coach would call for the kids to do as many reps as possible of a specific exercise, changing it up about every 20 seconds. The motions for the shoulder workout, as we called, were similar to what you would do in the weight room: standing chest fly, military press, tricep extension. Have a variety of movements in mind, change them up every 20–45 seconds, crank up the music and build the strength. The intensity of this work-out is virtually limitless. Rest of the shoulder muscles can be thrown in by having the wrestlers hold the weights while they do lunges, or do up-downs, or level changes.

But the key to this workout was that every wrestler was doing it at once. All wrestlers policed each other and made sure that maximum effort was being expended, and for 9 minutes the whole team was working together to build strength. To top it off it didn't cost the coach his budget for the year.

Step two: Team Wondersticks. The wonderstick, was a bit more costly, but added another way of training as a team. Your local hardware, or plumbing supplier is the place to go. As a team we bought four and five foot lengths of PVC plastic plumbing pipe in both 2" and 4" diameters. Don't forget the end caps, plumbers glue, and duct tape. The wonder-stick, sarcastically named by the wrestlers for the lack of joy they had when faced with the workout, was really a miniature weight bar.

After purchasing the materials we glued one end cap on the PVC in place and held it firmly in place with plenty of extra duct tape. Then, we mixed standard post-hole concrete and began to fill the PVC pipe. The 2" PVC with just concrete, weighed 35 pounds. To increase the weight of the bar we dropped knuckle-pins and other heavy iron objects into the pipe and let the concrete fill and settle around them. With this technique the 2" wonder-sticks weighed upwards of 55-60 pounds. Once filled we set the sticks upright to let the concrete dry and then glued the end cap in place. We did the same with the 4" PVC, but be careful adding too much iron to those wonder-sticks. With the extra diameter gripping them can be real tough. Some of the 4" wonder-sticks weighed upwards of a hundred pounds. All of these were neatly contained in very durable PVC piping. They were usable on the wrestling mats and did not make a mess.

The sections were four and five feet long, just short of an actual barbell. However, the wonder-stick really forced wrestlers to squeeze. Again, the diameter was 2 and 4 inches. When in use the wrestlers constantly had to grip the stick to go through the exercises.

The wonder-stick workout was in the neighborhood of 10-15 minutes. With wrestlers working in pairs. One wrestler would do a series of reps for example, 10 hang clean reps, 10 lat rows, and 10 military presses. Then, the other wrestler would do the same. Both wrestlers, would spot each other. The wonder-stick workout worked well, since our weight room did not have near as many stations as the 30 wonder-sticks provided. Of course, the wonder-sticks did have a financial cost, in the area of four dollars each. But, overall the wonder-sticks provided the team another way of strength training together.

Step three: Get out the towels. Towel workouts are simple and relatively low in cost. A few dollars for a new heavy-duty shower towel, or perhaps you can get some parents to donate some old beach towels. Once, there is enough towels to accommodate two wrestlers per towel, it is time to start adding in the towel workout into your practice time. The different exercises are limitless. With two wrestlers working as resistance against each other, all sorts of exercises can be done. While some exercises will focus more on biceps or lats all of the exercises will force wrestlers to engage in exercises that promote a powerful grip.

Wrestlers can work on a standing curl, with one wrestler kneeling in front of the other pulling down on the towel while the other holds the center of the towel and does a number of repetitions, then they can exchange places. The wrestlers can work on the pulling strength working the towel back and forth for a series of reps in two man hand saw motion, much like two lumberjacks cutting through a fallen tree. The tricep curl can be done with the resistance wrestler standing behind the other, while the wrestler does the standing tricep extension. Again the possibilities are limitless and the work-out potential can only be diminished by one wrestler not providing enough resistance for the other.

Cary Kolat and Sammie Henson employed this towel workout at the end of practices before heading off to Sydney to wrestle in the Olympics. All the while they were less than thirty feet from the state of the art weight room adjoined to the wrestling room on the campus at the Olympic Training Center. The weight room is filled with every gadget and machine you could possibly want, but two world class wrestlers pushed each other through hundreds of repetitions using a simple towel. I'm sure they've spent plenty of time in the weight room pumping conventional iron, but the workout they went through was no less impressive, and in many ways it was superior.

To provide more strength training for your team look for creative ways to provide strength building workouts into your regular wrestling practice. Three simple solutions are the knuckle-pin work outs, the wonder-sticks, and the towel workouts. All would be beneficial to any high school wrestling team. And, each can be provided for an entire team at a low cost for the coach. Strength is fundamental cornerstone of the sport of wrestling, as a coach help your wrestlers build that strength by using these creative means.

PERIODIZATION OF RESISTANCE TRAINING

The use of periodized resistance training has been shown to be superior to constant training methods (Fleck and Kraemer, 2004). Periodized training involves the planned variation in the intensity of exercises and in the volume of a workout. Typically one periodizes large muscle group exercises. However, variation schemes can be created for smaller muscle groups. One must consider the type of periodized program to use. In general there are two basic types, which have developed. Linear and non-linear periodized protocols for maximal strength and power development. Below are some of the basic differences between linear and non-linear periodization approaches to resistance training. With the need for rest and recovery and the long seasons in wrestling, non-linear programs are becoming quite popular.

Classic Linear Models

Classic periodization methods utilize a progressive increase in the intensity with small variations in each 2 to 4 week microcycle. For example a classic 4 cycle linear periodized program (4 weeks for each cycle) would be:

Classic Linear Periodized Program	
MicroCycle 1	**MicroCycle 2**
3–5 sets of 12–15 RM	4–5 sets of 8–10 RM
MicroCycle 3	**MicroCycle 4**
3–4 sets of 4–6 RM	3–5 sets of 1–3 RM

You can see that there is some variation within each microcycle due to the repetition range of each cycle. Still, the general trend for the 16 week program is a steady linear increase in the intensity of the training program. Due to the straight line increase in the intensity of the program it has been termed "linear" periodized training.

The volume of the training program will also vary with the classic program starting with a higher initial volume and as the intensity of the program increases the volume gradually decreases. The drop off between the

intensity and volume of exercise can become less as the training status of the athlete advances. In other words, advanced athletes can tolerate higher volumes of exercise during the heavy and very heavy microcycles.

It is very important to point out here that one must be very careful not to progress too quickly to train with high volumes of heavy weights. Pushing too hard can lead to the potential for a serious overtraining syndrome. Overtraining can compromise progress for months. While it takes a great deal of excessive work to produce such an overtraining effect, highly motivated trainees can easily make the mistake out of shear desire to make gains and see progress in their training. So it is important to monitor the stress of your workouts for your exercise and the total conditioning program. Remember exercises within a program can interact to compromise each other too.

The purpose of the high volume exercise in the early microcycles has been thought to promote the muscle hypertrophy needed to eventually enhance strength in the later phases of training. Thus the late cycles of training are linked to the early cycles of training and enhance each other as strength gains are related to size changes in the muscle. Programs that attempt to gain strength without the needed muscle tissue are limited in their potential.

The increases in the intensity of the periodized program then start to develop the needed nervous system adaptations for enhanced motor unit recruitment. This happens as the program progresses and heavier resistances are used. Heavier weights demand high threshold motor units to become involved in the force production process. With the associated increase in muscle protein in the muscles from the early cycle training force production of the motor units are enhanced. Here again one sees a integration of the different parts of the 16 week training program.

A 16 week program in reality is called a mesocycle and a year training program (macrocycle) is made up of several mesocycles. Each mesocycle attempt to progress the body's muscle hypertrophy and strength upward toward one's theoretical genetic maximum. Thus, the theoretical basis for a linear method of periodization consists of developing hypertrophy followed by improved nerve function and strength. This is repeated again and again with each mesocycle and progress is made in the training program.

Non-Linear Periodized Programs

More recently, the concept of non-linear periodized training programs have been developed to maintain variation in the training stimulus. However, non-linear periodized training makes implementation of the program possible due to schedule or competitive demands. The non-linear program allows for variation in the intensity and volume within each week over the course of the training program (e.g., 16 weeks). The change in the intensity and volume of training will vary within the week. An example of a non-linear periodized training program over a 16 week mesocycle would be:

Non-Linear Periodized Program
This protocol uses a 6 day rotation with one day rest between workouts.

Monday	Wednesday
4 sets 12–15 RM	4 sets of 8–10 RM
Friday	**Monday**
3–4 sets of 4–6 RM	4–5 sets of 1–3 RM
Monday	**Wednesday**
Power Day	2 sets of 12–15 RM

The variation in training is much greater within the week. One can easily see that intensity spans over a maximum of a 14 RM range (possible 1 RM sets versus 15 RM sets in the week cycle). This span in training variation appears to be as effective as linear programs. One can also add a "power" training day where loads may be from 30–45% of 1 RM and release of the mass is allowed of no deceleration exists with the movement of the joint(s). Medicine ball plyometrics and other lower body plyometrics are also performed here as well.

Different from the linear programs, one trains the different components of muscle size and strength within the same week. Different from the linear methods, non-linear programs attempt to train both the hypertrophy and neural aspects of strength within the same week. Thus, one is working at two different physiological adaptations together within the same 7 to 10 day period of the 16 week mesocycle. This appears possible and may be more conducive to many individual's schedules especially when competitions, travel or other schedule conflicts can make the traditional linear method difficult to adhere to.

In this program one just rotates through the different protocols. The workout rotates between very heavy, heavy, moderate and light training sessions. If one misses the Monday workout the rotation order is just pushed forward meaning one just performs the rotated workout scheduled. For example, if the light 12–15 workout was scheduled for Monday and you miss it you just perform it on Wednesday and continue with the rotation sequence. In this way no workout stimulus is missed in the training program. One can also say that a mesocycle will be completed when a certain number of workouts are completed (e.g., 48) and not use training weeks to set the program length.

Again the primary exercises are typically periodized but one can also use a 2 cycle program to vary the small muscle group exercises. For example in the "triceps pushdown" one could rotate between the moderate (8–10 RM) and the heavy (4–6 RM) cycle intensities. This would provide the hypertrophy needed for such isolated muscles of a joint but also provide the strength needed to support heavier workouts of the large muscle groups.

In conclusion, two different approaches can be used to periodize your training program, more specifically, linear and non-linear program schedules. The programs appear to accomplish the same effect and are superior to constant training programs (2). It appears that this is accomplished by training either the hypertrophy component first and then the neural strength component second in the linear method and both components within a 7–10 day time period in the non-linear method. The key to workout success is variation and different approaches can be used over the year to accomplish this training need.

EXAMPLE RESISTANCE TRAINING PROTOCOL FOR WRESTLING

Many programs can be used to condition for wrestling. For younger wrestlers one never uses resistance lower then a 6 RM. Other considerations for younger wrestlers will be given at the end of the chapter (Kraemer and Fleck, 2005). It is interesting to note that excessive running by wrestlers to make weight can dramatically reduce their power capabilities and may be counterproductive to their wrestling success. High intensity running should be limited with cross training and other forms of anaerobic training such as interval sprint training used and appropriate recovery allowed for (Fleck and Kraemer, 2004).

Off-Season Program

The exercises are performed in the order listed. Italics indicate exercises that can be periodized (strength/power or undulating model) in this phase. Some whole body exercises are done at the end of the workout to prepare the body for exerting effort under conditions of fatigue which is a very common feature of wrestling. Strict attention to exercise technique is needed in such workouts. Spotters must be especially aware of this in these types of workout designs.

Warm-Up—general exercise consisting of jogging or cycling for 5–10 minutes followed by a general stretching routine. Perform exercises in the order listed.

Monday and Friday	Wednesday
Bench Press	* *Power Cleans*
Squat	*Dumbbell Incline Press
Shrugs	Lunges
	Leg Curls
4-way Neck Exercise	* *Seated Rows*
Sit Ups	Abdominal crunches
Seated Military	*Lat Pull Down
Arm Curls	Isometric Grip Exercises (6 second holds)
* *Hang Pulls*	Standing Calf Raises
Stiff Leg Deadlift	* *Deadlift*
	Reverse Arm Curls

Frequency & Approximate Time

* 3 training sessions per week with at least 1 day separating sessions
* 40–60 minutes per session

Additional Injury-Prevention Exercises

● Neck exercises which
● elbow exercises
● Low back machine exercise
● Various wrist exercises

Additional or Replacement Exercises

* Front Squats
* Plyometrics for power day exercises
* Wrist curls or wrist roller

Off-Season Program Notes

* Format: set-repetition
* Number of sets: 3 for each exercise
* Resistance: Periodized resistances for the * exercises, other exercises 10–12 RM
* Rest period between sets and exercises: 2 to 3 minutes for heavy lifts, and 1–2 minutes for lighter lifts >10 repetitions.
* Repetitions per set for abdominal exercises: 20 to 25

Pre-Season Program

Warm-Up—general exercise consisting of jogging or cycling for 5–10 minutes followed by a general stretching routine. Exercises should be performed in the order listed.

Monday/Friday CIRCUIT	Wednesday Maintenance Strength Power
Squats	Bench Press
Bench Press	Squats
Seated Rows	Power Cleans
Sit Ups	Deadlift
Arm Curls	Leg Curls
Upright Rows	4-way Neck Exercises
Hang Pull the ground	Isometric Grip Exercises (6 second hold)
Sit ups	Sit Ups
Leg Curls	

The exercises are performed in the order listed in the circuit.

Frequency & Approximate Time

* 2 training sessions per week with at least 1 day separating sessions. Two days a week for 6 weeks prior to the season will be dedicated to developing the wrestler's ability to tolerate and buffer lactic acid. The other day will be used to maintain strength and power capabilities.
* 30–45 minutes per session

Additional Injury-Prevention Exercises

● Knee extension
● Split squats
● Front Squats

Additional or Replacement Exercises

* Lat pull-down
* Seated row
* Arm curls
* Shoulder Press

Advanced Exercises

* Power Cleans

Pre-Season Program Notes

* Format: circuit and set format where appropriate to the workout
* Number of circuits and sets: 2 to 3
* Resistance: The Wednesday workout should be done in a circuit fashion where a set of 10 repetitions are performed with 2 minutes of rest or less between exercises. 10–12 RM,
* Rest period between sets and exercises: 1–2 minutes
* Repetitions per set for abdominal exercises: 20 to 30

Other: The whole body lift using a hang pull is used to simulate the need for whole body lifting under conditions of great fatigue in a match.

In-Season Program

Perform the exercises in the order listed.
Warm-Up—general exercise consisting of jogging or cycling for 5–10 minutes followed by a general stretching routine.

Workout 1	Workout 2
*Hang Pulls	*Power Cleans
*Back squat	*Leg press
*Bench press	Neck Exercises
*Dumbbell overhead press	Isometric Grip/ Wrist Exercises
Lat pull-down	*Seated Rows
Knee curl	*Stiff Leg Deadlift
Reverse elbow curl	*Arm Curls
*Calf raise	Jump Squats

Abdominal or twisting abdominal exercise for both workouts

Frequency & Approximate Time

* 1 to 2 training sessions per week with at least 1 day separating sessions depending upon match schedule.
* 30–35 minutes per session

Additional Injury-Prevention Exercises

* Internal/External rotator cuff exercises

Additional or Replacement Exercises

* Incline dumbbell bench press
Lunge
* Deadlift

Advanced Exercises

● The trainee performs no more than 3–5 repetitions per set
● Rest should be 2–3 minutes between sets and exercises

In-Season Program Notes

● Format: circuit
● Number of circuits: 1–2 based on schedule

Resistance: Varied for * exercises with 3–5 RM 8–10 RM, and 12–15 RM with undulating periodized model can also be used for multi-joint large muscle group exercises.

Strength Training

Nowhere else in sports is the need for total body strength as evident as it is in wrestling. The ability to push, pull, and stabilize with the upper body and torso and to perform lifts with the body weight of a competitor by using the legs are movements occurring regularly during every 6-minute match. Therefore, strength development should include a variety of exercises that will improve those skills. It is also important to remember that both unilateral and bilateral exercises should be chosen for the program. Compared with circuit resistance training, the rest periods are longer (2–4 minutes) and require heavier loading (6RM and lower). Multi-joint exercises are necessary to develop the strength of the myriad movements integral to wrestling and should be performed with multi-planar actions. Not all the exercises listed below can tolerate 6RM loading and should be considered supplemental lifts to overall strength development. Example exercises would include the following:

- Chest: bench press, incline press, decline press.
- Upper back: lat pull-down, pull-ups, rows.
- Lower back: good morning exercise, deadlift, hyperextensions, thighs, squats, split squats, linear and lateral lunges.
- Hamstrings: stiff-leg deadlift, standing leg curls.
- Arms: arm curls, tricep extensions, wrist curls.
- Small group exercises, wrist curls, etc can be started at the 10–12 RM resistance for variation and range to a lighter resistance 20–22 RM for loading variations.
- Repetitions per set for abdominal exercises: 20 to 30

Other Conditioning Profiles

Plyometric Training

In conjunction with traditional power development using Olympic lifts, plyometric exercises can add another dimension to the improvement of dynamic movements needed in wrestling. Although the intensity of plyometric exercises is not yet clearly established in the literature, exercise progression needs to advance from less challenging (e.g., 2-legged take-off and landing in place) to highly difficult (e.g., 1-legged take-off and landing with rotation). Similar to performing Olympic lifts, plyometric drills must be performed with maximal effort.

It is important to remember that increasing the number of repetitions within a set is not the most appropriate avenue to vary the training load, for the power or velocity of the movement may decrease. Therefore, it is recommended to carefully plan to use higher repetitions only when power endurance is targeted. Both upper- and lower-body plyometric exercises exist, which will benefit wrestling performance. Such exercises include the following:

- Upper body: medicine ball exercises such as the chest pass, scoop toss, and clean toss; plyometric push-ups.
- Lower body: jumps in place, bounds for distance.
- Core: over-unders, dynamic tubing pulls, hip toss.

Injury Prevention and Isometric Training

The ankles, knees, back, shoulders, and neck are typical sites for injury in wrestling. Although many of the exercises prescribed within a wrestling workout will address aspects of injury prevention, specific drills may be added to target specific weaknesses. Loading can be varied (typically moderate to light); however, care must be taken when exercising these areas of the body. Some exercise suggestions include the following:

- Rotator-cuff exercises.
- Neck exercises.
- Core stability and flexibility.
- Isometric bear hug.
- Isometric hand-grip exercises.
- Rope climb.

WEIGHT TRAINING SAFETY FOR YOUNG WRESTLERS

The National Strength and Conditioning Association, and the American Orthopaedic Society for Sports Medicine, and American Academy of Pediatrics all suggest that children can get positive benefits from participation in a properly prescribed and supervised resistance training program. The major benefits are related to:

Young wrestlers can benefit from a resistance training program.

- Increased muscular strength and local muscular endurance (i.e., the ability of a muscle(s) to perform multiple repetitions against a given resistance)
- Decreased injuries in sports & recreational activities
- Improved performance capacity in sports and recreational activities

This is especially important for young wrestlers. While professionals have supported the use of resistance exercise programs in children, they have cautioned parents, teachers, and coaches about the need for proper program design, competent supervision, and correct teaching of exercise techniques. These areas are paramount for safe and effective resistance training programs for children. Some of the benefits (e.g., performance enhancement in preadolescence) (Kraemer and Fleck, 2005) need further study to explain on anecdotal and clinical impressions. However, greater understanding has started to diminish the unrealistic fears about children and resistance training. The need for continuous training may be an important factor when prepubescents participate in resistance training. It is interesting to note that in prepubescents, growth rates are so great that without continued training any strength advantage due to training disappears quickly. After a summer of no training the advantage in strength achieved by resistance training is lost as children naturally become stronger. Such data suggests that continued training may be necessary to gain and keep increased muscle strength in the prepubescent child.

Programs for Younger Wrestlers

The development of a prepubescent resistance training program should follow the same steps as that of a program for adults. However, the following questions also need to be considered prior to having a child begin a resistance training program:

1. Is the child psychologically and physically ready to participate in a resistance exercise training program? Typically if in a wrestling program there is almost a need to help prepare the young wrester's body for the demands of the sport.
2. What resistance training program should the child follow?
3. Are the proper lifting techniques for each exercise in the program understood?
4. Are the safety spotting techniques for each lift in the program understood?
5. Are the safety concerns of each piece of equipment used in the program understood?
6. Does the resistance training equipment "fit" the child properly?
7. Does the child have a balanced physical exercise training program (i.e., participate in cardiovascular activities and other sports in addition to resistance training)

For younger wrestlers the following principles should be used for their weight room training.

1. Find a competent instructor
2. Set realistic goals
3. Wait until the child is ready
4. Warm up and cool down
5. Use spotters
6. Use proper lifting technique
7. Wear appropriate shoes
8. Use only equipment in good condition
9. Don't hyperventilate (breath in and out fast)
10. Don't continue lifting if you feel pain
11. Exercise 3 times per week
12. Don't cheat on your technique to lift heavier weights
13. Don't lift more weight than you can lift safely

SIDEBAR: Strength Training for Young Athletes

Scott Riewald, PhD, CSCS, NSCA-CPT and Keith Cinea, MS, CSCS, NSCA-CPT
National Strength and Conditioning Association Education Department

Introduction

More and more, coaches and parents are asking the question, "When is it safe for my child to start strength training?" Several other questions, such as "What exercises should young athletes perform?" and "How often should they engage in strength training?" quickly follow. This article is designed to shed some light on these, and other, questions and dispel some common 'myths' surrounding youth strength training.

Let's define some terms... So that we are all on the same page, it is important that we define some common terms that will be used throughout this article.

The National Strength and Conditioning Association (NSCA) defines youth as a child who has not yet reached, or is going through, physical maturity. Recognize that not all children progress through puberty at the same time or at the same rate. Three athletes of the same chronological age (i.e. all are 12 years old) can differ by ± two years in biological age (differences with respect to maturity). Even though you have three twelve year olds, maturity wise they can range in age from 10–14.

Strength training is synonymous with the term 'resistance training' and is defined as a specialized form of conditioning that is used to increase one's ability to produce or resist force. Strength training uses the principle of progressive overload to force the body (muscles, bones, tendons, etc.) to adapt in order to be able to produce and/ or resist larger forces. Strength training is not power lifting nor is it bodybuilding or trying to lift the most weight you can. Strength training is a tool that can augment sport performance through improved strength and motor control.

Is youth strength training safe?

The risk of injury is probably the primary concern of any coach or parent who has a child beginning a strength training program. Any exercise or activity carries with it some risk of injury—even a child running in the backyard can suffer an injury. It is unrealistic, therefore, to assume that injuries will never occur. However, this risk of injury can be minimized substantially by following a few simple guidelines. Specifically, appropriate training and competent instruction/ supervision are the two keys to minimizing all injuries.

Both the NSCA and the American Academy of Pediatrics state that youth strength training can be safe and effective if:

- A **competent coach** who is skilled in program design supervises **every** strength training session and,
- Proper technique is taught and required.

Even with this information, several safety concerns still exist. Two of the most common concerns raised by parents and coaches, damage to growth plates and overuse/soft-tissue injuries, are addressed below.

Concern #1: Does strength training damage growth plates in bones?

Most parents and coaches are hesitant to begin strength training with young athletes for fear of damaging the bones and possibly stunting growth. Almost everyone has heard a story of some child experiencing stunted growth after damaging a bone's growth plate from lifting weights. This story could be considered an "urban legend"—a story that everyone has heard, but no one knows if it is in fact true.

Before going any further, let's define the term growth plate. In children, all bone growth occurs at a region of cartilage near the ends of the bone. This region is weaker than 'mature bone' and may be at a greater risk for injury. If the growth plate is damaged there is a chance that growth in the bone will be stunted.

The fact is that no growth plate fractures have been documented in athletes who engage in a resistance training program that includes **"an appropriately prescribed training regimen and competent instruction."** The risk of injury to the growth plates can be further minimized by not allowing the athletes to lift weight over their heads or perform maximum effort lifts (i.e. performing one repetition lifting as much weight as they can). **A general rule of thumb when working with younger athletes is to have them only exercise with weights that they can lift six times or more.** Growth plate injuries should be taken seriously because they can happen. However, with proper care, the risk can be virtually eliminated.

Concern #2: Do overuse injuries occur with strength training?

The potential for repetitive use injuries to the soft tissue (muscle, tendons, ligaments) of the body is another concern for young athletes entering a strength training program. These types of injuries do occur. The majority (40–70 percent) of strength training related soft-tissue injuries are muscles strains with the lower back being the most frequently injured area. Again, these types of injuries can be minimized by following a few simple guidelines:

- Teach the athletes proper technique for each exercise that is performed.
- Supervise every strength training session.
- Do not have the athletes train with maximal or near-maximal loads.
- Avoid using resistive devices that are supposed to improve vertical jump height. These may contribute to injury of the lower back.

Does strength training work for young athletes?

Benefits of Youth Strength Training

- Improved strength and coordination.
- Increased muscle endurance.
- Improved sport performance.
- Increased bone density.
- Improved heath.
- Improved bone strength/ bone density.
- Reduced risk for injury.
- Improved self-image and self-confidence.

Yes, strength training can benefit young athletes. Some of these benefits are highlighted in the accompanying table. Most people believe that testosterone (a steroid produced naturally in the body that plays a role in increased muscle mass and, consequently, increased strength) is necessary to build strength. However, there are also other mechanisms that can produce strength gains. Since young athletes (and female athletes) do not produce large amounts of testosterone the mechanism behind the strength gains differs from what is seen in adults. Resistance training helps to improve motor control and strength by "teaching" muscles how to work together in a coordinated manner. Even within a muscle, strength training helps to synchronize the contraction of individual fibers which leads to improvements in strength without gaining any additional muscle mass. Therefore, do not expect a young athlete to develop much new muscle mass when they begin strength training, since testosterone and other hormones that are required for the building of new muscle mass is not present in large quantities.

Designing a Strength training Program

Probably the best way to introduce athletes to the wonderful world of strength training is to have them perform 'body-weight' exercises. As you might guess, these exercises use the athlete's own body weight as the resistance. These exercises can include:

- Push ups,
- Pull ups,
- Sit ups (crunches, bicycles, etc),
- Back extensions,
- Body weight lunges or squats,
- Step-ups, and
- Dips.

The benefits of these exercises are several-fold. First, this type of exercise is inexpensive and easy to implement. Second, these exercises strengthen the core muscles of the body (the core is defined as the muscles surrounding the body's center of mass—namely the abs, lower back, and hip musculature) that help to stabilize the body. It is important to develop a solid strength base in these muscles before progressing on to more advanced exercises.

The initial goal of any program should be to build some muscular endurance. Start out slowly, initially performing one set of 15 repetitions. As the athletes develop, strive to complete three sets of each exercise, each containing six-15 repetitions, three times a week as part of the regular program. As an athlete matures physically and emotionally, you can begin to introduce more complex exercises (multijoint lifts, free weights, low intensity plyometric as examples) into the program. However, even the most basic multi-joint exercise requires a solid strength base in the body's core musculature to minimize the risk of injury. If strength training is a part of the overall training program, it is important to make it consistent—when strength training is stopped, detraining (a loss of strength and the strength associated benefits) will occur.

Questions to ask before starting a strength training program

There are several questions you should ask yourself (or the strength coach if that is not you) before embarking on a strength training plan for your young athletes.

Is the athlete physically and emotionally mature enough to engage in a strength training program?

As mentioned, you want to start young athletes on a program that centers on muscular endurance and building strength in the core muscles of the body. As an athlete matures, he or she can progress on to more complex exercises, such as multi-joint exercises or lifting free weights. Athletes need to show the maturity, both physical and mental, to advance to these more complex exercises. Keep in mind that athletes of the same 'chronological age' can differ by as much as ± two years physically or mentally. Also keep in mind that females mature as much as two years earlier than males.

If machines or equipment are being used, is it sized appropriately for a young athlete?

Most equipment in strength and conditioning facility will be sized to meet the needs of an adult and not a young athlete. Make sure you can adjust any equipment to the size of the child. If you cannot, then do not perform the exercise until the child "grows into" the equipment. When the need arises for "size appropriate" equipment, dumbbells and most free weights can be used. Dumbbells and free weights allow you to 1) accommodate for differences in the size of the athletes and 2) eliminate the need for purchasing junior/ youth equipment.

Is the program going to be properly run and supervised?

Proper supervision and teaching are essential to running a safe and injury-free strength training program. The NSCA recommends a 1:10 coach to athlete ratio for young athletes. Strength training is more than just throwing a bunch of exercises together; a program should be carefully tailored to the needs of the athlete and the sport.

NSCA's Recommendations for Youth Strength training

- All athletes should be taught proper exercise and spotting technique. Exercises should initially be taught with no load to allow proper technique to be learned.
- All training sessions should be supervised by an experienced fitness professional.
- Each child should be physically and emotionally prepared to participate in a strength training program. Also consider the athlete's maturity level when introducing more advanced exercises.
- Children should have realistic expectations/goals.
- The exercise area should be safe and free from hazards.
- Every exercise session should be preceded by approximately five-10 minutes of a general warm-up, followed by several sport specific warm-up exercises performed at a light intensity.
- Equipment should be properly sized for a child.
- Begin lifting, preferably, with body weight exercises. Athletes can also engage in basic machine exercises if they use light loads that allow the athlete to complete 12–15 repetitions.
- The program should progress to ultimately encourage athletes to perform one-three sets of the exercises on two-three non-consecutive days. Each set should consist of six-15 repetitions.
- Never increase the load being lifted by more than five percent for upper body or 10 percent for lower body exercises.
- Competition between children should be discouraged since this may lead to athletes performing maximum lifts.
- Strength training should be stopped at any sign of injury and the child should be evaluated prior to re-entering the strength program.
- Never force a child to participate in a resistance-training program.
- Keep the program fun.

References

NSCA Quick Series Guide to Weight Training for Kids: A summary of The National Strength and Conditioning Association's Youth Strength Summit. Savannah, GA. July 1999.

American Academy of Pediatrics Committee on Sports Medicine and Fitness, Policy Statement on Strength Training by children and adolescents. *Pediatrics* 107(6): 1470–72. June 2001.

Faigenbaum AD, WJ Kraemer, B Cahill, J Chandler, J Dziados, LD Elfrink, E Forman, M Gaudiose, L Michelli, M Nitka, and S Roberts. Youth resistance training: NSCA Position Statement Paper and Literature Review. Strength and Conditioning 18(6): 62–75. December 1996.

With new weight loss guidelines nation wide it is important that the young wrestler not limit their body mass so as to hinder future growth and development. Resistance training can help the young wrestler attain optimal strength, power and endurance for the sport at a given weight so starvation weight loss practices and using exercise just to cut weight is not recommended for the optimal maturity and growth of the wrestler over time. In a recent study it was shown that years of abusive weight loss practices promotes chronic dehydration and abnormal fluid regulatory systems in both high school and college wrestlers who have undertaken the practice of making dramatic weight cuts prior to each match.

Developmental Differences

Physical and emotional differences in children can be observed. Some children are big, others are smaller. One child may become very upset and another not really concerned about a missed shot in a game. The physical differences are due to different genetic potentials and growth rates. It is important for adults to realize that children are not just "little adults." Furthermore, despite a similar age, all children (e.g., 12 years) are not equal physically or emotionally. Understanding some of the basic principles involved with growth and development will allow the development of more realistic expectations for children. This will also help when developing goals and exercise progressions in resistance training programs. It is important that the exercise program matches the physical and emotional level of the child.

Many aspects are involved in the growth and development of a child. It is not based on one single factor such as height. Many factors influence fitness gains including genetic potential, nutrition and sleep.

Maturation has been defined as the progress toward adulthood. Several areas can be considered when examining the maturation of the child.

- Physical size
- Bone maturity
- Reproductive maturity
- Emotional maturity

Each of these areas can be clinically evaluated. It is common for the family physician to make various assessments as to the development of a child in these areas. Each individual has a chronological age and a physiological age. It is the physiological age which is the most important and determines the functional capabilities and performance for that person and this should be considered when developing a resistance program.

Designing Individualized Resistance Training Programs for Children

The design of the total conditioning program, as well as the resistance program, should consider the following needs of all children.

1. Conditioning of all fitness components.
2. Balanced choice of exercises for the upper and lower body development.
3. Balanced exercise choice for muscles on both sides of each joint.
4. Use of body part as well as structural exercises.

After the needs analysis, but before beginning a resistance training program, children, like all individuals, should be examined by a physician. This is to insure awareness of any physical problems present that need to be considered in the design of the program. For example, if a child has Osgood-Schlatter disease, exercises involving extreme bending of the knee may be contraindicated. The child should begin with a basic resistance training program which exercises all the major muscle groups of the body and muscles around each joint of the body. Warm-up and flexibility exercises should be performed prior to and after each training session. Additional sports specific exercises and exercises based on individual need can be added to the program after the child has learned basic lifting techniques. Individualizing a program requires considering the strengths, weaknesses, and goals of each lifter.

General fitness requires training of all major muscle groups. Successful performance of a particular sport skill is dependent upon the strength and power of particular muscle groups and not the gender of the participant. This is true for adults as well as children. Programs designed for collegiate or professional athletes should not be performed by prepubescents or pubescents. The ability of these athletes to improve in strength using these programs is in part due to their years of resistance training experience. Many times, these programs involve lifting very heavy resistances (1–3 RM) which as previously discussed, may result in injury to prepubescents. Again, resistances should not go heavier then a 6 RM (See Kraemer and Fleck, 2005). Forcing prepubescents or pubescents to perform programs designed for mature gifted athletes will overstress prepubescents and may result in injury, over use, or over training phenomenon.

SUMMARY

Conditioning programs for wrestling must address the different features of the sport demands. Strength and power are important as well as the ability to produce these forces under extreme fatigue. Proper weight management is vital to the training success of the wrestler. The ability to buffer acid in the muscle and blood is important and requires conditioning programs in the weight room that address this before one takes the mat to improve performance and prevent injury. Younger wrestlers must develop the toleration to any conditioning program gradually including wrestling practice itself. Proper periodization of the resistance training program is also vital for conditioning success. Ultimately the development of a resistance training conditioning program is one that has multiple components in it and integrates it over the different phases of the season with proper rest and recovery allowed. A scientific approach to the resistance training program can help to develop a wrestler's potential for success on the mat.

16
Optimal Performance Weight

Eileen Bowker

QUESTIONS TO CONSIDER
- What is the lowest allowable percent body fat for a high school wrestler?
- How can a proper wrestling weight be determined?
- What is the best recommended way to lose weight?
- What is the recommended percent ratio of protein, carbohydrates, and fat in a wrestlers' diet?

INTRODUCTION

Wrestling is a sport defined by the existence of weight classes. Although the intent of the weight classes is to equalize competition by limiting body weight differences among competitors, health problems associated with attempts by wrestlers to rapidly lose weight have attracted the attention of professional organizations. Exercise science research has repeatedly demonstrated that rapid weight loss can also adversely affect athletic performance.

In 1997, three collegiate wrestlers tragically died while engaging in unsafe weight loss practices. Billy Jack Saylor, 19 of Campbell University, died of a heart attack, Joe LaRosa, 22 of the University of Wisconsin-LaCrosse and Jeff Reese, 21, of the University of Michigan both died by metabolic derangement. These deaths demanded that parents, coaches, Certified Athletic Trainers and physicians evaluate weight certification, weight maintenance and nutritional habits of youth, high school, college and Olympic wrestling programs. The NCAA made immediate changes to rules specific to weight cutting, weigh ins and weight classes.

The National Federation of State High School Associations (NFHS) Medical Advisory Committee released a strong recommendation suggesting that all 50 state high school athletic associations should have a comprehensive weight management program in place. These new rule changes and policies have brought about a much needed change in the sport of wrestling.

BACKGROUND

It has been speculated by historians that wrestling began either as a means of survival, a test of courage or a demonstration of supremacy. The sport has evolved into many forms. Its history is easily traced to the dawn of mankind.

As the sport evolved, weight classes were instituted. Unfortunately, traditionally this has meant an excess (>5% of an athlete's total weight) loss of fat early in the season. However, weight classifications provide the structure for safe and equitable competition.

The NFHS core requirements for weight management in wrestling should consist of the following:

1. Hydration testing
2. Body Composition Assessment
3. Establishment of a lowest allowable weight class for each wrestler
4. Establishment of a weight loss plan for each wrestler
5. Establishment of a nutrition education program specific to wrestling

The National Wrestling Coaches Association has developed an Optimal Performance Calculator—OPC that enables programs to meet these needs.

Weight certification is a very individual process. It is the wrestler that needs to know where he or she will be the most effective. The lowest weight possible is not always the strongest.

HYDRATION TESTING

There are many different ways to assess hydration in wrestlers. One of the easiest and most practical methods is to measure the specific gravity of urine. Urine specific gravity is elevated whenever there has been excessive loss of water through sweating, vomiting, diarrhea or elevated body temperature. Thus the higher the urine specific gravity number the more dehydrated the wrestler is.

The two most commonly used methods to assess urine specific gravity are reagent strips and refractometer. Both methods are acceptable measures of urine specific gravity, however refractometry is considered the gold standard.

An athlete must be hydrated in order to undergo the body composition assessment. Generally a specific gravity of 1.020 is acceptable.

BODY COMPOSITION ASSESSMENT

Because most interscholastic wrestlers are experiencing growth, the selection of a weight class should be determined with the assistance of body composition analysis. Although methods for assessing body composition have been available for years, their use has not been widely accepted or employed. This state of affairs is changing.

There are several methods to determine percent body fat. Underwater weighing is considered most accurate, but is not easily available. Skin Calipers that use folds of skin from several body positions that are measured and then put into mathematical calculations are commonly used. Newer to the sport are bioimpedance scales that send waves through the skin and measure fat and hydration levels and Air Displacement units. It is important to monitor percentages so that a wrestler does not become under fat.

At the present time, Lohman's skinfold equation appears to be most desirable and practical for use in mass testing because its total error of measurement is the lowest of the anthropometric equations evaluated for use with Caucasian interscholastic wrestlers. Regardless of the method of equation used, it is essential that wrestlers have their body fat percentages determined before the season begins and before they initiate any program to make or maintain body weight. It is recommended that wrestlers under 16 years of age maintain at least 7% body fat, while older wrestlers may drop to 5%.

Seven percent body fat is considered the *lowest* healthy level of fat content for teenage males. Fifteen percent for females. Body fat measurements can help you determine how much fat you can lose in order to drop to 7%. Keep in mind that 7% is not a magic number. It is just a guideline to follow. Most wrestlers perform very well at a higher percentage of body fat. So, if you are now 10% body fat, there is no reason to believe that you'll wrestle better at 7% body fat. Many health care professionals will be able to help you determine your minimal wrestling weight.

The goal of safe weight loss is to *lose excess fat weight*. Not all fat on your body can be considered "excess" fat. A certain amount of fat is essential for use as energy, to act as a shock absorber for your internal organs, to insulate your body from the cold, and to store certain nutrients.

MANAGING WEIGHT

There are more than a few factors to consider when deciding the "best" wrestling weight, but the most important is: How much weight can you safely lose and still perform well? The weight class you choose should not be so low that you have to sacrifice good nutrition for the sake of making weight. In addition to the adverse physical effects of trying to cut too much weight, unhealthy weight loss practices affect you psychologically; the more you worry about your weight, the less you concentrate on your wrestling. Here is how to determine your "minimum" safe weight for competition.

Weight control presents one of wrestling's greatest challenges. Wrestling's good name has been tainted by ill-advised weight loss practices. Historically, wrestlers have severely restricted their food intake while exercising strenuously each day. The end result was a state of semi starvation. This semi-starvation results in muscular weakness, lethargy and inability to concentrate. Dehydration is/was used to shed the last few pounds to reach a desired weight class.

Research has demonstrated over and over again that rapid weight loss is detrimental to physiological (the inside of the body) function and individual performance requirements of wrestling. Rapid weight loss through semi-starvation actually breaks down muscle. Dehydration decreases strength and muscular endurance and increases the risk of heat illnesses.

Since the NCAA rule changes in 1998 scientists have reported that the new rules are achieving the desired result. There has been a significant decrease in weight cutting of college wrestlers and a decrease in the amount of rapid regain. It is believed the the domination of rule changes and the education of the student athlete have had a positive effect on the sport.

"Wrestling is better today than it ever was. Don't let any old timer tell you different," said John Smith, Oklahoma State University head coach, 6 time world champion while he was addressing the new weight rules to coaches at the USA Wrestling Silver Clinic in Ohio, June 2001.

Wrestling is beginning to see wrestlers compete closer to their natural body weight. This is evident at the college level and should begin to occur at the high school level.

NUTRITION

Nutrition is one component in the training of wrestlers in which most people are mis-informed or misunderstood. The sport is plagued with stories of rapid weight loss and miracle diets. This information is generally passed from wrestler to wrestler and is misleading and dangerous. A wrestler must take the time to learn the facts about diet and dietary habits in order to achieve their Optimal Performance Weight.

A competitive athlete approaches food as the fuel for their workout and their matches. There are three focal points in maintaining Optimal Performance Weight and meeting nutritional needs. The three points are:

1. A balanced diet at a sustaining caloric level.
2. Adequate fluid intake.
3. A high energy output to attain and maintain an optimal performance.

THE WRESTLER'S DIET

A diet is simply the food that you eat. Food provides nutrients to fuel the body. However, the scientific facts are simple: poor nutrition will hamper performance. The body cannot function at its best when it lacks vital nutrients. Consider these points.

- To grow naturally and increase strength, wrestlers need the same nutrients as other teenagers, but need *more* calories to meet the demands of daily training.
- Fasting causes the body to use muscle proteins for energy even if fat is available. This limits muscle growth and strength development.
- A proper diet will help wrestlers lose fat weight without sacrificing muscle tissue or becoming dehydrated.
- Dehydration is a major cause of losses in strength and endurance.
- Losing weight *rapidly* results in a loss of both muscle tissue and water.
- Losing weight *gradually* (2–3 lbs/week) is the best way to lose fat and keep muscle.
- Proper training includes practicing proper nutrition *every day.*
- Practicing good nutrition and proper weight control methods is vital to achieving peak physical performance.

SIDEBAR: Something to chew on

Ted Witulski/USA Wrestling

With the start of every high school season, there is always renewed interest in nutrition. Whether the focus is on dropping to a lower weight or staying strong through a proper diet, wrestlers always have many questions on what they should eat.

Judy Nelson, Nutrition Coordinator for the United States Olympic Committee helps America's elite athletes achieve success at the highest levels of competition. USA Wrestling's coaching staff relies on her expertise on a regular basis. Her suggestions should be high priorities for wrestlers and coaches trying to establish proper nutrition in a daily diet.

Step one: Switch to skim

Switching to skim milk can make a dramatic difference in caloric and fat intake for any individual. In an eight ounce glass of reduced fat 2% milk there is 122 calories with 4.7 grams of fat. In low fat 1% milk, there is 102 calories and 2.5 grams of fat. A wrestler that switches to skim milk takes in 86 calories and .4 grams of fat per eight ounce glass.

Clearly there is a benefit in switching over to skim milk. An eight ounce glass is generally smaller than what most people consume in a sitting these days. So, the benefit can be even further magnified.

Step two: Lots of fruit

In speaking to Ms Nelson about the importance of fruit in a diet, she sees benefits varying from fruit to fruit. "Bananas and oranges are very important because of the Vitamin C they provide. Melons are high in Vitamin A and blueberries are also great." So, when adding fruit to a diet variety can be an important factor to consider.

Step three: Juice over pop

Pop provides nothing of value for a wrestler's body to run off of. There are no nutrients to digest. Further, youthful consumers have gotten hooked on oversized drinks. A wrestler should definitely consider the numbers before they grab a soda. Eight ounces of pop has about 140 calories. The "average" pop serving has increased in size, with many people drinking as much as 24 ounces of pop in one sitting. Using a caloric intake of 4200 calories a day, 24 ounces of pop would be 420 calories or nearly 20 percent of the energy intake for the day. Throw in the fact that it has no nutritional value, coaches and wrestlers should see that fruit juice is a much better beverage to reach for.

Step four: Baked Potatoes

Baked potatoes are an easily prepared food that should become a staple in a wrestler's diet. Don't forget to eat the skin though. According to Nelson, the baked potato has almost no fat and a minimal amount of sodium with a good supply of complex carbohydrates.

Of course a wrestler's nutritional training can run afoul if the potato is loaded down with condiments like butter and sour cream. A wrestling secret in eating a potato is adding water to the potato. Wrestlers know that baked potatoes can be dry, so the best thing to do is re-hydrate it. After breaking it open and smashing it with a fork pour a little more water on it and it won't taste as dry.

Step five: Maintain variety

Once again Judy Nelson's nutritional point is very simple. "No one food has everything a wrestler needs." Variety in food, even in a specific food group is important. Don't rely on one food, to supply all of the vitamins and nutrients needed for day to day health. Remove the junk from the diet, but maintain variety.

Step six: Lots of water

Staying properly hydrated is difficult for the average person. For an active athlete it can be very hard to stay hydrated without a conscious effort. Nelson offers that fluid needs can be estimated at 1 milliliter per calorie. So in a 3000 calorie a day diet an individual would need to consume three liters of fluid.

Generally speaking water is overlooked as an important part of good nutrition. One old standard is 64 ounces of water consumption a day. Although Nelson states that this is not very scientific, it is probably well above what most wrestlers are consuming daily. Clearly wrestlers work hard and perspire significantly so wrestlers should work to replace the lost fluid. Water replacement is a critical part of a nutritional plan for a wrestler.

Step seven: The secret of egg whites

Wrestlers need to understand where hunger pains come from. Foods that are high in sugar, for example, are broken down quickly after consumption. So, while a candy bar might taste good, its satisfaction is limited because it is broken down before other foods that contain higher amounts of protein.

If wrestlers want to maintain a fuller feeling for a longer duration they need to look to having a diet with good protein. Egg whites are a common source of quality protein. Additionally, egg whites contain no fat. Throw the yolk away, that's a whole other topic.

Wrestlers can prepare egg whites easily by boiling up a dozen eggs and storing them in the refrigerator. Egg whites contain about 3.5 grams of protein each. Encourage wrestlers to make use of this source of protein.

Step eight: High fiber is highly important

Again variety is certainly important for wrestlers focusing on proper nutrition. Fiber is one part of a good daily diet. Judy Nelson encourages wrestlers to make a high fiber cereal part of their daily food consumption. Cereals like All Bran and breads can be good sources of fiber. In checking the nutrition panel on cereal or bread try to find a product that has at least three grams of fiber per serving. Don't be deceived by the packaging or the name, make sure to check the nutritional outline.

Step Nine: Don't rely on meat

Protein is a highly important element for good nutrition for athletes. But a person does not have to rely only on meat to get good sources of protein. There are many soy -based products and dairy products that can work just as well as red meat does for protein. Wrestlers should consider trying legumes such as black beans and pinto beans as protein sources. Again variety can help in nutrition and make it easier to maintain a positive outlook when a person watches what they eat.

Step Ten: Plan for after the weigh-in

Wrestlers after making weight need to focus on foods that will help recover and won't adversely effect performance. Foods with fat are definitely slower digesting. Carbohydrates can be easier on a wrestler's stomach. Foods like applesauce, crackers, and cereal can be easily digested and aid in recovery. After making weight don't let a lapse in judgement effect your performance, plan ahead and shoot for smaller portions spread throughout the tournament day.

Reaching a high level of achievement requires mental focus on all aspects of a wrestler's performance. Proper nutrition can be an area that can really help a wrestler attain their goals. Of course being a wrestler, in a junk food culture will hold anyone back. So, please take the ten simple suggestions to heart. Make use of the same nutritional training that athletes in the Olympics rely on.

FOOD GROUPS

Wrestlers can achieve a balanced diet by eating foods from the four basic food groups. The training table guidelines listed below indicate the minimum number of servings from each food group for each day. The menus in Supplement A are consistent with these recommendations.

- **Meat Group**: This group includes high protein foods: meats, poultry, fish, eggs, legumes (such as dry beans and lentils), and nuts. Choose lean meats, fish, and poultry (without skin) to help keep your fat intake low. Remember to keep portion sizes moderate.
- **Dairy Group**: This group is rich in protein, calcium, and other nutrients needed for healthy bones and muscles. Choose products labeled "low-fat" or "non-fat" to get the full nutritional value without the extra fat calories found in whole milk products.
- **Fruit/Vegetable Group**: This group includes all fresh, frozen, canned, and dried fruits and vegetables and juices. This food group is loaded with vitamins and minerals and fiber. Foods in this group are mostly composed of carbohydrates.
- **Grain Group**: This group is the main source of complex carbohydrates and fiber. It includes grains such as oats, rice, and wheat, and the breads, cereals, noodles, and pasta made from them.

Calories

A "calorie" is a unit used to describe the energy content of foods. Your body requires energy, and the food you eat supplies that energy. When you take in more food calories than you use, those extra calories are stored as fat, and you gain weight. Weight loss occurs when you consume fewer calories than you use. This causes your body to utilize its stored fat for energy, and you lose weight as a result. Losing weight gradually helps assure that mostly fat will be lost. Losing weight too quickly will cause you to lose muscle and water in addition to fat, sapping your strength and endurance in the process. Gradual weight loss is best accomplished by combining your training with a *slight reduction (500 calories per day)* in food intake. Remember, your body requires a certain amount of energy and nutrients just to keep you alive and healthy.

For this reason, *your caloric intake should not fall below 1,700–2,000 calories per day*. If you decrease your intake below this your body will not allow you to lose weight.

In planning your diet, it will be helpful to estimate how many calories you need each day. Caloric needs differ from wrestler to wrestler depending upon body size and activity level. You can estimate the minimum number of calories you need each day by using the graph in Figure 16-1. Supplement A contains examples of **2,000 calorie menus** to help you plan your diet. Supplement B can help you plan to eat wisely at fast-food restaurants.

Training Table Guidelines

Group	Minimum Servings/Day	Serving Sizes
Meat	2	2–4 oz. cooked meat (total 5–7 oz./day)
Milk	4	1 cup
Fruit/Vegetable	4	1/2 cup cooked 1 cup raw 1 med. size piece fruit 1/2 cup juice
Grain	4–6	1 slice bread 1 cup cereal 1/2 cup pasta

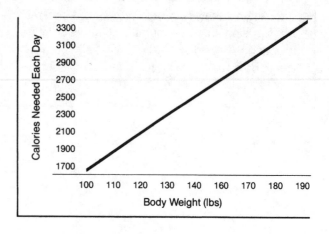

Figure 16-1. Determine the minimum number of calories for your goal weight.

Nutrients

Your body depends upon a constant supply of nutrients to keep it functioning. There are six essential groups of nutrients your body needs every day: water, carbohydrates, protein, fats, vitamins, and minerals. These nutrients work together to build and fuel your body.

Hydration

The most important nutrient for any athlete is water. Your body is 60–70% water. Water is absolutely essential for optimal health and peak performance. It is well documented that maintaining hydration is critical for optimal performance. You may be surprised to know that dehydration is a major cause of decreased performance. Some wrestlers are more sensitive to dehydration than others. A fluid loss of 2–3% of your weight can quickly occur during intense training. Even modest levels of dehydration should be avoided because dehydration harms performance.

It is important to drink plenty of fluid during practice and between matches. Not only will you feel better, but you may also find you have more endurance. During physical activity, thirst is not an adequate signal of the need for fluid. Follow the fluid guidelines listed below:

- Weigh-in before and after training to monitor fluid loss. Drink two cups of fluid for every pound of body weight lost.
- Remind athletes to drink plenty of water or other appropriate beverages.
- Hydrate before and after exercise.
- Make cool beverages available to athletes during and after practice.
- A fluid replacement sports drink with 6–8% carbohydrate is ideal for replenishing fluids.
- Have athletes note the color of their urine. When properly hydrated urine should be pale yellow.
- Avoid beverages containing alcohol and caffeine, as they promote dehydration.

Carbohydrates

Carbohydrates are the main food source of energy for your body and should make up 55–65% of the total calories you consume.

There are two forms of carbohydrates—starches (complex carbohydrates) and sugar (simple carbohydrates). When you consume carbohydrates they are changed to a simple sugar called glucose. This occurs during digestion. Glucose is the body's main source of energy. If there is an excess of glucose, the body converts it to glycogen and stores it for later use. Excellent sources of carbohydrates include breads, pasta, cereals, fruits, and vegetables. If you do not eat enough carbohydrates you will not have energy.

Fats

Everyone needs a little fat in their diets, and wrestlers are no exception. Fat should make up about 20–30% of the calories you consume. Fat helps the body store vitamins A, D, E, and K. Most of the fat we consume is naturally found in foods (meats, nuts, and dairy products) or added during the preparation of food (e.g. fried foods). Sources of additional fat include margarine, peanut butter, and salad dressings.

Proteins

Protein is used for growth and repair of all the cells in your body. Proteins also help regulate the bodies' fluid balance. Good sources of protein are meat, fish, and poultry. Many plant foods, like beans and nuts, are good protein sources too. However, nuts are also high in fat and should be eaten only in small quantities. Your diet should provide 12–15% of its calories as protein.

Vitamins and Minerals

If you eat a balanced diet from the four basic food groups, you will consume all the vitamins and minerals your body needs. Including ample portions of fresh fruits and vegetables in your diet will help ensure an adequate intake of vitamins and minerals. Vitamin and mineral supplements are usually unnecessary, but if you like to have the added "insurance" of taking a supplement, choose a vitamin and mineral supplement that does not exceed 100% of the Recommended Daily Allowance (RDA) for each nutrient.

Eating Before Training or Competition

When you eat can often be as important as *what* you eat before competition and between matches in a tournament. When you eat a regular meal, it takes about three hours for the food to be completely digested and absorbed. As a result, meals are best eaten three to four hours before competition. A properly-formulated sports drink can be consumed before, during, and following training or competition to help minimize dehydration and provide a source of energy to working muscles.

SUMMARY

Research has shown that practicing proper methods of weight control are essential to maximizing your athletic performance. Peak physical performance can only occur when the body is supplied with an adequate amount of essential nutrients. Using improper methods of weight control will decrease your level of performance. The Wrestler's Diet provides the necessary information to help you achieve the highest level of performance possible. The psychological advantages of maintaining good nutritional practices are great: you'll wrestle better if you feel good physically and mentally. You will also wrestle better knowing that you have done *everything* possible to be at your best.

In order to not just survive, but to thrive as a sport, we must say goodbye to the days of the sauna, sweat boxes, rubber suits and the semi-starved state of participation. Maintaining Optimal Performance Weight is the victory off the mat.

SUPPLEMENT A: Sample Menus and Snacks (2,000 Calories)

Breakfast

Blender Drink
Banana, 1	100
Milk, 1 cup 2%	120
Peanut Butter, 1t	95
Toast, 1 slice	70
Jam, 1t	15
Calories	**400**

Lunch

Hamburger on Bun
Bun	120
Grnd Beef, 2 oz	120
Catsup, 1T	20
French Fries	220
Milk, 1 cup 2%	120
Oatmeal Raisin Cookies (2) (2½" diameter)	120
Calories	**760**

Dinner

Roast Pork, 3 oz.
Roast Pork, 3 oz.	220
Baked Potato	100
Broccoli, 1 stalk	20
Margarine, 2t	70
Bread, 1 slice	70
Sliced peaches, 1 cup	130
Milk, 1 cup 2%	120
Calories	**730**

Snack
Lo-cal Pudding, 1 cup	130
Total Calories	**2020**

Breakfast
Grapefruit juice, 6 oz.	75
Unsweetened Cereal, 1 cup	110
Banana, 1 medium	100
Milk, 1 cup 2%	120
Toast, 1 slice	70
Margarine, 1t	35
Jam, 1t	15
Calories	**525**

Lunch

Chicken Salad Sandwich
Bread, 2 slices	140
Chicken Breast, 2 oz.	120
Lo Cal Dressing, 1T	30
Milk, 1 cup 2%	120
Apple, 1 medium	80
Calories	**490**

Dinner
Chili, 2 cups	600
Saltine Crackers, 12	160
Milk, 1 cup 2%	120
Carrot & Celery Sticks	10
Calories	**890**

Snack
Frozen Yogurt, 4 oz.	120
Total Calories	**2025**

Breakfast
Apple Juice, 6 oz.	90
Oatmeal, 1 cup	145
Raisins, 1T	30
Milk, 1 cup 2%	120
Toast, 1 slice	70
Margarine	35
Calories	**490**

Lunch

"Sloppy Joe"
Hamburger Filling, 2 oz.	200
Bun	140
Carrot & Celery Sticks	10
Milk, 1 cup 2%	120
Chocolate Chip Cookie, 1 small	50
Calories	**520**

Dinner

Turkey Tacos
Taco Shells, 3	210
Picante Sauce, 2 oz.	30
American Cheese, 4 oz. shredded	220
Ground Turkey, 4 oz.	310
Lettuce, Onion, Tomato, etc.	10
Milk, 1 cup 2%	120
Calories	**900**

Snack
Orange, 1 medium	80
Total Calories	**1990**

Breakfast

Orange Juice, 6 oz.	80
English Muffin	140
Peanut Butter, 1T	90
Banana, 1 medium	100
Milk, 1cup 2%	120
Calories	**530**

Breakfast

French Toast, 2 slices	300
Syrup, 2 oz.	200
Strawberries, 4 oz., unsweetened	25
Milk, 1 cut 2%	120
Calories	**645**

Breakfast

Cantaloupe, ¼	60
Egg, poached	75
Toast, 2 slices	140
Margarine, 1t	35
Jam, 2t	30
Milk, 1 cup 2%	120
Calories	**460**

Lunch

Cheese Pizza, 2 slices	400
Milk, 1 cup 2%	120
Apple, 1 medium	80
Calories	**600**

Lunch

Turkey Sandwich	
Bread, 2 slices	140
Turkey Breast, 3 oz.	105
Lettuce, Tomato Slices	5
Lo-cal Mayonnaise, 1T	30
Milk, 1 cup 2%	120
Calories	**400**

Lunch

Tuna Pocket	
Pita Bread, 1	120
Tuna, 3 oz.	100
Lo-cal Mayonnaise, 2T	60
Lettuce, tomato slices	5
Pretzels, 1 oz.	110
Milk, 1 cup 2%	120
Calories	**515**

Dinner

Chicken & Noodles, 1 cup	300
Cooked Carrots, ½ cup	25
Lettuce Salad	10
Dressing, 1T	60
Milk, 1 cup 2%	120
Calories	**515**

Dinner

Beef Stew, 2 cups	400
Dinner Roll, 1	70
Margarine, 1t	35
Applesauce, 4 oz.	55
Milk, 1 cup 2%	120
Lo-cal Pudding, 1 cup	130
Vanilla Wafers, 6	100
Calories	**910**

Dinner

Broiled Turkey Breast, 3 oz.	130
Wild Rice Pilaf, 1 cup	270
Spinach Salad	15
Dressing, 1T	60
Angel Food Cake, 1 slice	125
Chocolate Syrup, 2T	75
Milk, 1 cup 2%	120
Calories	**795**

Snack

Milk, 1 cup 2%	120
Fig Bars, 5	250
Calories	**370**

Snack

Popcorn, 2 cups, no butter	60
Diet Soda, 12 oz.	0
Calories	**60**

Snack

Pineapple, 1 cup	150
Graham Crackers, 3 squares	80
Calories	**230**

Total Calories	**2015**

Total Calories	**2015**

Total Calories	**2000**

SUPPLEMENT B: Eating Out Wisely

You can maintain your training diet when eating at a restaurant if you are careful about what you order. Pay attention to how foods are prepared. Choose food that is baked, broiled, boiled, or poached. Avoid food that is breaded, fried, or served in gravy. Limit your use of butter, margarine, mayonnaise, sour cream, cream cheese, and regular salad dressings. Instead, use barbeque sauce, ketchup, mustard, relish, and vegetables for toppings. Do not be afraid to ask for food served "your way"; ask for extra vegetables in sandwiches or on pizza, skip the extra cheese or extra meat, request skim or 2% milk, and specify the toppings you want.

When you know you will be eating out, carefully choose low-fat foods for your other meals that day. Also, take along your own fresh fruit to munch on after the meal instead of ordering desserts.

When eating a meal at a fast food restaurant, don't make it a dietary disaster. A typical fast food meal is high in fat and low in calcium, vitamin C, and vitamin A. It is difficult to choose a high-carbohydrate meal at a fast food restaurant. Beware or you can eat half of your caloric allotment in one meal. Satisfy your hunger and nutritional needs by using the menus listed as guidelines. For a higher carbohydrate diet, order additional servings of the food items in bold.

	Calories	Protein	Carbo-hydrate	Fat
Breakfasts				
McDonald's				
Plain English muffin (2)	747	17%	56%	25%
Strawberry jam (1 packet)				
Scrambled egg (1)				
Orange juice (6 ounces)				
2% milk (1 carton)				
or Hot Cakes with butter* and ½ syrup packet	650	11%	66%	25%
Orange juice (6 ounces)				
2% milk (1 carton)				
*If still hungry, recommend ordering plain english muffin.				
Family Style Restaurant (Perkins, Village Inn)				
Buttermilk pancakes 5" (3)	761	12%	67%	20%
Butter (1 pat)				
Egg (1)				
Syrup (3 tablespoons)				
Orange juice (6 ounces)				
Usually comes with two eggs. Order one instead. Poached, soft- or hard-boiled is recommended.				
or *Cold Cereal* with 2% milk (4 ounces)	668	15%	58%	26%
Egg (1)				
English muffin				
Butter (1 pat)				
Jelly (1 packet)				
Orange juice (4 ounces)				
Lunch/Dinner				
McDonald's				
Chicken sandwich with BBQ sauce	677	23%	51%	25%
Side salad				
½ packet low-calorie vinegar and oil dressing				
Orange juice (6 ounces)				
2% milk (1 carton)				

	Calories	Protein	Carbo-hydrate	Fat
Lunch/Dinner				
Wendy's				
Chicken breast sandwich on multigrain bread (no mayonnaise)	719	22%	53%	25%
Baked potato				
Sour cream (1 packet)				
2% milk				
or Chili (8 ounces)	1,016	16%	57%	25%
Baked potato, plain				
Frosty (small)				
Side salad: ¼ cup lettuce, ¼ cup fresh veggies, ¼ cup cottage cheese				
Arby's				
Jr. Roast Beef on multigrain bread with lettuce and tomato (no mayonnaise or horseradish)	695	22%	51%	27%
Side salad*				
2% milk				
or Arby's Regular Roast Beef or ham and cheese sandwich	970	20%	52%	30%
Side salad*				
Vanilla shake				
*½ cup lettuce, 1 cup fresh veggies, ½ cup garbanzo beans, ¼ cup cottage cheese, 2 tablespoons low-calorie dressing				
Taco Bell				
2 tostadas*	1,040	18%	56%	27%
1 bean burrito				
2 plain tortillas				
2% milk				
or 1 tostada*	1,105	18%	55%	28%
2 bean burritos				
1 plain tortilla				
2% milk				
or 3 tostadas*	785	19%	53%	28%
1 plain tortilla				
2% milk				
*If possible, ask that tostada shell be plain, not fried.				
Pizza Hut*				
Large Spaghetti with meat sauce	1,023	19%	61%	20%
Breadsticks				
2% milk				
or ½ medium onion, green pepper and cheese pizza (thin crust)	1,126	20%	55%	25%
2 breadsticks				
2% milk				
*Pizza Hut does have a salad bar.				
Family Style Restaurant (Perkins, Village Inn)				
Baked fish	1,100	25%	51%	23%
Baked potato with sour cream (1 tablespoon)				
1 muffin				
Salad bar (1 cup lettuce)				
2% milk (8 ounces)				
Sherbet (½ cup)				

17
Prevention of Common Sports Injuries

Eileen Bowker

QUESTIONS TO CONSIDER

- What effect can warm-ups, cool downs, and conditioning have on preventing injuries?
- How can facilities be made safer for wrestling?
- What role does teaching wrestlers safety, appropriate sport techniques, and proper drills have in injury prevention?
- What injury prevention techniques can be implemented over the course of a season?

A thorough warm-up prior to wrestling practice will help to decrease possible injuries.

INTRODUCTION

Most sport involves the application of large muscular forces and physical contact at all levels of competition. All of the muscular force and physical contact cannot be eliminated from sport. However, if you follow several steps aimed at preventing injuries, you can make athletics safer.

As a coach, you are responsible for doing everything reasonable to allow participants to compete in an environment that is healthy and safe.

AVOIDING NEEDLESS INJURIES

It is our responsibility to have the usual safety mechanisms in place:

1. Set policies and procedures for practices and competition
2. Safety check of facilities and equipment
3. Selection of age appropriate activities
4. Proper warm up, flexibility and conditioning programs
5. An emergency action plan
6. Completed health history forms
7. Emergency numbers and Medical Release forms in the first aid kit

These are some of the areas of concern that usually come to our attention as we approach the season.

A proper warm-down consisting of thorough stretching and massage will facilitate a strong and injury free body.

SET POLICIES AND PROCEDURES FOR PRACTICES AND COMPETITION

Communicating with the parents of your athletes at the start of the season is imperative to avoid miscommunication and establish policies and procedures. For example children should never be left unattended. Parents should not leave their athlete at practice unless a coach or staff person has arrived. Also they should be on time to pick their child up after an event. Do you have permission to transport a child? Do you take daily attendance? Who should the parent inform if there has been an injury that has not been reported? Take time to establish these and other procedures and you should have good communication throughout the season.

SAFETY CHECK OF FACILITIES AND EQUIPMENT

Next let us consider the rooms-wrestling area (cafeteria, stage, pool balcony), the gymnasium (for sprints and endurance runs), the shower and locker room. All of these areas must be considered or we will lose athletes for short periods of time from "needless injuries." It goes without saying that the areas should be safe, but what does that actually mean? What kinds of concerns need to be considered?

The Wrestling Room

A wrestling mat should be in good condition. It should have a smooth firm surface, free of holes or cracks. Mat tape should be used to keep the mats from separating. Walls, bleachers or any area surrounding the wrestling mat should also be padded for safety.

Mats should be disinfected daily before and after practice to decrease the growth of infectious diseases. When possible mats should be stored flat or allowed to dry completely before being stored.

Wondering what to do with the old mats or the competition mat? Before you spend $4,000 on a mat storage device, consider putting one mat under the other. They stay flat and the shock absorbency can aid in the reduction of contusion and compression injuries. Protect the underside of matting with corn starch and talcum powder when placing mats against mats and mats over floor tile. This must be done to protect the mat surface. Rubber floor mats or even plywood (especially supported by 2 x 4's) will offer some additional shock absorbency.

The Shower Room

We need to be aware that a major defense against the contraction of disease is personal hygiene. Make sure the wrestlers shower immediately after practice and that they use soap which has the ability to attack the source of the problem. They must wash their hands, especially under the fingernail area, and all the other cracks and crevices on their body with soap and lots of hot water. Check out the shower room—do you have soap available? Is it the type they use to get under their fingernails? Is it the kind that is strong enough to attack the typical infectious agents that collect around the mat and on our bodies?

AGE APPROPRIATE ACTIVITIES

The instructions you provide during practices on how to perform specific sport skills have an influence on the risks of injuries to your athletes and their opponents. Teach your athletes the proper ways to perform specific techniques, and *never* teach athletes how to intentionally foul opponents. An improper technique often results in a greater chance of injury to the performer than does the correct technique. Acceptable techniques in sports usually evolve with safety as a concern.

You should promote fair and safe participation in practices and contests with strict enforcement of the rules to encourage skill as the primary factor in determining the outcome.

Drills that you select or design for your practices and the ways in which they are carried out have an influence on the risks of injuries to your athletes. Drills should be selected and designed with safety as a primary feature. Before implementing a new drill into your practice, several safety questions should be considered.

1. Is the drill appropriate for the level of maturation of the athletes?
2. Are the athletes sufficiently skilled to comply with the requirements of the drill?
3. Are the athletes sufficiently conditioned to handle the stress of participation in the drill?
4. Are other, less risky drills available to achieve the same practice results?
5. Can the drill be modified to make it less risky and yet achieve the desired training result?

Equipment and Apparel

A properly equipped and attired athlete is less likely to be injured. Therefore, it is important that you develop a list of essential equipment for your specific sport and distribute this information to your athletes and their parents. Parents should be informed during a pre-season parents' orientation meeting about appropriate equipment and apparel for their children. At the start of the first practice, restate to your athletes what you told their parents about appropriate equipment and apparel. Determine if:

1. All athletes have the essential protective equipment that is fitted properly (headgear, wrestling shoes, mouthguard, safety glasses)
2. All athletes are properly attired (long sleeve t-shirts, non abrasive materials, no belt loops or zippers, etc)

This type of inspection should be carried out regularly. Extra essential equipment should be included in the team's equipment bag for athletes who forget their equipment. Note that wearing jewelry is inappropriate during practices and contests. Also, if eyeglasses are essential, they should be safety glasses and worn with safety straps.

Proper Warmups

A warm-up at the beginning of your team's practices and before competition provides several important benefits. When warm-ups and stretching are completed, the skill-oriented drills on your practice plan or the formal drills before the match may begin. A warm-up period:

1. Increases the breathing rate, heart rate, and muscle temperature to exercise levels.
2. Reduces the risk of muscle pulls and strains.
3. Increases the shock-absorbing capabilities of the joints.
4. Prepares athletes mentally for practices and competition.

It is important to have an established, well planned, well organized warm-up procedure. This should include a jogging session with a large amount of basic motor fitness like skipping, hopping, galloping (single leg forward jogging), side shuffling, and backward jogging utilizing these and other basic movement patterns. During this time you can also evaluate your talent pool. The more related the footwork is to the sport, the better.

Flexibility must be included in every practice session. Again develop and monitor a program which increases the passive and active range of motion on both the front and the back of the body. All too often we stretch the back of the body (hamstrings and back muscles) without paying an equal amount of attention to the front of the body (quads and abdominal muscles). These anterior muscles must have a large range of motion so as to allow the successful completion of the back arch. The muscles of rotation of the trunk and hip area are also often overlooked. Standing rotary motion of the upper trunk countered by lower leg or foot sweeping motion in the opposite direction will assist in this rotary flexibility while also teaching the "foot sweep" motion. Remember you are helping your athletes gain better balance in some of these flexibility drills.

Stunts, tumbling, and mimetics are another aid in improving the wrestler's ability to avoid injury. Each practice in the early part of the season should include such items as:

1. Forward rolls, forward rolls-split legs, forward rolls-pike legs
2. Backward rolls, backward rolls-split legs, backward rolls-pike legs
3. Diving forward rolls

4. Back extensions
5. Shoulder rolls-right and left side
6. Cart wheels
7. Round offs
8. Round offs w/half twist

Mimetics are an old form of fun but valuable conditioning and motor ability activities. These activities include the bear crawl, seal walk, snake crawl, crab walk, reverse crab walk, and many others that you may be able to get from the school physical education instructors.

These activities serve a number of purposes, but here we are concerned about helping the wrestler learn how to move his body and its parts in new and challenging patterns of motion. Again, it provides us as coaches an opportunity to assess the motor ability of the athletes and help them learn to move, fall, and recover on the mat.

Moving through the above sequence will take about 30 minutes of practice, and it will get shorter as the athletes get used to the procedure. Perhaps this is the most important aspect—they get used to following a prescribed order for the beginning of practice. This can eliminate a lot of the "horse play" which often leads to "needless injury." In addition, it aids conditioning, motor development, motor fitness, balance, and self-esteem (when one learns to do something they previously could not perform).

Flexibility

After warming up the next step in practice should involve time spent on flexibility. Stretching is just another preventive measure to make certain that the body is ready for activity. Stretching takes each muscle through it's full range of motion in a controlled manner. Static stretching is the preferred method. This means that you take the muscle to its furthest point and hold that position for 15 seconds. This should be repeated twice for each large muscle group. Bouncing or ballistic stretching is no longer used.

Conditioning

The conditioning part of practice refers to the time spent working the cardiovascular (heart and lungs) system. Running, drilling and circuit training are just a few ways to increase heart and lung function. These activities should be sport specific and should never be used as punishment. Gradual increases will allow the athlete to make the adjustment from practice to practice.

Management of Practices and Contests

Every physical activity that occurs during practices and contests has some potential to result in an injury. Fortunately, most activities relating to practices and contests have only a rare chance in resulting in an injury. Injuries that do occur are the result of interactions between the situation in which the activity occurs and the physical status of the athlete. In addition to having an influence over the equipment, apparel, and facilities in reducing the risk of injuries, you have a major influence over the physical activities of your athletes during practices and contests. You can take several steps to properly manage the physical activities that occur at practices and contests to reduce the rate and severity of the injuries. These steps include the following:

Teaching Safety to Wrestlers

Whenever appropriate, inform your athletes about the potential risks of injury associated with performing certain sports activities and the methods for avoiding injury. By informing your athletes of these dangers and possibly establishing team rules that regulate their performance of high-risk activities, you will reduce the risk of injury to your wrestlers.

The key to teaching safety to your athletes is to prudently interject safety tips in your instruction whenever appropriate.

18
Prevention, First Aid and Handling of Injuries

Eileen Bowker

QUESTIONS TO CONSIDER

- What items belong in a well-stocked first-aid kit?
- What procedures should you follow when an injury occurs?
- What information should you have about your athletes in case they become injured?

Although wrestling is a physical sport, major injuries occur on an infrequent basis.

Paul is leading the defending state champion Ben by 1 point with 20 seconds remaining in the match. While Ben is trying to take Paul down with a double leg to win the match, he drives Paul out of bounds and violently collides with the score clock. As Paul's head struck the metal object, he slumped to the mat and lay motionless. The official, sensing the likelihood of injury, immediately signals Paul's coach to the corner to tend to the downed wrestler.

You must not rely on the likelihood that a serious injury will not occur to your athletes as an excuse for inadequate emergency preparation!

Watching from the corner, the first, and normal, reaction of a coach is to be frightened by the possible outcome of this violent collision. The sinking feeling in the stomach and the "Oh, no" message sent out by the brain when Paul went down have been felt by most coaches at some point.

If this, or some similar situation confronted you, what would you do? Are you prepared to act appropriately? As a coach of young athletes, it is your obligation to be able to deal with such an emergency. Before your first practice, you should: obtain medical information on your athletes, establish emergency procedures, and prepare to provide first aid.

INTRODUCTION

As a sport, wrestling takes precautions that make severe or serious injuries a rare occurrence. Wrestlers compete and usually train with individuals of approximately the same size. Age groups are set to limit the age discrepancies of competitors. Officials are placed on the mat to not only score the match but also to stop situations that they deem potentially dangerous. Practice and competition is done on a mat to cushion the landing. Still, because wrestling is a combative sport there is potential for serious injuries to occur.

Because of the contact nature of the sport of wrestling, there are potential situations for catastrophic injuries. The purpose of this chapter is to help the reader realize these situations, be aware of their causes, and understand the instructional responsibility of the coach.

A possible serious injury in wrestling is the fracture of the neck or back. Usually these types of injuries can be a rare occurrence by educating each wrestler on the rules of the sport. It is important that the coach has knowledge of the skill levels and physiological ages of the athletes being coached. Ask the question: "What can this group do safely?"

It is also important that the mat area and workout area are well padded and kept in repair. A coach should understand and use correct conditioning and weight training methods. Coaches should teach rules, know the human body, understand strength and conditioning techniques, and be aware of growth and development stages of young athletes.

A second area of potential danger is caused by lack of proper knowledge of weight control. Coaches should understand the human body and what happens if there is a change in water content, food intake, basal metabolism, or any drastic change to the system. Coaches must monitor each athlete to be alert to changes in weight. A coach should also be cognizant of changes in personality, school attendance, excessive nose bleeds, drop in grades, or lack of energy and strength.

A third area is in teaching technique. A coach must know the skill level of each athlete so that skills are not taught beyond the knowledge or physical ability of the athlete. For example, it would be poor practice to teach upper body throws to a physically immature boy. Further, the coach should understand the potential dangers involved with each technique as well as what makes a move legal or illegal (e.g., a throw versus a forceful throw).

MEDICAL INFORMATION

The completed Athlete's Medical Information (Supplement A) and Parental Instruction (Supplement B) forms should be in your possession whenever your athletes are under your supervision. Hopefully, the need to use this information will never arise. But, if an injury occurs, the information on these forms will help you and qualified medical personnel respond quickly. It is the responsibility of the coach to know of any and all special medical conditions that their athletes have and be familiar with their course of treatment.

EMERGENCY ACTION PLAN

As the coach of an injured athlete, you are responsible for the actions taken until the athlete is placed in the care of competent medical personnel, parents, or guardians. Parents and wrestlers expect you to know how to proceed. An Emergency Plan Form (Supplement C) has been developed to assist you in properly responding to an emergency.

The Emergency Action Plan Form provides directions for a number of people to carry out responsibilities in an emergency. One completed form is needed for each of the five individual parts listed below. The form also contains space for inserting site-specific information about emergency care.

Before the first practice, a number of responsible individuals must be assigned roles to carry out in an emergency. These roles are:

A. Attending to an injured athlete
B. Attending to the uninjured athletes
C. Calling for emergency medical assistance

Note that when a medical emergency occurs, all responsibilities must be addressed simultaneously.

Part A.

For most events, a physician or certified athletic trainer is not present to assist the coach in handling the medical aspects of an emergency. Thus, after taking charge of the situation and directing individuals to their assigned tasks, the coach is likely to be the person to attend to the injured athlete. After the injured wrestler is released to emergency medical personnel, the coach should complete the On-site Injury Report form (Supplement D). Also, if the injured athlete's parents or guardians are unaware of the emergency situation, information on the Athlete's Medical Information form should be used to contact them.

Part B.

Providing emergency care includes knowledge and skill in cardiopulmonary resuscitation (CPR), controlling bleeding, attending to heat stroke, attending to shock, and knowing how to use an allergic reaction kit. This knowledge and skill are beyond the scope of USAW Bronze Certification and should be obtained through Red Cross courses offered in most communities. When emergency medical personnel arrive, responsibility for the injured athlete should be transferred to these professionals. The Athlete's Medical Information and Parental Instruction (Release) forms should be presented to the emergency medical personnel. The person designated on the Parental Instruction (Release) form (usually the coach) must accompany the injured athlete to the medical center.

Part C.

If the coach is attending the injured athlete, the uninjured athletes should be directed to a safe area within voice and vision of the coach. These responsibilities are assigned to the person in charge of the uninjured athletes. An accepted procedure for dismissing the uninjured athletes should also be developed.

Part D.

The responsibilities of the individual assigned to call for emergency medical assistance are covered here. This section also includes space for entering site-specific information for the location of the nearest telephone, emergency telephone number, directions to the injured athlete, and the location of the "flag" person. If known, the person calling for assistance should report the nature of the injury to the receptionist. After completing the call for assistance, this individual should privately report the status of emergency medical assistance to the person attending the injured athlete.

Part E.

Whether or not someone is needed to flag down and direct the emergency vehicle will depend on the site of the team's activities. If a flag person is needed, the procedures to follow are described here. In rare situations, where there is no telephone near the site of the injury, the flag person will be responsible for seeking emergency medical assistance.

Rehearsing emergency care procedures can be invaluable.

Immediate treatment of life-threatening injuries is extremely important. Being trained in basic first-aid and emergency procedures is invaluable and will give you more confidence when dealing with any type of injury.

PROVIDE FIRST AID

When an injury first occurs you must determine whether the injury is simple or serious. If the athlete is seriously injured, have your assistant coach, a parent, or a responsible athlete take the coins and the list of emergency telephone numbers from the first aid kit and call an ambulance. You should stay with the injured athlete until help arrives.

If the injury is less serious (simple) and does not require assistance from trained medical personnel, you may be able to move the athlete from the sport setting to an area where care can begin. Two important aids to properly care for an injured athlete include a first aid kit and ice.

The First Aid Kid

A well-stocked first aid kit does not have to be large, but it should contain the basic items that may be needed for appropriate care. The checklist in Figure 18-1 provides a guide for including commonly used supplies. Your certified athletic trainer or you may wish to add and subtract from the kit on the basis of your experience and/or local policies or guidelines.

A good rule of thumb for coaches is, "If you can't treat the problems by using the supplies in a well-stocked first aid kit, then it is too big a problem for you to handle." You should be able to handle bruises, small cuts, strains, and sprains. When fractures, dislocations, head, back, or neck injuries occur, call for professional medical assistance.

Ice

Having access to ice is unique to every local setting. Thus, every coach or certified athletic trainer may have to arrange for its provision in a different way. Ice, however, is very important to proper immediate care of many minor injuries and should, therefore, be readily available.

_____ white athletic tape	_____ plastic bags for ice
_____ sterile gauze pads	_____ coins for pay telephone
_____ Telfa no-stick pads	_____ emergency care phone numbers
_____ ace bandages	_____ list of emergency phone numbers
_____ Band-aids, assorted sizes	_____ cotton swabs
_____ foam rubber/moleskin	_____ scissors/knife
_____ tweezers	_____ safety pins
_____ disinfectant	_____ soap
_____ first aid cream	_____ sling

Figure 18-1. First aid kit checklist.

CARE OF MINOR INJURIES

R.I.C.E.

You should not attempt to care for anything except minor injuries (e.g., bruises, bumps, sprains). Many minor injuries can be cared for by using the rest, ice, compression, elevation formula (R.I.C.E) (see below).

Most minor injuries can benefit from using the R.I.C.E. formula for care.

When following the R.I.C.E. formula, ice should be kept on the injured area for *30* minutes and taken off for *30* minutes. Repeat this procedure three to four times. Icing should continue three times per day for the first *72* hours following the injury. After three days, extended care is necessary if the injury has not healed. At this time, options for care include: stretching and strengthening exercises, contrast treatments, and visiting a doctor for further diagnosis. When in doubt it is best to advise the athlete to seek attention from a medical professional.

MAINTAINING APPROPRIATE RECORDS

The immediate care you provide to an injured athlete is important to limit the extent of the injury and to set the stage for appropriate rehabilitation. However, immediate care is not the end of prudent action when an injury occurs. Two additional brief but valuable tasks should be completed. First, complete an on-site injury report form (Supplement D), and second, log the injury on the summary of season injuries form (Supplement E).

On-Site Injury Report Form

It is important for you or an athletic trainer to maintain a record of the injuries that occur to your athletes. This information may be helpful to guide delayed care or medical treatment and may be very important if any legal problems develop in connection with the injury. These records should be kept for several years following an injury. You should check on legal requirements in your state to determine how long these records should be kept. Always keep a copy and forward the original on to the appropriate person.

SUMMARY

This chapter attempts to acquaint you with various injuries associated with sport and how you should be prepared to deal with these injuries. If you have prepared your first aid kit, brought along the medical records, and have practiced your emergency action plan, you should be able to handle whatever situation arises. Follow the steps that are outlined for you, and remember—you are not a doctor. If you are in doubt about how to proceed to call for professional medical help. Do not make decisions about treatments if you are not qualified to make them.

Remember, react quickly and with confidence. Most injuries will be minor and the injured athlete will need only a little reassurance before they can be moved to the bench area. Injuries will always occur in sport. Therefore, you must prepare yourself to deal with whatever happens in a calm, responsible manner.

The **R.I.C.E.** formula for care of minor injuries involves the following steps:

R = **Rest.** Keep the player out of action.

I = **Ice.** Apply ice to the injured area.

C = **Compression.** Wrap an elastic bandage around the injured area and the ice bag to hold the bag in place. The bandage should not be so tight as to cut off blood flow to the injured area.

E = **Elevation.** Let gravity drain the excess fluid.

SIDEBAR: Asthma

More than 20 million Americans have asthma. Asthma is a disease of the lungs in which the airways become narrow or blocked. There is no cure for asthma, but asthma can be managed with proper preventative treatment.

When asthma occurs a person experiences difficulty breathing. An asthmatic may experience the following symptoms: shortness of breath, breathing trouble, coughing, wheezing and other symptoms. When an asthmatic episode is severe a person may need emergency treatment to restore normal breathing.

Many things can cause asthma. These things are called triggers. Triggers will vary from person to person. Some of the most common include allergens, irritants in the air, respiratory infections, exercise, weather, strong emotions and some medications.

Each case of asthma is unique. An asthmatic should keep track of the triggers and monitor their lung function. If an athlete is diagnosed with asthma they must be careful.

ASTHMA FACTS

✓ Asthma is the most common chronic condition among children.
✓ Asthma is more common among male children than female children.
✓ Asthma is more common among children (7–10%) than adults.
✓ Nearly 5 million asthma sufferers are under age 18. It is the most common chronic childhood disease, affecting more than one child in 20,
✓ Asthma is slightly more prevalent among African Americans than Caucasians
✓ Asthma accounts for one-quarter of the emergency room visits in the U.S.
✓ Nearly half of all the asthma hospitalizations are for children
✓ Asthma is the third-ranking cause of hospitalization of children
✓ Each day 14 Americans die from asthma.

SOME SYMPTOMS AND SIGNS OF ASTHMA

- Wheezing
- Chest tightness
- Coughing
- Difficult breathing and shortness of breath

SOME SIGNS OF A MORE SERIOUS EPISODE OF ASTHMA
WHICH REQUIRE PROMPT MEDICAL ATTENTION

- Breathlessness may cause the child to talk in one-to-two word phrases or not at all
- The child's neck muscles may tighten with each inhalation
- The child may have an increased rate of respiration at rest.
- The child's lips and nail beds may have a grayish or bluish color
- The child may exhibit chest retractions—Chest skin sucked in

FIRST AID

- Help the child to assume a comfortable position with shoulders relaxed.
- If the child has been prescribed an inhaler, have them use the inhaler.
- Talk to the child reassuringly and calmly. His or her anxiety can be lessened if you show you understand and know how to be helpful
- Encourage the child to drink fluids
- If the medications do not appear to be working effectively, notify the parent or guardian. Call for emergency care.

Athlete's Medical Information

(to be completed by parents/guardians and athlete)

Athlete's Name: _____ Athlete's Birthdate: _____

Parents' Names: _____ Date: _____

Address: _____

Phone No's.: (____)_____ (____)_____ (____)_____
                  (Home)   (Work)   (Other)

Who to contact in case of emergency (if parents cannot be immediately contacted):

Name: _____ Relationship: _____

Home Phone No.: (____)_____ Work Phone No.: (____)_____

Name: _____ Relationship: _____

Home Phone No.: (____)_____ Work Phone No.: (____)_____

Hospital preference: _____ Emergency Phone No.: (____)_____

Doctor preference: _____ Office Phone No.: (____)_____

MEDICAL HISTORY

Part I. Complete the following:

	Date	Doctor	Doctor's Phone No.
1. Last tetanus shot?	_____		
2. Last dental examination?	_____	_____	_____
3. Last eye examination?	_____	_____	_____

Part II. Has your child or did your child have any of the following?

General Conditions:	Circle one		Circle one or both		Injuries:	Circle one		Circle one or both	
1. Fainting spells/dizziness	Yes	No	Past	Present	1. Toes	Yes	No	Past	Present
2. Headaches	Yes	No	Past	Present	2. Feet	Yes	No	Past	Present
3. Convulsions/epilepsy	Yes	No	Past	Present	3. Ankles	Yes	No	Past	Present
4. Asthma	Yes	No	Past	Present	4. Lower legs	Yes	No	Past	Present
5. High blood pressure	Yes	No	Past	Present	5. Knees	Yes	No	Past	Present
6. Kidney problems	Yes	No	Past	Present	6. Thighs	Yes	No	Past	Present
7. Intestinal disorder	Yes	No	Past	Present	7. Hips	Yes	No	Past	Present
8. Hernia	Yes	No	Past	Present	8. Lower back	Yes	No	Past	Present
9. Diabetes	Yes	No	Past	Present	9. Upper back	Yes	No	Past	Present
10. Heart disease/disorder	Yes	No	Past	Present	10. Ribs	Yes	No	Past	Present
11. Dental plate	Yes	No	Past	Present	11. Abdomen	Yes	No	Past	Present
12. Poor vision	Yes	No	Past	Present	12. Chest	Yes	No	Past	Present
13. Poor hearing	Yes	No	Past	Present	13. Neck	Yes	No	Past	Present
14. Skin disorder	Yes	No	Past	Present	14. Fingers	Yes	No	Past	Present
15. Allergies	Yes	No			15. Hands	Yes	No	Past	Present
Specify:_____			Past	Present	16. Wrists	Yes	No	Past	Present
_____			Past	Present	17. Forearms	Yes	No	Past	Present
16. Joint dislocation or					18. Elbows	Yes	No	Past	Present
separations	Yes	No			19. Upper arms	Yes	No	Past	Present
Specify:_____			Past	Present	20. Shoulders	Yes	No	Past	Present
_____			Past	Present	21. Head	Yes	No	Past	Present
17. Serious or significant ill-					22. Serious or significant in-				
nesses not included above	Yes	No			juries not included above	Yes	No		
Specify:_____			Past	Present	Specify: _____			Past	Present
_____			Past	Present	_____			Past	Present
18. Others:_____			Past	Present	23. Others: _____			Past	Present
_____			Past	Present	_____			Past	Present

Part III. Circle appropriate response to each question. For each "Yes" response, provide additional information.

		Circle one	Additional information

1. Is you child currently taking any medication? If yes, describe medication, amount, and reason for taking.   Yes   No   _____

2. Does your child have any allergic reactions to medication, bee stings, food, etc.? If yes, describe agents that cause adverse reactions and describe these reactions.   Yes   No   _____

3. Does your child wear any appliances (e.g., glasses, contact lenses, hearing aid, false teeth, braces, etc.)? If yes, describe appliances.   Yes   No   _____

4. Has your child had any surgical operations? If yes, indicate site, explain the reason for the surgery, and describe the level of success.   Yes   No   _____

5. Has a physician placed any restrictions on your child's present activities? If yes, describe restrictions.   Yes   No   _____

6. Does your child have any existing and/or past medical or emotional conditions that require special concern and attention by a sports coach? If yes, explain.   Yes   No   _____

7. Does your child have any deformities (e.g., abnormal curvature of the spine, heart problems, one kidney, blindness in one eye, one testicle, etc.)? If yes, describe.   Yes   No   _____

8. Is there a history of serious family illnesses (e.g., diabetes, bleeding disorders, heart attack before age 50, etc.)? If yes, describe illnesses.   Yes   No   _____

9. Has your child lost consciousness or sustained a concussion?   Yes   No   _____

10. Has your child experienced fainting spells or dizziness while exercising?   Yes   No   _____

Part IV. Has your child or did your child have any of the following personal habits?

Personal Habit	Circle one		Circle one or both		Indicate extent or amount
1. Smoking	Yes	No	Past	Present	_____
2. Smokeless tobacco	Yes	No	Past	Present	_____
3. Alcohol	Yes	No	Past	Present	_____
4. Recreational drugs (e.g., marijuana, cocain, etc.)	Yes	No	Past	Present	_____
5. Steroids	Yes	No	Past	Present	_____
6. Others Specify: _____	Yes	No	Past	Present	_____
_____	Yes	No	Past	Present	_____
_____	Yes	No	Past	Present	_____

Part V. Please explain, below, any "Yes" responses in Parts II, III, and IV or any other concerns that have present implications for my coaching your child. Also, describe special first aid requirements, if appropriate. An additional sheet may be attached if necessary.

_____

_____

_____

_____

_____

_____

_____

SUPPLEMENT B: Parental Instruction

Parental Instruction Concerning Medical Treatment

Card No. _____

Wrestler's Name _____ Date of Birth _____

Parent/Guardian Name _____

Address _____

Telephone Numbers: Home: _____

                            Work: _____

Please indicate another person to contact in the event of an accident and we are unable to reach you:

Name _____ Telephone _____

Insurance Company _____

Policy Number _____

Is this athlete presently on medication? _____

If yes, please list medication(s) _____

_____

Drug Sensitivities _____

Other Allergies _____

Please read the alternative statements below and sign under the one that you choose.
DO NOT SIGN MORE THAN ONE!

1. If my child needs medical attention, it is my wish that I be contacted before any medical procedures are done on my child, unless immediate treatment is necessary to save my child's life or to prevent permanent injury.

    Signature of Parent/Guardian _____

    Date _____

2. If my child needs medical treatment while participating, it is my wish that the treatment be begun while efforts are being made to contact me. So that treatment is not delayed, I consent to any medical procedures that the physician believes needed, on the understanding that efforts will continue to be made to contact me. I accept responsibility for all cost related to such treatment.

    Signature of Parent/Guardian _____

    Date _____

Coach's Name _____

Club Name _____

EMERGENCY PLAN FORM*

Essential Items:

1. Well-stocked first aid kit
2. Medical forms for each athlete (Athlete's Medical Information, Athlete's Medical Information Summary, and Medical Release)
3. On-Site Injury Report form

PROCEDURES

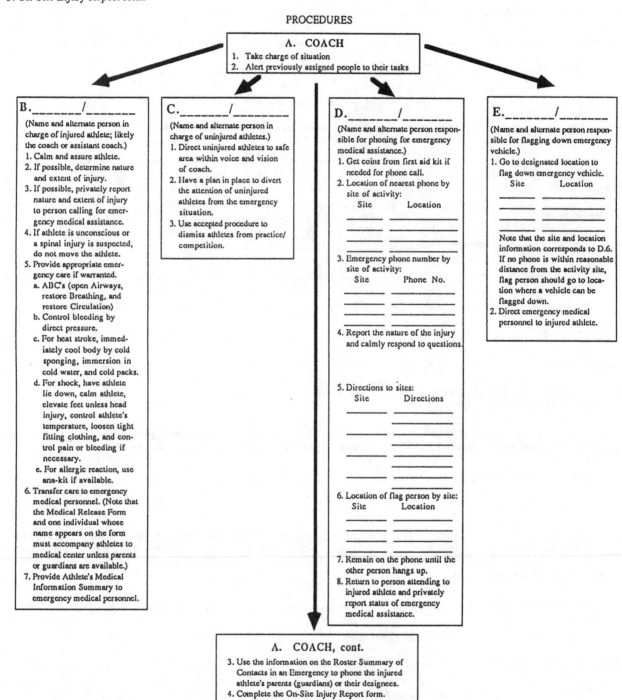

A. COACH
1. Take charge of situation
2. Alert previously assigned people to their tasks

B. _____ / _____
(Name and alternate person in charge of injured athlete; likely the coach or assistant coach.)
1. Calm and assure athlete.
2. If possible, determine nature and extent of injury.
3. If possible, privately report nature and extent of injury to person calling for emergency medical assistance.
4. If athlete is unconscious or a spinal injury is suspected, do not move the athlete.
5. Provide appropriate emergency care if warranted.
   a. ABC's (open Airways, restore Breathing, and restore Circulation)
   b. Control bleeding by direct pressure.
   c. For heat stroke, immediately cool body by cold sponging, immersion in cold water, and cold packs.
   d. For shock, have athlete lie down, calm athlete, elevate feet unless head injury, control athlete's temperature, loosen tight fitting clothing, and control pain or bleeding if necessary.
   e. For allergic reaction, use ana-kit if available.
6. Transfer care to emergency medical personnel. (Note that the Medical Release Form and one individual whose name appears on the form must accompany athletes to medical center unless parents or guardians are available.)
7. Provide Athlete's Medical Information Summary to emergency medical personnel.

C. _____ / _____
(Name and alternate person in charge of uninjured athletes.)
1. Direct uninjured athletes to safe area within voice and vision of coach.
2. Have a plan in place to divert the attention of uninjured athletes from the emergency situation.
3. Use accepted procedure to dismiss athletes from practice/competition.

D. _____ / _____
(Name and alternate person responsible for phoning for emergency medical assistance.)
1. Get coins from first aid kit if needed for phone call.
2. Location of nearest phone by site of activity:
   Site   Location
   _____   _____
   _____   _____
   _____   _____
3. Emergency phone number by site of activity:
   Site   Phone No.
   _____   _____
   _____   _____
   _____   _____
4. Report the nature of the injury and calmly respond to questions.
5. Directions to sites:
   Site   Directions
   _____   _____
   _____   _____
   _____   _____
6. Location of flag person by site:
   Site   Location
   _____   _____
   _____   _____
   _____   _____
7. Remain on the phone until the other person hangs up.
8. Return to person attending to injured athlete and privately report status of emergency medical assistance.

E. _____ / _____
(Name and alternate person responsible for flagging down emergency vehicle.)
1. Go to designated location to flag down emergency vehicle.
   Site   Location
   _____   _____
   _____   _____
   _____   _____

Note that the site and location information corresponds to D.6. If no phone is within reasonable distance from the activity site, flag person should go to location where a vehicle can be flagged down.
2. Direct emergency medical personnel to injured athlete.

A. COACH, cont.
3. Use the information on the Roster Summary of Contacts in an Emergency to phone the injured athlete's parents (guardians) or their designees.
4. Complete the On-Site Injury Report form.

*A minimum of 4 completed copies of this form is needed; one for each of the individuals with assigned tasks. Make sure that information is included at all practice and competition sites.

On-Site Injury Report Form

Name _____ Date of injury ___/___/___
　　　　　(Injured Player)　　　　　　　　　　　　　　　　　　　mo　day　yr

Address _____
　　　　　(Street)　　　　　　　　(City, State)　　　　　　　(Zip)

Telephone _____
　　　　　(Home)　　　　　　　　(Other)

Nature and extent of injury: _____

_____

How did the injury occur? _____

_____

Describe first aid given, including name(s) of attendee(s): _____

_____

Disposition:　　　　to hospital　　　　　to home　　　　　to physician

Other _____

_____

Was protective equipment worn?　　　_____ Yes　　　_____ No

Explanation: _____

_____

Condition of the playing surface _____

_____

Names and addresses of witnesses:

Name	Street	City	State	Tel.
Name	Street	City	State	Tel.
Name	Street	City	State	Tel.

Other comments: _____

_____

_____
　　Signed　　　　　　　　　Date　　　　　　　　　Title-Position

Summary of Season Injuries Form

Injury Type	First 4 Weeks	Middle Weeks	Last 4 Weeks	Total
1. Abrasion				
2. Back or Neck Injury				
3. Blisters				
4. Contusion				
5. Cramps				
6. Dental Injury				
7. Dislocation				
8. Eye Injury— Contusion				
9. Eye Injury— Foreign Object				
10. Fainting				
11. Fracture				
12. Head Injury Conscious				
13. Head Injury Unconscious				
14. Heat Exhaustion				
15. Heat Stroke				
16. Lacerations				
17. Loss of Wind				
18. Nose Bleed				
19. Plantar Fascitis				
20. Puncture Wound				
21. Shin Splints				
22. Shock				
23. Sprain				
24. Strain				
25. Others:				

Do you see a trend?   YES   NO

Steps to take to reduce injuries next season:

(1)_____

(2)_____

(3)_____

SUMMARY OF SEASON INJURIES

(4) _____
(5) _____
(6) _____
(7) _____
(8) _____
(9) _____
(10) _____
(11) _____
(12) _____
(13) _____
(14) _____
(15) _____
(16) _____
(17) _____
(18) _____
(19) _____
(20) _____
(21) _____
(22) _____
(23) _____
(24) _____
(25) _____
(26) _____
(27) _____
(28) _____
(29) _____
(30) _____
(31) _____
(32) _____
(33) _____
(34) _____

19
Contagious and Infectious Skin Diseases

Eileen Bowker

QUESTIONS TO CONSIDER

- Why are contagious diseases so common in the sport of wrestling?
- What are the two most common forms of the HIV virus transmittal?
- What is the difference between viral and bacterial skin diseases?
- What are some common conditions that mimic contagious diseases?

INTRODUCTION

The potential for skin infections in wrestling places special demands on the coach. The organisms causing skin infections are found everywhere, but the conditions under which wrestlers train and compete, make the prevalence of skin infection higher than in many other sports. Skin infections can have a huge negative impact on individual wrestlers, who can be held out of competition, and also, can create a negative impression of the sport among the general public. Wrestling is the ultimate in close, one-on-one competition. The constant skin-on-skin contact makes it imperative that wrestlers avoid contagious skin diseases. If a wrestler does contract a contagious skin disease, the coach should have a rudimentary knowledge of common conditions so that the problem can be dealt with in a quick and medically correct manner. Good coaching procedures will also contribute to prevention. As wrestling coaches, it is our responsibility and duty to approach this topic with the utmost urgency and seriousness. The unethical behavior of just one coach who allows an infected wrestler to compete will negatively effect our sport. There are three groups of microorganisms that cause the vast majority of skin infections in wrestlers. These are fungi (responsible for ringworm), bacteria (particularly those causing "staph" infections responsible for impetigo and boils), and viruses (responsible for herpes simplex).

FUNGAL SKIN DISEASES

Ringworm

Despite the name, ringworm is a plant. There are no worms! Ringworm is a common, itchy, red, scaly skin infection caused by one of several fungi that is common in our environment. This type of fungi that grows in skin, are called dermatophytes. They digest a protein in the skin called keratin. It is usually transmitted by direct skin-to-skin contact, but can be picked up by touching articles of clothing or mats that have the fungi on them. Growth of these fungi begins when the spores, which are like microscopic "seeds," enter the skin and begin to grow. The growth pattern for ringworm infections are circular patches with scaly, raised borders. Healing in the center produces the typical ring effect. However, rings are not always present. Some people can carry the spores without any itch or rash appearing. (See Figure 19-1).

In medical terms we use the word tinea to mean a fungal infection of the skin. There is tinea corporis (body), tinea capitis (head), tinea pedis (athlete's foot), and tinea cruris (jock itch). Ringworm in wrestlers is also referred to as tinea corporis galdiatorum. The conditions necessary for the growth of tinea include: a warm, moist, and dark environment; abrasions; and direct skin to skin contact. Sounds like a wrestling room! The results of a study of high school wrestling teams in Pennsylvania, showed 87% with at least one wrestler with ringworm. Historically, ringworm was often ignored or tolerated. Most cases do not have serious effects, but there has been, and rightfully so, a heightened awareness of the possible transmission of all diseases through competition.

The guidelines set forth by the National Federation of High School Associations (NFHS) require that a wrestler with a skin lesion (sore or rash) have a doctor's authorization to compete. This form states that the condition "is not communicable." The NFHS recommends that standard for this non-communicable state is reached after one week of treatment (two weeks if in the scalp). The NCAA has a standard of 72 hours post treatment. The NCAA also allows the covering of a single lesion, whereas this is not allowed in high schools. The facts are that we do not know at this time with certainty when this non-contagious stage is reached. It seems to be quite variable. Adding to this uncertainty is the fact that there are some people who carry the spores and do not show any outward symptoms, but can be the source of infection in others.

Thankfully, there are a variety of effective drugs. There are over the counter topical creams. Some of these anti-fungals include Desenex, Aftate, Cruex, and Tinactin. More recently, Lotrimin and Lamisil have been added to the arsenal. Lamisil is the medicine of choice named by a number of well-respected dermatologists. Wrestlers and trainers would be

smart to have a tube in their sport bags. According to Dr. Lawrence Johnson, a dermatologist from Geneva, IL who has worked with USA Wrestling, early lesions of the skin may be difficult to distinguish between herpes, dermatitis, early impetigo, or ringworm. Treatment by these medications are extremely safe, so even if the condition is misdiagnosed for a day by the wrestler, there is no risk posed by using the ointment. It is always very important to obtain a definite diagnosis by a dermatologist. There have been cases when, because of the itch involved, wrestlers will use a hydrocortisone cream. This drug can diminish the symptoms for a while, but the next flare-up will be severe.

Oral medications are also available. These are prescribed in cases involving the scalp, where there are multiple lesions, or sites of infection, in cases of multiple infections on a team, and used to prevent outbreaks in wrestlers who have a history of infection. Dr. BJ Anderson of Minneapolis, has written extensively on this subject and works with many wrestlers, recommends oral Lamisil. He feels that drugs like griseofulvin and fluconazole (Diflucan) are also effective, but for the combination of effectiveness and safety, it is hard to beat Lamisil. If these drugs are prescribed for a period greater than several weeks, liver function is monitored, as there can be some toxicity. A final consideration is that these drugs are not cheap!

The prevention of ringworm infections includes regular screening of wrestlers by a dermatologist, or an athletic trainer who has experience with skin diseases. While the use of products such as Kenshield may provide some benefit by providing an actual barrier to the spores, there is no evidence to suggest that it is superior to a program of inspection and quick response. Personal hygiene is of course important. This includes clean workout gear, and showering (including the scalp) right after wrestling. The mat surface should be kept disinfected. This includes reducing the tracking of spores into the area with foot traffic. Some coaches and trainers have their athletes put on their wrestling shoes at matside. To minimize the chance of abrasion, some coaches make sure that the practice gear is smooth, breathes (does not trap moisture), and is non-abrasive.

While mat surfaces have traditionally received a great amount of attention, studies attempting to cultivate cultures from the surfaces of mats have not been conclusive. Most research stresses the role of skin to skin contact. The vast majority of ringworm infections are found on the upper body. If the mat was the primary mode of transmission, this would not be the case. Anderson attributes the rise in cases of ringworm to the changes we have seen over the last generation, with more emphasis on wrestling on the feet in a contact position. He reviewed old footage and compared it to recent matches and found approximately a 30% increase in the amount of head to head, or tie-up contact.

Dr. Tom Kohl, of Reading, Pennsylvania has also done extensive research on skin infections in wrestling. Some of his most recent work has been in the area of ringworm "carriers." These are the people who do not exhibit infections, but carry the spores in their scalp, and can be big time transmitters of ringworm. Dr. Kohl, recommends the periodic team use of Nizoral AD shampoo. This shampoo is available over the counter, and has the anti-fungal medicine ketoconazole. He feels this may be effective with these "carriers" with teams experiencing persistent outbreaks.

Prophylactic drug therapy (this is the medical term used to describe the use of a drug to prevent contracting a disease) is being used by some dermatologists. These drugs are expensive. Anderson uses Lamisil, whereas Kohl uses a one time per week "pulse" dose of Diflucan. This prophylactic medication is used as teams approach tournament season.

Teams must align themselves with a dermatologist. Find a dermatologist who wants work with local wrestlers from surrounding teams. Oftentimes, these "team dermatologists" will see wrestlers referred to them after practice. Dermatologists who work with wrestling teams stress the need for informed, expert judgment in deciding on the appropriate course of action for individual wrestlers. The time in the season, the level of the wrestler, medical history, family concerns all of these factors and more go into a decision. Early in the season, he says he is more conservative. Some wrestlers may think that a lesion is ringworm, when in fact it is something else. There is also the possibility of infections with more than one type of organism. Get your team aligned with an expert who is familiar with wrestling!

Yeast

Yeast infections are red, bumpy, and scaly infections of hot, sweaty areas of skin caused by a tiny round fungus. The yeast that usually cause this problem are present on everyone's skin all the time anyway, but usually do not cause any problem in normal cool, smooth skin. With heat, sweat and irritation, the yeast proliferate on the surface of the skin and cause a rash. Wrestlers will more commonly get a yeast infection from their own heat and sweat versus actually contracting it from another wrestler. There can be extreme itching and discomfort in infected areas. Many of the normal ringworm antifungus creams work well for yeast, and in bad infections there are prescription oral antibiotics. Keeping the skin as cool and dry as possible during practice, along with cooling down immediately after practice with a shower is quite helpful in preventing this infection. A wrestler with a severe yeast infection should probably stay out of any hot, sweaty activities for a few days and allow the infection to clear. If the wrestler has an important match, he can participate as long as the yeast infection is in a covered area, like the groin or buttocks.

Tinea Versicolor

Tinea Versicolor is a common, fairly harmless, superficial fungus infection of the skin. It can cause temporary discoloration of the skin, and if it gets bad, quite a bit of itching. This disease is considered very harmless and is more often caused by an overgrowth of a person's normal fungus on the skin rather than being caught from another wrestler. This fungus is a natural inhabitant of the skin and is not related to the ringworm fungus. It occurs most commonly on the trunk but can be involved in other areas. It can be treated by nonprescription

SIDEBAR: Against All Odds
U.S. Wrestler Finds the Strength to Move on After Facing Death

"I doubt you'll have use of your body from the neck down. You may not even survive the operation."

Those are numbing words. It's about the last thing anyone would want to hear before going into surgery. But that's exactly what Sam Kline, a former All-America wrestler from West Virginia University and one of America's brightest prospects at 74 kgs, heard from his doctor before having an emergency operation on his spine in early June.

"I got real calm," Sam said. "I wasn't freaked out going into surgery. I knew whatever God had in store for me, I'd be able to handle. They rolled me in and put me out, and I don't remember being nervous about waking up."

Perhaps it was his faith in God that gave him his serene outlook. Or maybe it was the nurse that. It all started the morning of June 6th.

Sam had been training at a regular pace at the U.S. Olympic Training Center in Colorado Springs, Colo. and was pleased with his progress. He had strained a rib in practice a few weeks prior, but didn't think much of it. It hadn't affected his training. He got up that Wednesday morning to take a swim and later in the day took a nap. That's when he noticed that something wasn't quite right.

"I woke up from a nap after swimming with a little bit of back pain," he said. "I took a little stretch to walk it off and it wouldn't go away. It kept getting worse."

Sam wasn't too concerned, but he went to the training room to get some ice before grabbing dinner in the cafeteria. But, by about 8 p.m. he couldn't take the pain anymore and ended up going to the emergency room at the neighboring Memorial Hospital. He got a shot of pain medication and blew the pain off as a muscle spasm and went back to his room at the training center to sleep for the night.

Thursday rolled around, and things weren't better so he went to the training room to get more pain medication for his back. The trainers denied him any pain relievers, but gave him some muscle relaxers and sent him back to his room for the day. He still didn't think anything serious was wrong.

"I went back and took some of the muscle relaxers and they were doing nothing for me," Sam said. "I sat down on the couch and there was only one position I could get comfortable in. I would sit crooked on the couch. It wasn't really comfortable, it was just the only thing I could stand."

"I sat there for close to 10 hours. People kept coming in to talk to me and my roommates and they'd come back five or six hours later and say 'God, Kline, what are you doing here in the same spot?' I was really struggling."

Sam didn't sleep a wink that night. He just lay in bed as the pain kept pulsing through his body. When he rolled out of bed Friday morning he could hardly walk. He struggled over to the training center, and after one look at him, the trainers gave him some pain medication.

Later that afternoon Sam was feeling better, so much better, in fact, that he went out to see a friend. Finally, after three days of pain, he was starting to feel better. He was able to get a good night's sleep. Everything seemed fine. That relief wouldn't last long, though.

"I woke up Saturday and went to the training room and they wanted to stretch me out, they wanted me to lie on my back," Sam said. "And now the pain that was in the lower part of my back started to spread out to my hips and to the upper part of my shoulder. It was really intense, I couldn't even lie down."

Sam had developed a temperature. The trainers weren't concerned about it, though, because it wasn't abnormally high. He went back to his room to take a nap. Once again, he woke up in worse shape than he was when he went to sleep.

"When I woke up, I couldn't get out of bed by myself," Sam said. "I couldn't use my legs. I could move them, but I couldn't use them. I couldn't support my weight."

Sam was beginning to realize that his condition was more serious than he originally thought. He called the trainers and they sent a doctor over to check him out. That doctor happened to be five-time Olympic gold medalist Eric Heiden. Heiden, who was only at the Olympic Training Center for a couple of weeks to help work with the athletes, told Sam to get to the hospital immediately.

"Just getting down to the car to go to the hospital was incredibly painful," Sam said. "I made it to the hospital and they barely even checked me it into the room and they started sedating me and working on trying to figure out what the problem was."

The doctors performed an MRI and Sam waited anxiously for the results as his condition worsened. What had started out as a small pain in his back had taken over his body. He couldn't move his legs at all anymore and he could feel it consuming his upper body as his arm began to stiffen. He wasn't too concerned, though. Dr. Heiden had told Sam that it was probably an infection in his spine that could be treated with an IV. Sam couldn't focus on being worried anyway.

"I was in so much pain that it was taking up most of the space in my mind," Sam said. "I was just trying to control that."

Sam's doctor came back with a surprising report. Sam needed another MRI. The abnormality in his spine was so large that the first MRI didn't detect it all. By the time the doctor came back with the results from the second MRI, it was 2 a.m. and the news wasn't good. Sam wasn't prepared for what the he was about to hear.

"He came in and he just kind of shook his head at me and he said this is very serious," Sam said. "First, he tested my strength in my hand. The strength in my arms was terrible.

"I asked the doctor if I'd ever wrestle again. He said absolutely not. I asked if I'd ever walk again. He didn't know." That's when the doctor laid it all on the table for Sam.

"I doubt you'll have use of your body from your neck down and I don't know if you'll survive this operation," said the doctor.

"All right doc, how about something positive," Sam asked, looking for a glimmer of hope.

"I can't really think of anything positive to say," was his response. "I'd spend more time with you, but time is of the essence. We need to operate immediately. I'm going to prep the operating room. You need to have surgery right now."

Now, what had originally been self diagnosed as a muscle spasm had gone far beyond what anybody could have imagined. Not only was Sam's wrestling career on the line, but his life was.

"That hit me pretty hard," Sam said in retrospect. "A lot of thoughts started running through my mind. I really couldn't focus on much."

Then a ray of light came to Sam just before he was wheeled into the operating room. A nurse who had overheard the conversation between Sam and his doctor went over to Sam and reassured him.

"You're in good hands," the nurse said to Sam. "A lot of people come in here in dire circumstances that shouldn't make it and they do make it. You have to have a positive attitude."

Then the nurse and Sam prayed together.

Sam had prepared himself for whatever was going to happen to him on that operating table as the surgeons performed a spinal lamenectomy. He wasn't nervous, even though the hospital didn't have a full surgical staff on hand to perform such a complex operation. He was reassured that Dr. Heiden, an orthopaedic surgeon, just happened to be at the training center at the time and was able to assist with the surgery.

Sam was at peace before the doctors cut an incision up the length of his entire spine up to his neck. The infection that had been incubating in his body for the past three weeks literally oozed out of his back. The doctors cut pieces out of 18 of Sam's vertebrae to access and rid the remainder of the infection from around his spine.

What Sam hadn't realized, is that when he strained his rib three weeks prior, he had torn a ligament in his back. When that happened, a pool of blood formed at the base of his spine, similar to a bruise. Somewhere along the line, Sam got scratched and Staph bacteria, which is common on human skin, entered his body and found its way to the pool of blood. Then the bacteria gained strength and created a Staph infection that fed off of its new home. After building up strength, the infection started to make its way of Sam's spine, and that's when he began to feel the pain.

By the time of the surgery, the infection had made its way up to Sam's neck. Without the surgery that night, the infection would have made it to Sam's brain, where it could not have been stopped.

The next thing Sam remembered after praying was waking up groggy in the middle of a hallway.

"When I woke up, I was being wheeled down a hall and started to move my arms and legs immediately," Sam said. "When the doctor looked down he almost ran into the wall he was so surprised. He pulled me into a room and tested my strength. They were really pleased with my strength reactions."

"We go against odds like this all the time and lose," said the doctor. "It's really nice to finally win one."

Sam had beaten the odds- and in no time at all. He was determined to continue surprising people. And that he did. Not only did he have use of his arms immediately after his surgery. With the help of his friend and fellow wrestler Aaron Simpson, Sam was able to walk on the second day. With the support of his coaches, his friends and his family, Sam was out of the hospital a week later, attending the game for the USA Wrestling's staff softball team. All this after the doctor told him he probably wouldn't walk again.

"I started to contemplate things and I realized this is one of the best things that's ever happened to me in my life," Sam said. "I felt like a medical miracle. I think it's a strong example of faith in God and trusting in his strength."

Sam Kline made a full recovery from the staph infection but was not able to wrestle again. Skin infections and contagious diseases are important issues that wrestling coaches must be aware of. Make a constant and consistent effort to teach the youth and parents about the importance of good hygiene.

anti-yeast, anti-fungus creams, or in bad cases an antibiotic can be prescribed by a physician. Keeping the skin cool and dry and clean will often prevent this eruption from occurring. (See Figure 19-2).

BACTERIAL SKIN DISEASES

Impetigo

Impetigo is a honey colored, crusty, oozing, superficial skin infection usually caused by the staph or strep bacteria. These germs are commonly found in the environment and even on normal skin. Usually, clean dry skin is a good barrier and keeps these germs out. Whenever the skin has a break, the barrier function of the skin is lost and then these bacteria can invade the skin and cause infection. Impetigo usually starts in an area that has a cut, scratch, scrape, abrasion, or burn. If these lesions are not quickly treated, the infection can appear within a couple days. It can then spread quite easily in the local area and even on distant skin sites. This disease can be transmitted directly from skin-to-skin contact, or indirectly if the infection gets on the mat or other wrestling gear. The rash can cause itching, burning, or pain. Early in the course of the disease this can be treated with hydrogen peroxide or an over-the-counter antibiotic ointment. This infection is a perfect example where an "ounce of prevention is worth a pound of cure." All cuts and open areas of the skin should be treated with peroxide or an antibiotic ointment. Most of these ointments can be suggested by the team physician and kept in the coach's medical box. After practice all wrestlers should shower gently and thoroughly. Any reasonable soap should be sufficient. Any wrestler with impetigo should not be engaged in active wrestling until all of the sites have completely dried up and he gets a doctor's okay to resume contact wrestling. This usually occurs in 7–14 days. (See Figure 19-3).

Folliculitis

Folliculitis is a common infection of the hair follicles caused by either common bacteria like staph and strep or less common germs. The pustules can pop up in a day or two after contacting another wrestler with the infection, or, these sores can pop up from one's own bacteria on the skin if the skin is irritated or excessively hot and sweaty. These bumps can itch and burn, and the pustules can be small or exceedingly large and deep. Mild cases can be treated with hydrogen peroxide, alcohol, or external antibiotic creams. Oral antibiotics can be used for severe cases. Folliculitis can be prevented by having meticulous hygiene on the mat. After practice the wrestler should shower immediately to cool off the skin and get clean. A wrestler should be very careful with shaving his beard area. Clean clothes should be worn every day at practice. The wrestler should not compete until all the pustules are dried up and flat, with no redness or pus.

Conjunctivitis

Conjunctivitis is a common, contagious infection of the eyes. It can be spread from direct contact with the pus from another wrestler's eye or from the mat or other objects that have gotten the pus on them. The infection can arise one or two days after contact. The eyes can be red and painful and sensitive to light. A common lay term for this infection is "pink eye." Antibiotic eye drops prescribed by a doctor usually clear the infection quickly. A wrestler with pink eye should not be allowed in the wrestling room until the eye infection is completely clear.

MRSA (Methicillin Resistant Staphylococcus Aureus)

Coaches and athletes in all sports should be aware of a strain of staph bacteria that is resistant to most antibiotics. It is a fast moving infection that can begin as a simple sore. It can quickly spread with catastrophic results. Many of the coaching practices that are made for prevention of infection pertain to this infection as well. Do not ignore scrapes or abrasions of the skin. These must be cleaned and covered. Maintain good personal hygiene with frequent hand washing. This extends to the locker room

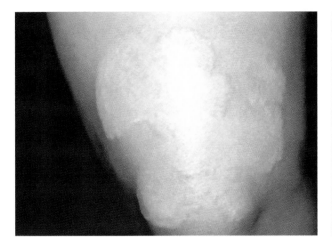

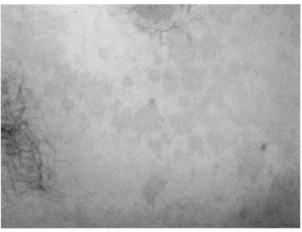

Figure 19-1. Ringworm fungus on knee.

Figure 19-2. Tinea versicolor on chest.

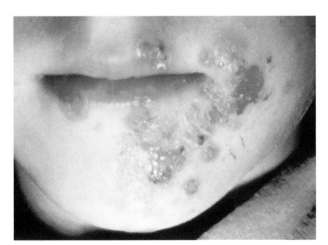

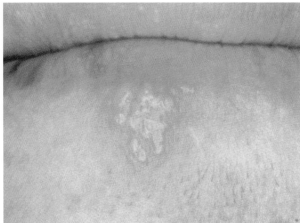

Figure 19-3. Impetigo on mouth.

Figure 19-4. Herpes simplex on lower lip.

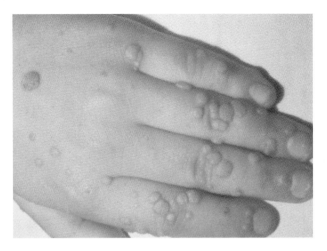

Figure 19-5. Warts on hands and fingers.

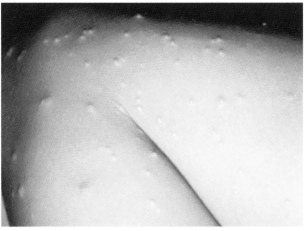

Figure 19-6. Molluscum contagiosum on leg.

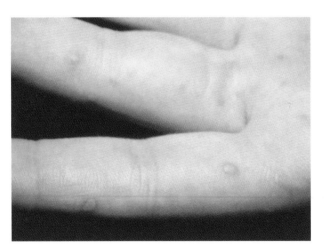

Figure 19-7. Hand-foot-mouth disease.

Figure 19-8. Psoriasis.

where care must be taken in not sharing towels, gear, or coming in contact with bandages and band aids of other athletes. Do not ignore seemingly insignificant abnormalities in the skin that seem to be worsening.

VIRAL SKIN DISEASES

Herpes Simplex

Herpes is a very common blistery, viral eruption seen on the skin or mucous membranes. Nicknames for this eruption are "cold sores" and "fever blisters." When one wrestler gives it to another wrestler, this is called Herpes Gladiatorum. The most common area for this virus is on the lips, but it can occur absolutely anywhere on the skin. The infection is most commonly found on the side of the face because of the wrestling tie-up. It usually begins with tingling sensation. Small red bumps usually form, which become clusters of tiny blisters filled with a cloudy fluid. The skin surrounding this area is usually reddened and inflamed and is associated with throbbing, stinging, and pain. There may be flu-like symptoms. Nearby lymph nodes can also swell and cause great discomfort. The blisters soon collapse and form yellow-brown scabs. This usually takes 2–4 days. Wrestlers should not return to the mats until the sores have healed. This is usually 5–10 days. Some doctors encourage the use of drying agents, such as Benzoyl Peroxide, to speed up this process.

The virus enters the body through an open area in the skin or mucous membranes. It travels up the nerve to the central nervous system. The virus then never completely leaves the nerves in the backbone for the rest of the person's life. Periodically the virus can activate and leave the central nervous system. It will travel back out the nerves to the skin and manifest as blisters.

There is no vaccine to prevent a person from contracting this disease, but there are antiviral drugs (Acyclovir) which can help. These antibiotics, available as a cream, or pills, do not eradicate the virus from the body, but greatly diminish the severity of episodes. If a wrestler suffers from frequent "cold sores," these medications can be taken in pill form several days prior to a wrestling meet to prevent an eruption. (See Figure 19-4).

Warts

Warts are scaly, rough, tan contagious bumps that occur on the skin and mucous membranes. Warts are caused by a virus. The bumps usually cause no problem but they can get quite large and irritated and split open, bleed, and hurt. If left untreated, warts can spontaneously clear, but it could take months or many years for that to happen. Some people are extremely prone to have this virus and the virus can persist for decades. After contact with the skin the virus may take weeks or months to grow.

Since there are no wart vaccines or antibiotics, these bumps are frozen, burned, lasered, or treated with acids. Because warts are considered rather harmless, a wrestler does not have to miss practice or meets. To prevent spread of this nuisance condition the wrestler should have all warts thoroughly covered with clothing or tape. (See Figure 19-5).

Molluscum Contagiosum

Molluscum Contagiosum is a harmless communicable viral skin disease. It manifests as small, pearly, tan bumps occurring anywhere on the skin, including the face. Usually these little bumps have no symptoms but they easily get rubbed and irritated and then they can itch, burn, or bleed, and look bad. The bumps can pop up either a few days or up to two months after direct contact with the skin rash or indirectly with clothing or articles that have touched the rash. This disease can last a few months or several years before it spontaneously clears. Since this condition is not really harmful or dangerous, it does not have to be treated in an athlete who is in a noncontact sport. Wrestlers should be treated immediately so that this virus does not spread to the whole team and to opponents. There is no vaccine or internal antibiotics for this virus. The bumps are killed with external therapies, such as acids, scraping, burning, freezing, and blister solutions. (See Figure 19-6).

BLOOD-BORNE PATHOGENS

HIV/AIDS

HIV/AIDS is a disease that weakens the immune system and makes the person extremely susceptible to a variety of infections and cancerous problems. However, it is important to note that there has never been a documented case of HIV/AIDS being contracted through the sport of wrestling. This disease is caused by the human immuno-deficiency virus (HIV). The first case was reported to the United States Centers for Disease Control in 1981. Since then, millions of people worldwide have become infected with HIV, and hundreds of thousands have died from this disease. The symptoms and signs vary depending upon which organ system in the body is a problem at the time.

The virus is usually transmitted via close sexual contact or sharing of needles by drug abusers. The worry for sports is that an HIV positive athlete might transfer the disease via blood during contact during competition or practice. It is generally agreed among experts that the likelihood of transmission of blood-borne pathogens-such as the human immuno-deficiency virus (HIV) and hepatitis B through athletics is extremely low. A person can have the virus in the system and not be aware of it for months or years. So all sports have now implemented the use of "universal precautions" when handling bodily fluids. For wrestling, this means stopping the contest during any bleeding, the use of gloves while giving treatment and cleaning up any blood on the mat. Cleaning up blood on the mat can be done with a spray of germicidal solution or diluted household bleach (10 parts water to one part bleach). Disposal of the cleanup supplies should be done in appropriately labeled bags. Blood cleanup "kits" can be purchased or stocked by a trainer, and should be available in the wrestling area during both competition and practice.

Hepatitis B

Hepatitis is a term that means inflammation of the liver. There are many causes of liver inflammation, such as viral, chemicals, drugs, alcohol, and anatomical problems like gall bladder disease. One common cause of hepatitis is a virus called hepatitis B. The gestational period for this disease is one to three months after contact. It is commonly transmitted via exposure to blood. The most common cases involve sharing dirty, intravenous needles or unsafe sexual activity. There is the same concern from this blood borne pathogen that exposure to blood during a contest might transmit this disease. A vaccine for hepatitis B is now being given to young people. Policemen, teachers, coaches, medical personnel and other workers who are exposed to blood now regularly get the vaccine.

MISCELLANEOUS CONTAGIOUS DISEASES

Scabies

Scabies is an extremely itchy, blistery, contagious, oozy skin infestation caused by a tiny mite. This mite burrows under the top layer of skin, where it lays eggs. The eggs hatch and baby mites move around the skin and burrow in other areas. The itching is very intense. Thus, the name scabies, which is derived from the Latin word scabere, which means to itch and scratch. As the infestation progresses, large blisters, hives, blotchy skin, eczema, and other allergic manifestations can occur on the skin. The patient will scratch open his itchy skin and cause deep, bloody grooves that can get infected with bacteria and fungi. The diagnosis can be proven by taking a scraping from a suspicious area and finding the tiny mite under the microscope. Once the diagnosis is proven, an appropriate insecticide lotion can be applied to the skin and the rash can come under pretty good control after only a couple treatments. Sometimes cortisone pills or lotions, and anti-itch medicines are required to help speed up the resolution of the rash. Scabies is contracted from close skin-to-skin contact. It can easily be spread around a wrestling room. Often it takes several weeks after contracting this mite before the person actually realizes that they have a problem. The moment a wrestler is suspected of having scabies, he must be seen by a physician and treated appropriately. He must not return to competitive wrestling until he is deemed to be free of mites.

Pediculosis

Pediculosis is the medical name for a superficial infection by little bugs called lice. The three different types of Pediculosis infections are head lice, body lice, and pubic lice. The head lice by definition occur mostly on the scalp, but sometimes they can occur on the eye lashes and brows, and, on males, even on the chest hair. Symptoms can occur several days after the lice gets on the scalp. The louse lays an egg sac called a nit on the base of the hair shaft. The nit is a smooth, white blob that adheres strongly to the shaft. The lice are brown and often very difficult to find in the scalp, but the white nit is often much easier to find. As time passes this infestation can cause severe itching of the scalp. The person will scratch and cause open sores on the scalp that easily get infected. That can cause swelling of the neck lymph nodes and neck stiffness and tenderness. Treatment can be with a prescription lotion or shampoo, such as Lindane, or many of the non-prescription, over-the-counter medicines are quite adequate also. These are available at all pharmacies. A wrestler with head lice should be kept out of practices until cleared by their physician.

Body lice is not very common. It is seen during wars when soldiers are not able to change clothes frequently and are living in close contact with other soldiers. Soldiers call body lice "cooties." This louse can live off of the skin on clothing for long periods of time. With this disease it is important to clean or fumigate all clothing that might be infested with the louse. The skin can be treated with Lindane, or other anti-louse agents. It is not likely that a wrestling coach will ever come across this problem.

Pubic lice infections are called "crabs" because this louse is very flat and looks like a crab. The rash can cause extreme itching and if the wrestler scratches, he can cause open sores

that can get infected just like head lice infections. Any of the above medicines can easily clear up this infestation. It is not likely that a wrestler will contract this disease from another wrestler, as it requires close, skin-to-skin contact and most of the time the wrestler will be adequately dressed to prevent transmission. However, in practice it is much more contagious.

Hand-Foot and Mouth Disease

This is a unique viral illness with an eruption that occurs classically on the hands, soles and in the mouth. It occurs more commonly in young children than adults. This is not to be confused with the serious hoof and mouth disease of cattle. The disease manifests with small red spots on the hand, foot and mouth. Most persons do not feel very ill and can continue with their daily activities. A minority of patients can get quite ill with high fever, headache, loss of appetite, and other symptoms resembling severe flu. The gestation is one or two weeks after contact. There is no medical treatment for this disorder other than rest, fluids and pain medicines. A wrestler with this disease should be kept out of the wrestling room for about 1–2 weeks on the average. (See Figure 19-7).

CONDITIONS THAT CAN MIMIC CONTAGIOUS DISEASES

Psoriasis

Psoriasis is a rather common, harmless, red, scaly skin rash. The cause is unknown. The presentation is quite variable. Some patients have only a few, tiny, pink scaly patches of rash on their body. Others can be almost completely covered by a terribly thick, itchy, crusty rash. It is felt to be a disease of healthy people, but in rare cases it can seem to cause an associated arthritis. Psoriasis is usually a lifelong problem, but it can wax and wane through the person's life. The onset can be at any age. The therapy must be individualized to be appropriate for each person's age, health, and degree of skin involvement. There is no cure, but with an aggressive approach most psoriasis can be managed. There is no prevention as this is some sort of a genetically built-in tendency. Psoriasis is not contagious to other wrestlers. Most people with psoriasis do not take up wrestling as a sport because they are embarrassed by the rash, or they worry that the chronic trauma to the rash will make it worse. A wrestler with psoriasis can compete almost anytime they desire to, and feels their psoriasis is controlled enough to withstand the physical trauma of wrestling. (See Figure 19-8).

Eczema

Eczema is an itchy, scaly, harmless, non-contagious skin rash. Eczema often starts in early childhood and is commonly associated with allergies, hayfever, and asthma. The exact cause is unknown, but each patient can often pinpoint factors that worsen it. Some children outgrow eczema, but many continue to have it to one degree or another well into adulthood. Eczema is usually quite itchy and uncomfortable. It often interferes with sleeping and with concentration. If the rash itches, then the patient often scratches vigorously. This can open up the skin and cause crusting and bleeding and secondary bacterial skin infections. The long-term outcome is variable. Since there is no cure, a variety of creams, ointments, pills, and shots are used to control this disease. Eczema is not contagious but any secondary skin infection might be. Most persons with severe eczema do not wrestle because the intense heat and sweat makes the eczema far too itchy. Those patients with eczema who do desire to compete in wrestling can do so with a well thought out plan of treatment that would be designed with the help of a doctor, the coach, and parents.

Infection Prevention Program
(adapted from Dr. Craig S. Kimmel-Twelve Step Infection Prevention Program)

1) Check skin daily for breaks or abnormalities. Depending on the age of the athletes, it can involve the wrestler, the coach, parent, trainer, and team physician. Education of all of these parties is essential!

2) Make sure that all wounds are reported, examined, cleaned, and appropriately treated. Cover all wounds, including scrapes, scratches, and cuts securely before wrestling.

3) Have a physician evaluate any skin lesion or infection. Wrestlers with infections must be cleared before returning to the mat. If possible, align your team with a knowledgeable and interested physician or dermatologist.

4) Wrestlers should take a thorough, but gentle shower after all practices. Wash hands frequently.

5) Avoid abrasive uniforms

6) Never share equipment, uniforms, kneepads, headgear, water bottles, or towels.

7) Keep uniforms and workout gear clean. This includes headgear and kneepads.

8) Wear long sleeve workout shirts.

9) Keep nails trimmed.

10) Do not share combs, soap, razors, or other toiletries.

11) If a sore is present, dry this area last, to avoid spreading to other parts of the body with the towel.

12) Mats, the surrounding area, and locker rooms must be sanitized/disinfected daily! Keeping the mats clean also includes keeping the bottoms of wrestling shoes clean (put them on in the mat area) and keeping people with street shoes off of the mats.

Acne

Acne is a very common pustular eruption seen from puberty and extending into the adult years. The pimples are seen mostly on the face but can be seen on the neck, chest, back, and shoulders. The pimples can be quite small or huge, deep, and cause severe scarring. Often there is an excess of oiliness and blackheads. In severe cases the patient can run a fever and have swollen lymph nodes. Acne can have its onset at any age but it usually does not start until after puberty. There are a variety of treatments that can control this condition. The heat, sweat, and rubbing of wrestling might aggravate acne. Acne is not contagious. The pustules are usually sterile. Most persons with ordinary acne can compete. If the acne is cystic and the lesions can easily break open and bleed, then the wrestler must have those areas completely covered with clothing and gauze or tape, or consider not wrestling until their acne is better controlled.

Managing these conditions requires working with the wrestler's dermatologist. Cracks in the skin can lead to secondary infection. Additionally, the wrestler should carry a written note from a doctor describing the condition and location. Many states have forms for this purpose.

20
Principles for Training Your Wrestlers

Tyler Brandt

QUESTIONS TO CONSIDER

- What are the differences between immediate, short-term and long-term energy?
- What is periodization?
- What are the differences between a macrocycle, mesocycle and microcycle?

The training we put athletes through is done to teach them the sport and to improve their performance. Through the years, coaches, teachers and sport scientists have identified some key principles and concepts that can guide coaches to safely and effectively train athletes. These basic principles form the basis for this chapter, and can be successfully applied by coaches at all levels.

Principle of Adaptation

We know that our body undergos changes as a result of participating in a sport. Our body adapts to the particular demands placed upon it. When the body encounters a stress to which it is not accustomed, over a period of time it responds so as to better meet this new stress. Just by doing the sport, these changes will occur. A person who takes up cycling and will experience an increase in the strength and endurance of the thigh muscles; a kayaker will experience similar changes in the upper body muscles; soccer and basketball players will find increases in their ability to run harder for longer

periods of time; and wrestlers will get stronger and larger neck muscles because of the unique stress applied to this region. During the earliest stage, the body will react by becoming sore and there may even be a decrease in performance, but this is followed by an adaptation which overshoots the starting performance level. Effective coaches take advantage of these adaptations by planning training sessions which will maximize the desired adaptations. Conversely, failure to use the basic training principles and concepts can also have a negative impact on sport performance.

Principle of Progressive Overload

Two important concepts are the foundation for all sports training—**overload** and **progression**. Overload is the stress mentioned in the previous paragraph to which the body is unaccustomed. A beginning wrestler engages in some activities where their partner is pushing the head down to execute a half-nelson. The first response will be soreness, but is quickly followed by an increase in the strength of these muscles allowing for a stronger resistance to this applied pressure. Coaches will further increase this overload by using specific exercises that strengthen the neck musculature to even higher levels.

Principle of Specificity

Training adaptations are specific to the type of activity performed. For example, a swimmer must swim, or runner has to run, in order to effectively adapt to their particular sport. These adaptations are also specific to the manner in which the activity is done. If the runner is a sprinter, the training would emphasize shorter sprints, rather than the slower, longer distances of the distance runner. The weight training of a shot-putter would emphasize low repetitions done explosively, rather than slow actions with a high number of repetitions. The principle of specificity dictates that the training program must stress the physiological systems that are critical for top performance in the sport in order to get the necessary specific training adaptations.

In order to apply this principle, one has to have an understanding of the needs for the sport, along with a basic understanding of how the body produces energy for movement. During physical activity, the energy output from the working muscles can be 120 times higher than when at rest. Depending on the intensity and duration of the activity, the relative contributions of the body's various means for energy production will be different. There are three main energy systems our body's use to supply the energy for activity.

Immediate Energy: The ATP-CP System is an immediate source of energy for muscles, used within the first 5-15 seconds of activity. The energy is provided from the bonds in the phosphates adenosine triphosphate (ATP) and creatine phosphate (CP) stored in the muscles. There is enough stored energy from these sources to sustain all-out exercise for less than 10 seconds. Brief, maximal efforts such as the beginning of a sprint, a maximum lift in weight lifting, or a double leg takedown, use energy from these stored phophagens.

Short-Term Energy: The Lactic Acid System (also called Anaerobic or Glycolytic system) is an intermediate source of energy for high intensity activity and is used from the time that the stored energy already present in ATP and CP is used up (about 6 seconds in all-out activity) and can extend up to two minutes. This short term system actually "recharges" the ATP high energy bonds for further use. When ATP is used to transfer the stored energy to the muscles for work, one of the high energy phosphate bonds is broken and energy is released. This leaves adenosine diphosphate (ADP), and phosphate. The energy to recharge ADP back into ATP comes mainly from the sugar glucose. This blood sugar is also stored, and available in muscles as the chemical called glycogen. When glucose is split to recharge ADP under intense conditions, it results in the formation of lactic acid. This short-term energy pathway, along with the energy that is already present in the immediate system, probably supplies about 90% of the energy for wrestling. Competitive, or live wrestling, uses an an all-out effort from a large amount of muscle mass.

Why can we only use this system for only 1 to 2 minutes? As was stated, an intermediate by-product of this short-term energy system is lactic acid. (Accumulation of lactic acid can increase to 25 times that over rest or light activity). This acidification inhibits or shuts down the enzymes which control these glycolytic (sugar splitting) reactions in the body. We have to stop, or at least lower the intensity of the activity.

Long-Term Energy: The Aerobic System (also called oxidative system) is a long-term source of energy and can be employed for hours. It uses a constant supply of oxygen which can keep pace with the intensity of the activity. This is also the energy pathway used to complete the entire breakdown of glucose to water and carbon dioxide (CO_2), which during use of the anaerobic system ends with the temporary by-product of lactic acid.

Training the appropriate energy system results in physiological changes which will allow for greater energy production in the manner most suitable for the sport. Wrestling is an intense, short burst, explosive sport using predominately anaerobic energy sources (early in the match from the immediate system, then predominately from the glycolytic, or lactic acid system). However, it is a "mixed" sport, in that all three systems are used in both competition and training. While wrestlers do not need the endurance of a distance runner, a well-developed aerobic system will allow for some recovery of the lactic acid system following a flurry, or a break in the action. It also will allow for the most effective use of practice time.

Defining the needs of the sport is the first step in designing a good training program. We need to identify the factors that contribute towards success in wrestling. The next step would be to plan training activities that develop these factors, along with training the appropriate energy system. Some important components for wrestling are:

- Technique
- Aerobic Capacity or cardiovascular endurance
- Anaerobic Capacity—this means explosive, high intensity activity
- Strength-both static and dynamic
- Strength Endurance
- Explosive Power
- Power Endurance
- Tactics & Strategy
- Flexibility
- Speed & Quickness
- Balance & Kinesthetic Awareness

Components of the Training Program are the variables that the coach can manipulate in planning workouts. These are **frequency** (the number workouts per week), **intensity** (the difficulty or pace of the training), and **duration** (the length of time of the training activity). **Volume** is a function of frequency and duration and gives the overall amount of training. **Interval Training** is a technique used by coaches to vary these components in individual workouts, and as the season goes on. This can mean lengthening the duration of live wrestling, decreasing the rest interval, and increasing the intensity of the wrestling. This can be accomplished through more challenging partners, wrestling when pre-fatigued, and establishing the number of attacks that must be initiated in a particular time, to name a few methods.

Principle of Hard/Easy and Variability

Many athletes train hard every time they workout. Many coaches follow this regimen as well. Sport scientists are finding that continual hard training with little variation from high intensity and high volumes can lead to less than optimal adaptation, or worse yet, a decrease in performance. This can also explain the success and popularity of "cross-training" used to break up the routine.

Principle of Periodization is defined as the gradual cycling of the components of the training program so as to achieve top levels of fitness/performance at the right time of the year. The term **peaking** is used to describe this situation. It makes no sense to be in this peak state for early season dual meets and to be worn out by the time important tournaments come toward the end of the season. Application of periodization requires planning in advance. Some coaches of elite athletes begin their planning around the four-year Olympic quadrennium. More frequently, one begins with an annual cycle. In periodization terminology, this is referred to as a **macrocycle**. This macrocycle is further divided into 1–3 **mesocycles** which represent the most important competitions. Because of a shorter season, a plan for high school team might have just one mesocycle, built around the end of the season state tournament series. It could also add an additional mesocycle that builds towards important summer competitions. The guiding principle is to begin with a high volume of more general activities and gradually move towards a decrease in volume and an increase in intensity with more specific drills and exercises. Each mesocycle is broken down into periods of preparation, competition, and transition. In the **preparation** phase practices consist of a higher number of repetitions in drilling and exercises. There may be more technique work performed at a slower speed. Aerobic work may take the form of distance runs. Volume is gradually built up to high levels. It is

SIDEBAR:
Tyler Brandt

One of the most common questions that wrestling coaches ask is "How do you peak wrestlers for the State tournament?" This question is not easily answered. To properly peak a wrestler many questions must be answered first. Is the wrestler a multi sport athlete? Is the wrestler a year round athlete? What type of weight program is the wrestler involved in? It is critical to know these answers to be able to determine the proper training program. We will talk about the year round wrestler and the in season only wrestler.

The terms that need to be known are macrocycle, mesocycle, microcycle, active rest, progressive overload, plateau, overtraining, and the energy systems that produce the fuel that move the body.

A macrocycle is a period of time, usually three to four months and is the base time frame of the program. You need to decide whether you will have three or four macrocycles in a year. A mesocycle works within the macrocycle and consists of a four to six week program that is more specific. The mesocycle holds sport specific training regiments involving large technical periods along with heavy conditioning sessions. Finally, there is the microcycle; this is a short one to two week session that has very specific goals in mind. The incorporation of microcycles occurs before competition or when a distinct problem has been detected and immediate and insistent correction is needed.

Active rest means exactly that, wrestlers need to rest but stay active. During a period of active rest, no wrestler should be competing in any sport. In addition, intense training should not be occurring. Activities like pick-up games of football, non-competitive games of racquetball, rounds of golf, swimming, or any other activity, as long as it is not organized sports competition. Progressive overload holds that to increase strength an athlete must continually increase the load put on the body. A gradual increase of weight, time, distance, frequency, or intensity is an acceptable type of increase to stress the body systems to create an increase in the system being trained. A plateau occurs when a wrestler or athlete has not cycled properly, has overtrained, or has not progressively overloaded their system. When a wrestler stops seeing increases or gains in their training regiment, even though they continue to train, is a sign that they have hit a plateau and a change in the workout is needed. When a wrestler over trains, their body will act similar to an athlete that has hit burnout. The wrestler will not respond well to weight training, conditioning, or other sport related workouts. This occurs when the same workout continues for long periods of time, which is another important reason to maintain an annual plan.

The importance of the energy systems is even greater than most coach's think. The body has three systems, the ATP-PC system, the Anaerobic system or muscle glycogen system, and the Aerobic system. The ATP-PC system utilizes creatin phosphate that is located in the muscle belly for energy production. This is an immediate source of fuel and last approximately 7–10 seconds. The Anaerobic system burns sugar, or glycogen, from the muscle for its energy. This is also readily available but becomes depleted in approximately 3–6 minutes. The final energy system is the Aerobic system; the energy source is blood fat and oxygen. When the fat and the oxygen combine they combust and provide energy for work. Armed with this information we can now build a year round program that includes a seasonal peak for the State Wrestling Championships, as well as an off-season peak for Junior Nationals.

A macrocycle will last 3–4 months and will be the foundation of the annual plan.

A mesocycle consists of a 4–6 week program and is coordinated and built into the macrocycle.

A microcycle is a short cycle lasting only a week or two that is coordinated and built into the mesocycle, enhancing the structure of the macrocycle.

To begin the annual plan you must determine the major events that you or your wrestlers will be attending. For this example, we will select the High School state tournament and the Junior National Freestyle and Greco Roman wrestling tournament. The development and implementation of the correct cycles will now be applied.

Utilizing a backward design model a microcycle is needed one week prior to the state tournament.

With that in place, we know that a microcycle will be utilized the 2nd week of February. The placement of the microcycle determined that a mesocycle will be all of January and the 1st week of February. The macrocycle will then begin in the 2nd week of October and end in the 2nd week of February. With the High School season macrocycle set, the next macrocycle calendar to be developed is the off season championship calendar. Junior Nationals is the last week in July, which dictates the microcycle. The mesocycle the goes from the 3rd week of July to 3rd week of June. The macrocycle will be in place for the months of April through May. The annual calendar looks like this:

Month	Week	Cycle	Phase
August	1	Rest	
	2	Rest	
	3	Active Rest	
	4	Active Rest	
September	1	Preseason	Preparation
	2	Preseason	Preparation
	3	Preseason	Preparation
	4	Preseason	Preparation
October	1	Preseason	Preparation
	2	Macro 1/Meso 1	Preparation
	3	Macro 1/Meso 1	Preparation
	4	Macro 1/Meso 1	Preparation
November	1	Macro 1/Meso 1	Conditioning
	2	Macro 1/Meso 2	Conditioning
	3	Macro 1/Meso 2	Conditioning
	4	Macro 1/Meso 2	Conditioning
December	1	Macro 1/Meso 2	Conditioning
	2	Macro 1/Meso 2	Conditioning
	3	Macro 1/Meso 3	Conditioning
	4	Macro 1/Meso 3	Conditioning
January	1	Macro 1/Meso 3	Competition
	2	Macro 1/Meso 3	Competition
	3	Macro 1/Meso 3	Competition
	4	Macro 1/Micro 1	Competition Taper
February	1	Macro 1/Micro 1	Competition Taper
	2	Competition	
	3	Rest	
	4	Rest	
March	1	Active Rest	Base Building
	2	Active Rest	Base Building
	3	Macro 1/Meso 1	Preparation
	4	Macro 1/Meso 1	Preparation
April	1	Macro 1/Meso 1	Preparation
	2	Macro 1/Meso 1	Preparation
	3	Macro 1/Meso 1	Preparation
	4	Macro 1/Meso 2	Conditioning

Month	Week	Cycle	Phase
May	1	Macro 1/Meso 2	Conditioning
	2	Macro 1/Meso 2	Conditioning
	3	Macro 1/Meso 2	Conditioning
	4	Macro 1/Meso 2	Conditioning
June	1	Macro 1/Meso 3	Competition
	2	Macro 1/Meso 3	Competition
	3	Macro 1/Meso 3	Competition
	4	Macro 1/Meso 3	Competition
July	1	Macro 1/Meso 3	Competition
	2	Macro 1/Micro 1	Competition Taper
	3	Macro 1/Micro 1	Competition Taper
	4	Competition	

The Preparation Phase

This phase consists of extensive aerobic conditioning, timing of wrestling moves to build confidence, and light drilling and combat.

Aerobic Conditioning

Long runs based on time that average about 45 minutes to an hour three times a week are needed. Once a week a distance run of 6-8 miles or more is required.

Wrestling Room

The focus is on timing of the technical wrestling holds. Light controlled drilling and light bouts of combat will facilitate this phase. Light combat would consist of chain wrestling moves, movement matches, and multiple move drilling. This type of wrestling requires resistance for position but also facilitates successful execution. A heavy teaching and coaching emphasis is applied during this phase. It is essential that each wrestler is receiving large amounts of technical coaching to eliminate improper technique and problem areas.

The Conditioning Phase

Anaerobic Conditioning

Working this energy system allows the wrestler to build a strong conditioning base that is strictly used for wrestling. High intensity and low duration activities are the style of training. Sprints, agilities, and other activities that are done explosively for a short period of time.

Wrestling Room

Mastering the techniques that have previously been taught in the preparation phase is critical. Additional technique should be introduced at this time, the level of which is determined by the wrestler's capacity. The style of drilling should be designed to create maximum repetitions on previously taught wrestling moves in a non-stop format that is timed. The drilling sessions must be high intensity and the heart rate should reach well above the target heart rate zone. During this phase, large amounts of time should be dedicated to heavy combat. Round robin wrestling and Grind matches (wrestling matches lasting a minimum of 30 minutes) are excellent in this phase. It should be noted that long drilling sessions which incorporate multiple technical moves will facilitate technical mastery and anaerobic conditioning.

The Competition Phase

Anaerobic Conditioning

Entering the competition phase means the event that you are peaking for is imminent. Maintenance of the established anaerobic conditioning is of the utmost importance. At the start of this phase, a reduction in conditioning can begin. All relevant conditioning activities are applicable but the amount and duration can be reduced. Drilling sessions are best to keep anaerobic shape.

Wrestling Room

Duration of wrestling practices decrease during this phase while the intensity is at its all time high. Review of match preparation and strategy is critical. Focusing on specific match situations and their mastery is essential. Live wrestling should begin to decrease in this phase. By the time you reach the competition taper phase, live wrestling should be at a minimum to prevent any injury or re-injury close to competition. Situational wrestling bouts emphasizing match specific and wrestler specific areas of improvement are the most beneficial. Building confidence in shape and technique through drilling and mental skills practice will provide the optimum compliment at the end of the season. Practice sessions should be no longer than one and a half hours, including warm-up. The following matrix outlines the information provided in this section.

Preparation Phase

Conditioning	Strength	Wrestling	Coaching
Aerobic	Base Strength-Reps of 10 3–4 times per week	Controlled Drilling	Technical
Timed Runs: minimum 48 minutes/3X-week	Follow with Strength Training - High Load - Low rep	Chain Drilling	Low Intensity
Distance Run: 1 time per week 6-8 miles		Movement Matches	
		Light Combat	

Conditioning Phase

Conditioning	Strength	Wrestling	Coaching
Anaerobic	Strength Maintenance 6-8 Reps as heavy as they can go	Technical Learning	Technical
High Intensity & Low duration (sprints / agilities / push-ups / sit-ups / etc...)	Follow Circuit training	Technical Mastery	High Intensity
		High-Medium Drilling	Injury Prevention
		Heavy Combat	
		Grind Matches - 30 minute matches or more	

Competition Phase

Conditioning	Strength	Wrestling	Coaching
Anaerobic	Muscular Endurance	Technical Learning	Technical
High Intensity & Low duration (sprints / agilities / push-ups / sit-ups / etc...)	Circuit training: Start at :45 secs with :30 secs of rest. Progress to 1:45 secs with :30 secs rest	Match preparation	High Intensity
		Situational Strategy	Injury Prevention
		Medium Combat	Mental Rejuvenation
Start decreasing the intensity	Scale back times closer to competition	Heavy Drilling High Intensity - Short Duration	

important to note that there may be competition during this time, but it is not most important target of the training. As the **competition** phase begins, the intensity is elevated. There may be less emphasis on presenting new techniques, drilling is faster, there is more live wrestling, sprints replace distance runs. There may be reductions in rest intervals and fresh partners are rotated onto one wrestler. All of these methods increase the intensity.

What happens if the practices and training continue with both high volume and high intensity? A decrease in performance is a likely result. This phenomenon is called **overtraining**. An older term that used to describe this condition was "staleness." How can overtraining be avoided? Coaches must plan for allowing the wrestlers to recover. One technique is to apply the **principle of hard/easy**. Within the weekly cycle there can be a variation of intensity and volume, so that hard workouts are followed by an easier day, allowing for recovery from the breakdown that accompanies high intensity training and subsequent adaptation. Another training concept is that of **tapering**. This is part of the process discussed earlier, where volume is reduced and intensity is increased, but it is employed a bit closer to the actual important competitions. During a taper, practices can still be intense, but they are shorter. The morning workout may not be held. Recovery therapies, while always important, are now emphasized. These may include ice, massage, relaxation activities, more post-practice stretching, increased sleep, and optimal nutrition and hydration schedules. The need to make weight for wrestlers, makes the more dramatic pre-competition resting, seen in some runners and swimmers, more difficult to employ.

The **transitional phase** follows the competition and in an annual cycle where there is only one peak, or mesocycle, might be called the off-season. In a plan where there is to be another mesocycle or peak, this period is highlighted by less intense training, a higher volume of general training, and "active rest." Active rest could include playing other sports, light lifting, and rehabilitation from any nagging injuries.

An important note when discussing the cycling of intensities and the volume of the training load in a periodized scheme is that even though the plan may call for an easier period following one of high intensity, training does not return to the level of the previous cycle. It is more of a staircase model, where the training load builds on the previous level of adaptation, and goes to a higher level.

The final training principle, which makes us come back to the realization that coaching is still as much an art, as a science, is the **Principle of Individuality.** Because of our genetic make ups, not every person responds to training in exactly the same way. The adaptation response to a particular training regimen will not always be the same. Scientists have identified the concept of "responders" and "non-responders" in an athlete's adaptation to particular training programs. Ultimately, coaches must take into account the specific needs and abilities of their athletes as they plan their training programs.

21
Wrestling In The USA

Bob Dellinger, Director Emeritus
National Wrestling Hall of Fame

Note: *This work draws its title from a series of columns by wrestling historian Donald A. Sayenga. Much of this information was obtained from The Magnificent Scufflers by Charles Morrow Wilson © 1959, and from A Pictorial History of Wrestling by Graeme Kent © 1968.*

QUESTIONS TO CONSIDER

- Who were America's wrestling presidents?
- What collegiate program dominated the landscape at the start of collegiate wrestling?
- Why is the history of American wrestling important for coaches recruiting athletes to wrestle?

Wrestling already was an established sport among the Native Americans in the 15th and 16th Centuries, when the first Europeans began arriving on the North American continent. Little has been handed down about the various styles practiced, but they are thought to have varied greatly from tribe to tribe. There was a common thread of savagery that typified the pursuits of warriors.

The English in the Colonies and the French in Canada made wrestling a popular sport at their social gatherings in early pioneer days. Before long, practically every settlement had its own champion, and there would be contests between various title-holders.

During the 18th Century, wrestling appeared to have mellowed from its early ferocity into a legitimate spectator sport, a bit on the rough-and-ready side, but legitimate. It was the major physical contact sport among men of all classes (boxing did not catch on until near the end of the 19th Century after being popularized by famed Civil War veteran William Muldoon, himself an accomplished wrestler).

Perhaps the early finishing school for scufflers was the Rev. James Maury's Academy at Fredericksburg, Virginia, an institution which turned young gentry into scholars and, as in the case of young George Washington, into able wrestlers as well. At 18, the big, shy Washington apparently held a "collar and elbow" wrestling championship that was at least county-wide and possibly colony-wide. Washington never lost his touch. At the age of 47, ten years before he became the first President of the United States, the Commander of the Continental Armies still had enough left to defeat seven consecutive challengers from the Massachusetts Volunteers.

The "collar and elbow" style devised its name from the starting position. Standing face-to-face, each wrestler placed one hand behind his opponent's neck and the other behind his elbow. While doing away with such tactics as bull-like rushes, the position opened up many possible skill maneuvers.

Even more renowned for his wrestling skills was young Abraham Lincoln, who was the wrestling champion of his county as early as 1830, at the age of 21. Lincoln was an impressive physical specimen, thin but wiry and muscular, strengthened by hard work in the fields and towering to a mighty 6 feet, 4 inches in height.

It was at this time that Lincoln had his celebrated bout with Jack Armstrong, the local tough and county wrestling champion. Lincoln was keeping the store at New Salem, Illinois, when his boss backed him to out-wrestle the feared Armstrong. From the start, Lincoln proceeded to hand out a thrashing to the local champion. Frustrated by Lincoln's enormous reach, Armstrong started fouling his opponent. Lincoln stood it for a while, but eventually lost his temper. Picking up his opponent, the storekeeper dashed him to the ground and knocked him out. Armstrong recovered in time to keep his cronies from starting a free-for-all.

A couple of years later, while serving as captain of a company of the Illinois Volunteers, raised because of the Indian uprising by Black Hawk, Lincoln suffered his only recorded defeat in a wrestling bout. He fought a soldier from another unit and lost a rugged struggle by the odd fall. This time it was Lincoln who averted the free-for-all which seems to have been the customary follow-up to an individual wrestling bout.

Often forsaking the "common British" style of collar and elbow for the free-for-all style of the frontier, Lincoln undoubtedly was the roughest and toughest of the wrestling Presidents. Also known as "catch-as-catchcan," this style was more hand-to-hand combat than sport.

Lincoln progressed rapidly between the ages of 19, when he defended his stepbrother's river barge from Natchez thugs, throwing the potential high-jackers overboard, and 29, when he cautiously mentioned himself as possibly the second best wrestler in southern Illinois. Lincoln certainly did not achieve any national

fame as a wrestler, but his career was typical of the way the sport was conducted in the first half of the 19th Century.

It was also typical of the wrestling careers of the seventh President, Andrew Jackson; the 12th, Zachary Taylor; the 18th, Ulysses S. Grant; and the 21st, Chester A. Arthur. Taylor never wrestled against Lincoln, but he was a skilled competitor in collar and elbow during his service with the Illinois Volunteers for the Black Hawk uprising. He always favored wrestling as an army sport.

William Howard Taft, the heaviest wrestling President at his "best weight" of 225, was a lifelong follower of collar and elbow. Big Bill was intramural heavyweight champion at Yale, and was a fourth generation wrestler in the Taft family. He was the 27th President.

Perhaps the most enthusiastic of the wrestling Presidents was Taft's immediate predecessor, Theodore Roosevelt, who continued regular wrestling workouts throughout his term as Governor of New York. Roosevelt, of course, had an affinity for most kinds of strong physical exertion. The 30th President, Calvin Coolidge, was rated "tolerable good" as a wrestler by his father, old Colonel John, until at around 14, Cal took to "duding around and daydreaming about being a big-city lawyer."

As the 19th Century drew to a close, "organized" wrestling competition began to appear, often as an additional feature of other sporting events, such as gymnastics meets or boxing tournaments among the sporting clubs of the day. The first national competition was conducted in 1887, with L. Chenoweth of the Pastime Athletic Club winning the only weight class, 134 pounds. The Amateur Athletic Union formally sanctioned its first national tournament in 1888, continuing through 1982.

The first collegiate athlete to win a national championship was Winchester Osgood, a football star at the University of Pennsylvania. He won the 1895 National AAU title in the "heavyweight" class (for competitors over 158 pounds). But the 20th Century would be well into its third decade before collegiate wrestlers established any true national presence. Until then, the sport was dominated by club teams such as the National Turnverein of Newark; the

Schuylkill Navy Athletic Club, St. George's AC; Rochester AC; Pastime AC; Michigan AC; Chicago Central YMCA; Gary YMCA, Multnomah AC of Oregon, the Olympic Club of San Francisco and various ethnic groups such as the Norwegian Turnverein, German-American AC, Greek Olympic Club, Chicago Hebrew Association and Swedish-American AC.

The National Turnverein produced America's first true wrestling hero. George Nicholas Mehnert, competing at 115 or 125 pounds, won six National AAU championships from 1902-1908, losing only one of more than 100 bouts. He earned gold medals in the Olympic Games of 1904 and 1908, and that feat stood as an American record for 84 years. Mehnert's only loss was administered by George Dole, a student at Yale University, where collegiate wrestling was in its infancy. Dole also was an Olympic champion in the 1908 Games.

Under the leadership of such pioneer coaches as Charles Mayser at Yale, William "Billy" Sheridan at Lehigh, Dr. Raymond G. Clapp at the University of Nebraska and Hugo M. Otopalik at Iowa State University, wrestling began to gain a foothold in collegiate athletics.

But the driving force behind collegiate wrestling was young Edward Clark Gallagher at Oklahoma A&M College (now Oklahoma State University). A football and track star at A&M, he launched wrestling as a varsity sport just before World War I and built it into a dynasty during the 1920s. His teams were undefeated for 10 years, 1922–1931, and were virtually unchallenged.

When A&M hosted the National AAU tournament in 1925, Gallagher's varsity swept to the team championship. So total was his charges' domination, that the junior varsity and A&M 's unattached entries placed second, far ahead of the rest of the field. Together the two groups won almost all of the medals.

College wrestling was here to stay, and the sport changed dramatically in 1928 with the first championship tournament of the National Collegiate Athletic Association. Gallagher's wrestlers won four of the seven weight classes, and his Aggies were team champions for the first four years and 11 of 13. Except for a

pause every four years to notice the Olympic Games, the spotlight remained fixed on collegiate wrestling for at least the next half-century.

For most of the 20th Century, collegiate wrestling has been the most popular version of the sport in the United States, particularly in the Midwest (Iowa) and the Southwest (Oklahoma), and has been far more thoroughly documented than competition in the international styles. Dan Gable, the most prominent figure in American wrestling, won an Olympic gold medal at 149.5 pounds in 1972. But he is far better known for his 100 victories as a collegiate wrestler at Iowa State University and his 350-plus victories and 15 national team championships as a collegiate coach at the University of Iowa.

Not until the the late 1970s did USA participation in the World Championships and the Olympic Games become fully publicized and respected. The first of the "new giants" was Leroy Kemp, who followed his three NCAA championships at the University of Wisconsin with three World titles and four gold medals in the freestyle World Cup at 163 pounds.

In 1986, a young man with the improbable name of John Smith burst upon the international scene at age 22 by winning a gold medal in the Goodwill Games, defeating the Soviet star in Moscow on worldwide television. Smith, who won two NCAA titles and 90 straight victories for Oklahoma State University, went on to win six consecutive world-level championships, including Olympic gold medals in 1988 and 1992 at 136.5 pounds. He was the first wrestler in 63 years to win the James E. Sullivan Award as America's greatest athlete, and eventually has become widely recognized as this country's greatest wrestler ever. He since has become a championship-winning coach at Oklahoma State.

Another of the modern super-achievers is heavyweight Bruce Baumgartner, who ruled America's freestyle heavyweights for 15 consecutive years, 1982–1996, and became the first USA wrestler to win four Olympic medals, gold in 1984, silver in '88, gold again in 1992, and bronze in '96. Smith and Baumgartner are the first American wrestlers since Mehnert, back in 1904 and '08, to win two Olympic golds.

Others regarded as "giants" of the sport in the United States include Robin Reed of Oregon State, a 1924 Olympic gold medalist at 134 pounds, who never lost a match to any opponent of any size; skilled technicians such as Stanley Henson of Oklahoma State and Bill Koll of Northern Iowa; Danny Hodge of Oklahoma, an athlete of incredible strength who pinned almost all of his opponents; and a New York policeman, Henry Wittenberg, who won more than 300 matches in a row and collected gold and silver medals in the Olympics.

Consider, too, Jack VanBebber, who won three collegiate championships for Oklahoma State and an Olympic gold medal in 1932 at 158.5 pounds, a combined achievement unmatched for more than 50 years. Brothers John and Ben Peterson from the state of Wisconsin each won an Olympic gold and an Olympic silver in the Games of 1972 and '76, a feat matched by Oklahoman Kenny Monday in 1988–92.

Two more wrestling brothers, Dave and Mark Schultz, also attained lofty goals, both winning Olympic golds in 1984. Dave won seven world-class medals in all, including a gold in the 1983 World Championships, three silvers and two bronzes. He was on line to return to the Olympics in '96, but was murdered in January of that year. Mark was a gymnast in high school, but when he took up wrestling, he won three collegiate titles at Oklahoma and two World crowns.

The Banach twins, Ed and Lou, captured five collegiate championships for Iowa and also won gold medals in the 1984 Olympics. Wade Schalles of Clarion University posted career totals of 821 victories and 530 falls, earning a listing in the Guinness Book of World Records as the sport's all-time winning and pinning leader.

Though collegiate wrestling has had a profound impact on the sport in the United States, it is also worthy of note that many college wrestlers that failed to win a NCAA Title still went on to achieve glory on the international mats. John Peterson who wrestled at Wisconsin Stout in the NAIA attained an Olympic Gold in Montreal in '76, Kevin Jackson who won three All-American honors at LSU, before having to transfer to Iowa State be-

cause of the dropping of the program earned a runner-up finish as a senior, yet Jackson went on to win two World Titles as well as the Barcelona Games of '92. Another notable international Zeke Jones won a World Title and was crowned the World's Most Technical wrestler despite never standing atop the collegiate podium. Finally, the most improbable run on the international mats belongs to Rulon Gardner. Gardner never made the NCAA finals, but after oversleeping weigh-ins at the '96 Trials he finally made the Olympic Team in 2000 for the Sydney Games. Gardner faced the legendary, three-time Olympic Champion from Russia Alexander Kareline. Kareline having never previously lost an international match failed to win the clinch against Gardner, losing his last bout 1-0 and launching Gardner into international stardom.

College still remains a storied part of wrestling in the U.S., as noted by Cael Sanderson's remarkable career for the Iowa State Cyclones. Sanderson, a native of Heber City, Utah, broke out his freshman year and kept on winning. He surpassed Gable's consecutive victory mark and when he was finished in the NCAAs he tallied 159 consecutive wins versus no losses. Sanderson then won a Silver medal at the World Championships in New York City's Madison Square Gardens, before grabbing the Olympic Gold at the Athens Olympic Games of 2004.

In the early part of this century, professional wrestling, a legitimate sport, was popular in the United States, reaching its peak in the 1920s and '30s. With the advent of television, professional "wrestling" degenerated into a prearranged display of rough and tumble antics, and no longer is a competitive sport. The names of legitimate professional champions such Georges Hackenschmidt, Frank Gotch, Farmer Burns and Ed "Strangler" Lewis have been obscured by today's circus antics.

Regardless, the sport of wrestling has had a profound impact on the culture and history of United States. Many famous and outstanding Americans honed their character on the wrestling mats growing up. Politicians such as the Speaker of the House Dennis Hastert, Senator Lincoln Chafee, and Senator Paul Wellstone wrestled. Roone Arledge, the creator of Monday Night Football and ABC's Wide World of Sports was inducted into the Wrestling Hall of Fame in 1992. Actors and comedians such as Robin Williams, Jay Leno, Billy Baldwin, Tom Cruise, Al Franken, and Kirk Douglas participated in the sport as well. Other accomplished wrestlers include: author John Irving, astronaut Michael Collins, Secretary of Defense Donald Rumsfeld, General Norman Schwarzkopf, Dr. Norman E. Borlaug recipient of the 1970 Nobel Peace Prize, President of Charles Schwab David Pottruck, CEO of Goldman Sachs Stephen Friedman. The list of famed wrestlers is long, for more information on the latest inductees visit The Wrestling Hall of Fame.

Wrestling's proud history in the United States demonstrates what a strong impact a sport can have on the lives of people. Share this history with young people starting out with the sport and let them know of the strength of character that wrestling is centered on.

22
Title IX and Wrestling

Gary Abbott

What is Title IX?

Title IX is a federal law that prohibits discrimination based upon gender in educational programs. The law has been in effect for over 30 years, and has had a major impact on our society.

On June 22, 1972, Congress enacted Title IX, which simply says:

> "No person in the United States, shall, on the basis of sex, be excluded from participation in, be denied the benefits of, or be subjected to discrimination under any education program or activity receiving federal financial assistance..."

After the law was passed, it became the responsibility of our federal government, through its Executive Branch, to develop the regulations and procedures for enforcement of Title IX. The governmental agencies have changed over the years. In addition, numerous Title IX legal cases have been tried in U.S. courts, and have helped shape the current application of the law.

Why is Title IX important to sports?

When Title IX was passed by Congress, the public discussion concerning the law did not include sports. However, within a few years of its passage, college sports became an area of American society where the law was put to the test, and is an area where it has had a tremendous impact.

In fact, the application of Title IX within athletics has become such a public issue in re-

cent years that many people believe that it is a law about sports, rather than an educational statute. There have been some special interest organizations that have credited Title IX completely for all of the success in the advancement of opportunity for women in athletics.

As originally passed by Congress, it is hard to question the intent of the law. Why would anybody have any problems with a law against discrimination?

The first thing to understand is that at the time the law was passed, there were considerably more men involved in college athletics than women. When evaluating athletics, in most cases, the law would be applied to eliminating discrimination against women. It is true that there has been an explosive growth for sports opportunities for women and girls, which would be the desired result of this legislation.

However, in athletics, the present interpretation has had undesirable and unintended consequences. The application of the law has caused men's teams to be cut and the interpretation is continuing to threaten opportunity at an alarming rate that is unfair and damaging. Far too often, men are eliminated and no new opportunities are created for women, all in the name of Title IX enforcement.

What is the three-part test?

There have been administrative procedures and interpretations for Title IX that has evolved over time. The federal government developed ways to identify discrimination against women in sports, in order to find remedies. Initially, this was handled by the Department of Health, Education and Welfare, but is now the responsibility of the Office of Civil Rights (OCR), which is within the Department of Education.

In 1979, the OCR published a "policy interpretation" which established the current rules used to evaluate Title IX complaints in athletics. It is known as the "three part test," because there are three ways in which universities can comply with the law. They basically are:

- if participation is "substantially proportionate" to enrollment
- if a school can show a "history and continuing practice of program expansion" for women
- if a school can show that it accommodated the "interests and abilities" of women

Prong 1 is known as proportionality, and it has been the most controversial aspect of Title IX enforcement. In 1996, the OCR issued a clarification that made proportionality the most prominent of the three prongs, calling it the "safe harbor." This made proportionality the easiest way to comply.

Colleges that chose to use Prong 1 are immediately in compliance. They do not have to prove a pattern of expanded programs for women, nor have to prove that the interests of women had been met. In addition, many court decisions have used proportionality as the basis of their decisions, often deferring to the 1979 interpretation and the 1996 clarification. Lawyers often advise their clients not to take a risk in being sued, and to choose Prong 1.

Is proportionality a quota?

Yes. Proportionality, as being practiced in college athletics, is a quota.

It takes a head count of students on a campus by gender, then takes a head count of student athletes by gender. If these two numbers do not match up, you are not compliant with proportionality.

Under proportionality, you don't have to consider the other prongs, whether there is a practice of new opportunity or if you have met the interests of women students. All that matters under proportionality is whether you meet the numbers, if you achieve the quota.

What makes it destructive to men's athletics is that there are many more men athletes than women athletes at the college and high school levels. In addition, the courts have ruled that it is acceptable for colleges just to eliminate opportunity for men (without adding any more women) in order to get the numbers to work.

In practice, prongs two and three are temporary steps on the way to prong one, the gender quota. Prong two is a history of program expansion, basically progress towards the quota. Prong three concerns meeting women's interest, which is difficult to measure and ultimately which reflects progress towards the quota. At best, prong two and three are temporary. And as enrollment patterns change, Title IX compliance is a moving target. You can be in compliance today, but out of compliance within a few years.

This "quota" has been a reason that many schools have dropped men's teams, including wrestling teams. Some colleges have instituted "roster caps," limiting the number of males on each team, in order to keep the quota numbers under control. It has been proven that the number of opportunities for men athletes have been drastically reduced due to dropped programs or roster caps.

This was not the original intent of Congress when the law was passed. In fact, the discussion during the process was to make sure there were no quotas. The bill's sponsor in the Senate, Birch Bayh, stated that gender quotas were "exactly what this amendment intends to prohibit." House sponsor Albert Quie made it clear that Title IX "would provide that there shall be no quotas in the sex anti-discrimination title."

Why is Title IX important to wrestling?

Of the sports included in college athletics, men's wrestling has been affected as much or more than any other sport. There have been more than 425 college wrestling programs eliminated since Title IX was passed in 1972

(NCAA, NAIA, NJCAA, etc.). This constitutes up to 60% of the programs in existence at the time.

There have been those who defend the current enforcement of Title IX who suggest that these wrestling programs have been dropped because it is not popular, a "dying sport." The facts are exactly the opposite. Wrestling is growing on the youth and high school levels. Wrestling is the No. 6 sport for high school male participants. USA Wrestling continues to grow and has set new membership records in recent years. More and more young people are involved in wrestling, yet the number of opportunities to compete in college wrestling have been greatly reduced.

Based upon that fact, there is little wonder that the wrestling community has become actively involved in the public debate about Title IX.

Is this just an issue for wrestlers?

Not at all. In fact, all sports opportunities for men are at risk due to proportionality. While wrestling has been hit dramatically, most men's Olympic sports have similar stories. One sport, men's gymnastics, is down to less than 20 total varsity teams in the entire nation. This issue is also about swimming, track and field, tennis, golf, baseball and many other sports.

In the early 2000's, the wrestling community has actively protected its existing college programs, by battling the negative consequences of Title IX. This aggressive approach has help slow the loss of wrestling programs. However, there has also been a rapid increase in the number of programs cut in other men's sports, especially track and field, which have not been as involved or vocal on the issue.

What is really happening in college athletics?

The most current statistics show there are 367,653 college athletes in the NCAA. That includes 212,140 men and 155,513 women. The percentage is 58 percent men and 42 percent women. Just to get a 50-50 quota, you need a swing of 58,627 athletes. But with enrollment trends, the swing is actually much larger if you wish to be proportional. You can add a lot of women athletes. You can cut a lot of men athletes. Or you can do a combination of the two. With financial limitations, it is far more likely to see cuts than additions.

Many people who defend proportionality blame the problem on football, which has large squad sizes and budgets at some campuses. However, at many major universities, college football makes a profit and supports the other sports teams financially. And you could eliminate every NCAA football player, 58,090 of them, and you just get to about 50-50. Yet with the popularity of football, it is unlikely that these cuts will come in that sport. The target will remain the Olympic sports.

The loss of college sports opportunity is hurting the Olympic movement. The three sports that have the highest number of medal events and are the best performers for the USA at the Summer Olympic Games are track and field, swimming and wrestling, and these sports are being dropped for men at the college level at alarming rates.

There are many more women's teams total in the NCAA than men's teams. In 2004, there were 390 more women's teams in the NCAA than men. In almost every sport, there are more women's teams than men's teams in the same sport. Women are also allowed more scholarships than men in the same sports.

Trends of college enrollment indicate that soon women may be 60% of all college students. Most universities already have many more women students than men. If proportionality continues to be used to enforce Title IX, there will have to be even more cutbacks in men's sports programs over time in to reflect the changes in enrollment.

Title IX enforcement is not just a problem in colleges. There is an active effort to begin to use proportionality on the high school levels. There are many more boys than girls participating in high school athletics. Therefore, if the quota is used extensively on that level, many high schools may choose to eliminate boys teams in order to comply with Title IX, just like the colleges have done in the past. The high school wrestling teams in every community could become a target for elimination if this trend continues.

Nobody who defends wrestling or other Olympic sports is trying to eliminate Title IX, or take opportunities away from women athletes. Until the issue of lost opportunities for men is addressed, this will remain a charged issue and will not go away.

What is USA Wrestling's position on Title IX?

Based upon input from its membership and leadership, USA Wrestling has become actively involved in the Title IX issue. Some of these activities have included:

- Since 1995, USA Wrestling staff has been assigned to work on the issue.
- In 1997, USA Wrestling and the National Wrestling Coaches Association formed a Joint Task Force on Title IX.
- In 1999, an ad hoc committee on Title IX was created by the USA Wrestling Board of Directors.
- The USA Wrestling Board of Directors has approved funding of programs and activities concerning Title IX.
- In 2002 and 2003, USA Wrestling staff and volunteers were actively involved in the public hearings of the Commission on Opportunities in Athletics, which was created by the administration of George W. Bush to review the interpretation of the law.

In an effort to clarify its position on this important issue, provide guidance to its membership and to work with other sports with similar challenges, the USA Wrestling Executive Committee approved the following position statement in 1999.

OFFICIAL USA WRESTLING POSITION ON TITLE IX

CONSENSUS STATEMENT

As a national governing body of amateur sports, USA Wrestling is committed to equality for all to participate in athletics. We support Title IX, a law passed by Congress in 1972 to provide equal opportunity in educational programs. We believe that the positive benefits of athletic competition should be available to every person, regardless of gender. We strive to provide men and women athletes with the necessary resources, programs and support to achieve their dreams.

In this spirit of fairness, we oppose any and all interpretations and enforcement procedures that allow for the elimination of men's athletic opportunities to achieve Title IX compliance. The elimination of men's programs, as a method to reach a numerical quota, is wrong, and does nothing to develop sports opportunities for women or men. The original intent of Title IX was to provide athletic opportunities for all, not to deny opportunity from anybody.

CONSENSUS MISSION

As a national governing body of amateur sports, we are dedicated to preserve and promote opportunities for all to participate in athletics on the youth, high school, college and elite levels.

CONSENSUS GOALS
- To revise the current Title IX interpretation and enforcement, so all athletes receive fair opportunities to compete.
- To eliminate the use of quotas as a way to develop equal opportunity in sports.
- To protect and develop men's and women's Olympic sports programs on the college and high school level.
- To educate the public about the challenges faced by Olympic sports in colleges and high schools, and inform citizens how they can help affect change.
- To work directly with all sports facing similar challenges, in order to provide a more powerful and unified presence in the public forum.
- To publicize the positive values of Olympic sports in our society, and provide information about their powerful impact on America's youth.
- To educate coaches in all Olympic sports, by developing administrative and public relations skills, to help strengthen and perpetuate the programs at their institutions.

What can be done to help wrestling survive and reform Title IX?

There is a growing grassroots effort to reform Title IX. This became apparent during 2002 and 2003, when the federal Title IX hearings were held across the nation, and numerous people came out to testify about the negative impact of proportionality. The media is starting to report on these issues, and more people are understanding why the quota is wrong.

Remedies have included working to create changes on all three levels of government: judicial, legislative and administrative.

The courts have consistently ruled in favor of the current system, confirming proportionality. Congressmen and Senators have avoided the issue and have not taken action, not wanting to alienate women voters. The Executive branch, which is managed by the current U.S. President, has not made changes to the regulations to address the problems, and that includes both Democratic and Republican administrations. Therefore, people who seek Title IX change are working at all three levels to try to find a solution.

The biggest way that a coach can assist in the effort to reform the law and protect wrestling is to become educated about Title IX. Every wrestling coach should be able to explain this situation to other people, and if necessary defend their position. A coach should be able to share information about this to the athletes on the team, as well as for the parents of the wrestlers in the program.

Most people do not understand what is happening to sports opportunities due to Title IX enforcement. Others have an unbalanced understanding of the issue, only having heard the propaganda of special interest groups defending the quota. Education is the key to getting people involved in the issue and motivated to seek change.

There are times when the wrestling community or those working to protect sports opportunities may request help in their efforts. This could include writing letters to politicians and newspapers, making phone calls, signing petitions or sending e-mails. Getting involved and asking the adults in your program to also participate can make a big difference.

USA Wrestling has information on Title IX on its web site, TheMat.com (www.themat.com).

There are groups being organized to address Title IX reform. One such organization is the College Sports Council, which combines the resources of many sports including gymnastics, swimming, track and field and wrestling. You can find out more about the College Sports Council by visiting its web site at www.collegesportscouncil.org